The Jews of Moslem Spain

3

THE JEWS OF MOSLEM SPAIN

by

ELIYAHU ASHTOR

VOLUME 3

Translated from the Hebrew by
Aaron Klein and Jenny Machlowitz Klein

The Jewish Publication Society of America
PHILADELPHIA 1984/5745

Originally published in Hebrew by
Kiryat Sepher Ltd., Jerusalem

Library of Congress Cataloging in Publication Data
(Revised for volume III)

Ashtor, Eliyahu, 1914–
The Jews of Moslem Spain.

Translation of Korot ha-Yehudim bi-Sefarad ha-Muslemit.
Includes bibliographies and indexes.
1. Jews—Spain—History. 2. Spain—Ethnic relations.
I. Title.
DS135.S7A8313 1984 946'.004924 73–14081
ISBN 0–8276–0237–5 (v. 3)

Manufactured in the United States of America
Designed by
Sol Calvin Cohen

The translation of this book into English
was made possible through a grant from

THE ADOLF AMRAM FUND

CONTENTS

The Jews of Moslem Spain

3

1

THE GOLDEN AGE OF HEBREW LITERATURE

I

In the eleventh century scholars who were steeped in Jewish lore and familiar with all areas of Hebrew literature lived in every Jewish community on the Iberian Penninsula. Most of them were religious ministrants who had spent many years of their youth in school. There they had absorbed the heritage of their forefathers—men learned in the Bible and Talmud following the tradition of the *geonim,* the heads of the Babylonian Talmud schools whose responsa and other writings they used as guides. Throughout the entire first half of the eleventh century, the leaders and rabbis of the Spanish Jewish communities maintained close contact with the Near Eastern academies—particularly with the eminent heads of the Talmud schools in Iraq. The Spanish Jews sent contributions to them and also, as was the practice in former generations,[1] sought guidance from them and exchanged opinions with them in legal and religious matters.

Within a short time treatises written by Jewish scholars of all schools of thought and branches of Jewish literature began to reach Spain from the Near East, arousing a renewed consideration of old questions within Spain's Jewish communities. A treatise on Hebrew grammar written in the middle of the eleventh century, for example, relates how one Jacob, a Jewish scribe from the city of León in northern Spain, went to Palestine and, on his return from Jerusalem, brought with him a book by Abu'l-Faradj Hārūn, the Karaite grammarian of Jerusalem. While in the Holy City, Jacob had transcribed Abu'l-Faradj Hārūn's treatise himself.[2]

During the middle and second half of the eleventh century, there was a marked decline in the level of scholarship at the Babylonian schools, while Jewish scholars in Spain were already attaining quite high degrees of learning. Spanish Jews came to the Near East, where they were held in esteem as judges and teachers of talmudic law.

One of these was R. Isaac b. Samuel, the S'fārādī ("the Spaniard"), who is mentioned in many late eleventh- and early twelfth-century documents from the Egyptian capital discovered at the renowned Geniza of Fustat. A man of learning, Rabbi Isaac acquired an education that was both ramified and fundamental during his youth in Spain. In the ninth decade of the eleventh century, he left Spain and visited Palestine and Syria, reaching the city of Aleppo. He then settled in Egypt's capital. The broad knowledge Rabbi Isaac brought from Spain made a strong impression on the Jews of Egypt, who appointed him a member of the Jewish law court in Fustat. Letters and documents from 1088 to 1127 that refer to him as a judge show that he served in his appointed office for many years. The Jews of Egypt honored Rabbi Isaac greatly, bestowing upon him resounding titles such as "Master of the College," "Man of the Worthy Court," and the like. Notwithstanding all the honors he earned, the rabbi continued to view himself as a stranger in Egypt. He proudly stressed his Spanish origin and maintained correspondence with Spanish rabbis, to whom he addressed questions relating to Jewish law.[3]

Among his other accomplishments, R. Isaac b. Samuel produced a work that selected and summarized the best commentaries on the Early Prophets written up to that period. He cites, for example, the work of the *geonim* R. Saadya, R. Shérīra, and R. Hai—as well as the commentaries of Ḥayyūdj; Moses b. Samuel Ibn Djiḳatilla; Nathan b. Yéḥīel, author of the 'Ārūkh; and Yephet b. 'Alī, the Karaite from Basra. Although in his work Isaac did not add much of his own, he succeeded in redeeming from oblivion the notes and commentaries contained in the earlier works, thereby making more than a negligible contribution to biblical exegesis.[4]

Isaac b. Samuel was thus both a jurisconsult and a biblical exegete; but like many Jewish scholars in Moslem Spain during that era, he endeavored to acquire secular knowledge as well. In his commentary on the Book of Samuel, he cites at some length the interpretation of a Spanish Jew named Moses b. Joseph Ibn Kashkīl, who wrote his treatise when he dwelt in the city of al-Mahdiyya in 1079. According to Isaac b. Samuel, Moses Ibn Kashkīl was well versed in the study of Hebrew and also possessed ample knowledge in the exact sciences (the disciplines of philosophy).

A letter found in the Geniza at Fustat describes how in the middle of the eleventh century Moses Ibn Kashkīl, accompanied by the emissary of Ṣamṣām ad-daula, a Moslem ruler of Sicily, came to the court of the Fatimid Caliph of Egypt. In this letter, as in Isaac b. Samuel's commentary, Moses Ibn Kashkīl is portrayed as a distinguished scholar, at home in the Oral Law and the Talmud and learned in secular matters. Advocating the literal interpretation of the miracles related in the Holy Scripture, he challenged the rationalistic explanations of Samuel b. Ḥofnī.[5]

When the Normans conquered Sicily, Ibn Kashkīl departed for Tunisia. In his old age he went to Palestine, where, as we are informed by Isaac b. Samuel, he died in Acre.

The Jewish scholars in Spain fostered the study of all branches of Jewish literature. Most of them, of course, applied themselves diligently to studying talmudic law. Some, however, continued the tradition of allegorical interpretation and treated the biblical texts in the midrashic (homiletic) manner. And, although these scholars mainly occupied themselves with the study of the Talmud, they also did not neglect Arabic belles lettres and the lore of other nations. On the contrary, like most Spanish Jews, who aspired with all their might to absorb the values of the general culture and to amalgamate it with their own cultural heritage, they, too, found much of interest in Arabic stories, and introduced them into their literary creations.

During the era of the "provincial kings," a book was produced on Spanish soil that narrates the history of the Jews from their very beginnings in an attractive form and in fluent Hebrew. Called *Sefer ha-yāshār* (or *Tōl'dōt Adam* or *Sēfer ha-yāmīm ha-'arōkh*), it mainly portrays the lives of the Patriarchs, but it goes on to depict the history of the Jews up to the days of the Judges. Under the influence of Moslem literature, in which the history of Abraham holds so important a place, the book narrates the events in Abraham's life at great length, even mentioning two journeys he made to visit his son Ishmael. As in the Arabic *Tales of the Prophets,* a long chapter in the *Sefer ha-yāshār* is dedicated to the life of Joseph—one of the heroes of Moslem folklore. The author of the book primarily combines biblical materials with stories he heard told by Arabs, though he was also familiar with various earlier sources such as the *Book of Jubilees,* the treatise by Philo the Alexandrine on Joseph, and the *Testaments of the Patriarchs.* It was his purpose to give the reader an extensive and continuous portrait of Jewish history in which an early episode would explain the later events. He did indeed succeed in achieving his objective: The book came to have many readers over the generations, rewarding with pleasure those who perused it.[6]

Other works produced at that time by Jewish writers in Moslem Spain also demonstrate to what a large degree the Jewish intellectuals were rooted in Arabic culture. The profound influence of Arabic literature is conspicuous in the ennobled type of Jew found in many of their works who is both loyal to the heritage of his forebears and permeated with the general culture.

The Jewish spiritual leaders never failed to read the commentaries of scholars of other faiths, such as Christian clergymen,[7] and were in constant touch with them. After the fashion of Spaniards who delighted in disputations, they would debate on matters of religion. A distinguished Jewish grammarian who produced his treatises in the middle of the eleventh century tells of his debates with the Christians hinging on the correct interpretation of biblical passages.[8]

Within the area of the exact sciences the contact between Jewish and Arabic scholars developed into collaboration. Treatises by Jewish scholars on the natural sciences all derived from the classical works of the Arabs. The calculation of the "cycles" in the Jewish calendar drawn up by Ḥasan b. Mar Ḥasan, the Jewish astronomer from Cordova, was made in accordance with the system of the renowned Arab astronomer al-Battānī.[9] In the eleventh century quite a number of Jewish intellectuals from Spain were astronomers, and all of them depended upon the tables and studies of the Arabs. These scholars—such as the physician Judah Ibn Rakufial, who wrote a treatise on the Jewish calendar in that period—were permeated with the Arabs' points of view on scientific matters and included them in their writings.[10]

Arabic was the Spanish Jews' language of both speech and thought, and as a matter of course there abounded among them men endowed with literary talent who put their abilities to the test in the branch of literature that was most highly esteemed—poetry. A large compilation of the annals and literature of the Arabs in Spain cites verses composed by a Jewish poet from Seville named Nissīm. According to the author of the collection, Nissīm was renowned especially for his "girdle poems."[11] Jewish women, too, acquired a reputation for their verse. One of these was Ḳasmūna bat Ismā'īl. Her father, himself a poet, taught her the art of Arabic poetry. He would compose one stanza of a poem and require her to continue composing in the same vein. Ḳasmūna, who was especially distinguished for her delicacy of feeling and great talent for expression, became a well-known poetess in Arabic whose verse was praised long after her death. A later Arabic writer describes how Ḳasmūna, having reached marriageable age, expressed her desire for a man. Looking into the mirror one day, she spontaneously broke into verse:

I see a garden in which the time for the gleaner has come
But I do not see the hand of the ingatherer reaching out therein.

The Arab writer went on to report that when Ḳasmūna's father heard these words, he began to seek a husband deserving of her.[12]

Another clear sign of the great influence exerted by Arabic culture on Jewish intellectuals in Spain was the extensive interest displayed in the study of Hebrew grammar. Just as the Arabs ascribed much importance to a perfect knowledge of their language, including all its rules and principles, and just as they would discuss its problems at their gatherings, so did the Jewish intellectuals concern themselves seriously with the structure of the language of the Bible. Hence at their social gatherings they discussed questions of Hebrew grammar and philological interpretations of biblical verses—all with the fervor of Spaniards in the discussion of any topic.[13] In the large communities circles of intellectuals particularly interested in the study of grammar looked forward avidly to receiving any new treatise.[14] Any innovations that a philologist brought forth prompted the experts to request that he adduce proofs,[15] and sometimes they were even induced to write a treatise in which they contradicted his novel opinions themselves.[16]

The influence of Hispano-Arabic culture on the intellectual life of the Jewish communities of Spain, in fact, expressed itself primarily in the development of Hebrew poetry, whose level mounted ever higher from one generation to another until it scaled the very heights of artistic creativity. As it was for the Arabs, so too did poetry become, for the Jews, the most beautiful means of expression in all things relating to etiquette and personal sentiments. Even a rabbinical scholar who wrote his colleague a letter would append some verse composed by him or would intersperse rhymes throughout the letter.[17]

The lines composed by such rabbinical scholars have been lost or forgotten, but the poems composed by gifted writers spread quickly, earned them great fame, and were gathered into *diwans* and preserved for hundreds of years. These were for the most part the creations of the greatest of the poets, who were intimates of community leaders and belonged to the upper classes of Jews in Spain. These poets' writings filled an important role in the social consciousness of the upper strata of Jewish society, for they demonstrated that Hebrew was no less eminent than other languages and that it could also be employed to express the sentiments and desires of the people of that era.

To be sure, the Hebrew poets had to work hard to adapt the archaic language of the Bible to poetry. In this they were aided by the grammarians, whose investigative activities paved the way for the development of verse and whose commentaries facilitated the understanding of the poems. But the achievements of the poets in this respect exceeded even the grammarians'. The Jewish poets of Spain were endowed with good taste, and, influenced by their Arab counterparts, they coined words and idioms that added new treasures to the language of the Bible, giving it the capacity to express entirely new concepts. The verses of many of the Hebrew poets—and more precisely, the gifted among them—bear the marked impress of the aristocratic society whose dignified mode of life they illuminate. The rhymed and metered words of the poets reflect conduct that is both restrained and refined; their rhymes are measured like the footsteps of the wealthy to whom they are dedicated, affording us a view into splendid houses and ornamental gardens.[18] Although some of these wealthy were men of learning well versed in the Hebrew tongue, there were others who were unable to appreciate the poems written in the language of the Bible. But they found satisfaction in the fact that their people had poetry like that of the Arabs. For this reason they willingly bestowed gifts on the Hebrew poets who appeared at their social gatherings alongside Arabic poets to recite their literary works.

In addition to the masterpieces of the preeminent Jewish poets, hundreds of thousands of Hebrew verses noted for the elegance and excellence of their content and style were composed in that era. A Hispano-Jewish writer of a much later period relates that in the days of Isaac Ibn Khalfōn—the late tenth and early eleventh centuries—the number of Hebrew poets in Spain was already large.[19] This was a direct outcome of the Hispano-Arabic way of life. Whereas in the Near East in those generations poetry was the esthetic delight of the persons of rank, in Spain it was the possession of all classes[20] and abilities. Even persons devoid of talent wrote poetry, and anyone who lacked even rudimentary ability would copy lines from the verse of a renowned poet for his own adornment.[21]

The genuine poets acquired a knowledge of all the ingredients of Arabic verse in order to imitate them and introduced previously unknown species of verse into Hebrew poetry. One such category was that of drinking songs encompassing all the delights of revelry. Drinking songs flourished among Spanish Arabs in the eleventh century, when the religious spirit among the ruling classes weakened. It is reported that even at the beginning of that epoch, Sanchol, the son and heir of al-Manṣūr, on hearing the cry of the *muezzin,* observed that it was better to be called to a wine feast. The Arab poets, who depended for their livelihood on the gifts of the wealthy, composed songs in which they celebrated the gardens in which the wine feasts were held, describing the trees and the flowerbeds, and sang the praises of the beautiful cups and their contents, which gladdened the heart of man.[22] The Hebrew poets, too, composed verse about the tables laden with fruits and embellished with flowers exuding a fine fragrance, and about the beauty of goblets and the hues of wine. One poet briefly sums up a description of a feast with these words:

Before me are the roses and all manner of spice
And in my cup, wine glistening like the sun. [23]

Circles of intellectuals who devoted themselves to philosophical meditation also abounded in the Jewish communities of eleventh-century Spain. They too followed in the footsteps of the Arabs—poring over books available to Arab philosophers and discussing the problems that engaged them. Their studies led to some controversy. According to a later tradition, Samuel the Nagid addressed an inquiry to the Gaon Rabbi Hai as to whether it is permissible and worthwhile to engage in philosophy, and the rabbi's response was in the negative.[24] Although this story may be apocryphal, it is certainly true that many of the Jewish intellectuals in the cities of Spain in that epoch were influenced by philosophic views, and that this provoked against them the wrath of the bigoted.[25] Some of these intellectuals freely professed religious skepticism, whereas others attempted to strike a compromise between the conclusions of the philosophers and religious belief, which is based on faith in divine revelation. It was the ideal of the latter group to reconcile Arabo-Hellenic science with Judaism, by basing Jewish thought on the systems of the philosophers and the cultural creations of the Jews on the principles of Arabic writers and scholars. In short, they sought to develop a Jewish culture that would dovetail with the great syncretic Arabic culture. In carrying over ideas, concepts, and points of view from the world of Arabic thought to Jewish literature, these intellectuals succeeded for the most part in choosing those conceptual elements that harmonized with the Jewish spirit—consequently retaining their spiritual identity and producing works of distinction.

II

It is commonly accepted that the cultural standard of a national group is measured on the one hand by its average intellectual level and on the other by the achievements of individuals—the masterworks of men blessed with talent. Judged by this standard, the eleventh century was the golden age in the history of the Spanish Jews. After many generations in which dedicated teachers labored to educate scholars, there emerged in that epoch from among the Jewish communities of Spain a host of preeminent intellectuals—poets and writers whose names are engraved in gold in the annals of Jewish literature.

One of the most distinguished of these was the philologist Abu 'l-Walīd Marwān Ibn Djanāḥ, the first man to write comprehensive treatises in the field of Hebrew grammar and Hebrew lexicography using the scientific method still current today. As is the habit of a genuine scientific scholar, he did not interlace his work with many details about his life; and even what we know of it from other sources is very meager.

The name of this man, who did so much more in the study of his language than any other grammarian, symbolizes the history of a people obliged to wander in alien lands. The name given him—the one by which he was known—was not a Hebrew name. He always refers to himself by the appellative Abu 'l-Walīd or by the Arabic name Marwān. However, like most Spanish Jews, he also had a Hebrew name—Jonah—and he was also called by the Latin name Marinus, a practice which had become accepted among the Jews in the days of the Roman Empire. Ibn Djanāḥ was his family name.[26]

Who his parents were, whether he came from a rich or poor family—on these matters he is silent. His birthplace was in Cordova, the capital of Spain in the lustrous days of Moslem rule; for this reason the appellation "al-Ḳurṭubī" is sometimes added to his name.[27] When Abu 'l-Walīd was born, in the late 990s,[28] there was still a large community in Cordova that included distinguished teachers and scholars. He did not spend his youth in the city of his birth, however, but in Lucena, the Jewish city southeast of the capital of the Spanish caliphs.[29]

In Lucena there were men of learning entirely preoccupied with talmudic law, students of the Hebrew language and biblical exegesis, and also intellectuals who cultivated the art of Hebrew poetry, which began to flourish in those days. Young Abu 'l-Walīd sat at the feet of all the masters who had won fame in the city. He studied the Talmud and the commentaries of the *geonim* but he was especially drawn to the study of Hebrew and biblical exegesis, already displaying that one-sidedness that distinguishes the characters of scholars and men of science throughout the generations. While he soon began to neglect the other areas of learning,[30] he delved very diligently into the study of Hebrew grammar.

Among the grammarians then living in Lucena, two became his teachers par excellence. The first was Isaac b. Levi b. Mar Saul,[31] with whom he studied for a long time. In keeping with the pattern of philological instruction in Arabic countries, Abu 'l-Walīd sat before him, reading from texts and collections of poetry. His teacher would then correct his errors and make comments.[32] Isaac b. Mar Saul's earnest approach to his subject and his exacting demands made a great impression on his young disciple. Long after he had studied with him, this quality in his master was etched upon his memory.[33] A gifted poet, Isaac b. Mar Saul took great liberties with his use of language in his poetry, that is, he used words not in accordance with their original meaning. This tendency on his part also influenced Abu 'l-Walīd, who explained certain linguistic phenomena as poetical figures of speech.[34]

Abu 'l-Walīd's other great teacher was Isaac Ibn Djiḳaṭilla,[35] regarded, along with Isaac b. Mar Saul, in Lucena at that time as being most erudite in the lore of Hebrew philology.[36] This teacher, too, had a marked influence upon the scientific method and the approach to research of the future grammarian. Isaac Ibn Djiḳatilla was an outstanding expert in the Arabic language, and it was no doubt he who spurred his talented disciple to acquire a full knowledge of Arabic language and literature and in particular to delve deeply into the writings of Arab grammarians. Abu 'l-Walīd became a distinguished Arabic stylist and seasoned his works with quotations from Arabic poetry.

Aside from these two distinguished teachers who determined, in large measure, the path he would tread in the future, Abu 'l-Walīd received instruction from the other teachers in Lucena, such as Abu'l-Walīd Ibn Ḥasdai, whose opinions he mentions in treatises he wrote some decades later.[37] However, even more important to him at the time were the writings of the great grammarian Ḥayyūdj. These opened for him new horizons in the laws governing Hebrew and in biblical exegesis.

To be sure, the young man from Cordova was endowed with a well-developed critical sense and did not accept others' views without reflecting upon them first and subjecting them to critical review. Even in his youth he set down in writing his comments and strictures on whatever his teachers had imparted to him and on what he found in books regarded as *the* texts against which no objections could be uttered.[38]

During the time he studied at Lucena, Abu 'l-Walīd also tried his hand at writing poems, as did many of the intellectuals in Lucena, "the city of song." His teacher Isaac b. Mar Saul in particular served as his model. But thanks to his critical faculty, Abu 'l-Walīd soon recognized that this was not his métier, whereupon he desisted from these experiments.[39] On the other hand the inclination to devote himself to the study of Hebrew grew stronger as he found that many, recognizing his linguistic talent, questioned him regarding the meaning of phrases in the Holy Scriptures.[40]

In the meantime he returned to Cordova to study medicine, since he did not wish to use his learning as a means to earn a living. Day and night, from the time of his return to the capital city, he pored over those writings of the Greek and Roman physicians that had been translated into Arabic, such as the works of Galen,[41] as well as the classical writings of the Arab physicians in the Near East that served as texts for study. He also accompanied physicians when they visited the sick. But beyond his preoccupation with the profession that would provide him with a livelihood, the young Abu 'l-Walīd did not forget the study of the Hebrew language he so loved. He made a proper distinction between the vocation he had chosen for himself and his life's dream in the field of investigation. The goal of his life he saw to be the writing of comprehensive books that would illuminate in a scientific way all the problems of

Hebrew grammar and include its entire vocabulary. Although Ḥayyūdj, who had laid the foundation for the scientific grammar of Hebrew, had already died when Abu 'l-Walīd reached Cordova,[42] there were many scholars of Hebrew philology there with whom he associated and exchanged opinions. One of these, Abū 'Umar Ibn Yaḳwā, tended to interpret the Bible in a free and critical manner.[43]

But even as Abu 'l-Walīd applied himself diligently to the study of medicine and devised plans for research in philology, the blue skies of Andalusia grew dark and the clouds that cast a pall of darkness over the world of the Spanish caliphate caused even tranquil scholars who had no interest in politics to break out of the normal pattern of their lives. The sons and heirs of al-Manṣūr, that ingenious tyrant, were forced to yield their ruling authority, civil war broke out between Andalusians and Berbers, Christian armies penetrated the plains of Andalusia, and the protracted siege of Cordova itself began, ending in 1013 with the Berber conquest of the city and a frightful slaughter. Even at the time of the siege, many of its inhabitants, including Jews, left the city; and after its conquest by the Berber forces, a stream of emigrants poured forth in every direction.

One of those who left the distressed city was Abu 'l-Walīd Ibn Djanāh.[44] After departing the city of his forebears, he wandered for a long time over the wide expanse of Spain from city to city, without settling in any of them.[45] During his years of wandering, Abu 'l-Walīd struggled with various difficulties: At times he found it hard to make a living or to adapt himself to an alien environment. More than once he thought that he had managed to settle in one location only to have the wheel of fate take a turn and compel him to seek another place to live. But the desire to learn ingrained in him was strong, and despite all the hardships that befell him, he continued his studies.

Because he was dependent upon small libraries that he discovered in various cities, Abu 'l-Walīd could not engage in systematic study, as he had in Cordova. However, at this time he began to study areas of knowledge that had formerly not occupied him at all. He studied the laws of logic from books he came upon in the libraries of Jewish and Moslem intellectuals. Through extensive perusal of treatises on this subject, he obtained considerable information regarding its principles and acquired the ability to frame definitions, to make his point in argument, and to carry on a discourse with clarity—qualities that became characteristic of him.[46] He also read the works of the Arabic philosophers based on Greek systems of thought—whether they presented the Greeks' views or endeavored to strike a compromise between them and religion based on faith in a revealed God and *creatio ex nihilo.*[47] However, the perusal of these books did not undermine Abu 'l-Walīd's pure faith; he remained loyal to the learning he had absorbed at the feet of his masters in Lucena. He readily accepted the Greco-Arabic systems of logic, but he shrank from philosophical speculation on metaphysical matters, vigorously opposing the view held by the philosophers who believe in the eternity of the world.[48] In general, he had no interest in considering the problems of creation, seeing them as beyond man's grasp, and he saw no advantage in wearying his mind over them. He sincerely believed it to be better for him to accept the words of the Holy Scriptures in their plain meaning than to destroy his faith by speculating on what is beyond comprehension.[49] True to his conservative outlook, he accepted the traditional text of Scripture, opposed emendations designed to clarify difficulties appearing therein, and depended upon the accepted interpretations of Jewish scholars in ancient times.[50]

Thus was his personality molded during the years of his wanderings. Even as he read philosophic treatises he came upon in the cities where he stayed briefly, his devotion to the traditional faith grew stronger, and in the course of time he became a representative of that current among the Spanish Jews that did not aspire to any compromise between religion and philosophy or rational faith. He was one of those who entered the garden of philosophy and remained unscathed.

After some years had passed, Abu 'l-Walīd settled in Saragossa, on the banks of the Ebro. Under the rule of the kings of the Tudjībid dynasty, it had become a flourishing city with a large Jewish community. Like many of the Jews of Cordova who had migrated to the provinces in northern Spain, Abu 'l-Walīd believed that in this city he would be able to make a living without difficulty and would also meet intellectuals and friends of learning. Although his chief desire was to abide serene and undisturbed in order to devote his free time to the study of Hebrew, it was necessary even for a man like him to have contact with scholars to whom he could unburden himself and report his discoveries, and from whom he could hear opinions. His hopes were not disappointed. Before many days had elapsed, he was already well known as a good doctor and was eagerly sought out by the sick.[51] He also became the father of a son named Aḥiya.[52] As is the way of erudite men whose custom it is to consider thoroughly those matters that concern them, he began to engage in a study connected with his occupation as a physician. He wrote a book called *Talkhīs* ("Digest") on simple remedies, indicating their names and the proper dosages to heal various ailments.[53] But the subject that really fascinated him remained the study of Hebrew. He continued to gather notes on the text of the Bible and the writings of grammarians who preceded him, and during his stay in Saragossa, which had a sizable Christian community, he also obtained and perused with much interest Christian translations of the Bible.[54]

After repeatedly examining the notes he had made over several years, Abu 'l-Walīd finally published his first book on the rules of Hebrew grammar—that is, he had copyists make several transcripts, which he distributed among friends interested in the subject. This first book,[55] which, like all his works, was written in Arabic, was called *Kitāb al-Mustalḥiḳ.* (It was translated into Hebrew and entitled *Sefer ha-hashlāma* or *Sefer ha-tōsĕfet,* "The Book of Supplement.")[56] Its purpose was to correct errors in Ḥayyūdj's two treatises dealing with verbs with a weak letter or gemmate verbs, and it also was intended to complete what Ḥayyūdj's works lacked. The entire scientific achievement of Abu 'l-Walīd is based on Ḥayyūdj's recognition that Hebrew words, like Arabic words, derive for the greatest part from triliteral roots; and Abu 'l-Walīd never denied his dependence on his great predecessor. He held him in great esteem and did not criticize him harshly; rather he stressed repeatedly that Ḥayyūdj's errors or omissions were due not to insufficient knowledge but to inadvertence or to his premature death.[57] Since it is a supplement to Ḥayyūdj's two treatises, *Kitāb al-Mustalḥiḳ* contains annotations to chapters in Ḥayyūdj's works arranged sequentially.

This first grammatical treatise by Abu 'l-Walīd renders all his virtues conspicuous. It is the product of most diligent and fundamental study. Abu 'l-Walīd avers that he went through the entire Bible eight times to gather material for his book,[58] and he mentions a number of times that he compared various manuscripts of Ḥayyūdj's treatises.[59] At the end of his book he counts the corrigenda and addenda he succeeded in introducing into it, as if to justify his work.

Sefer ha-hashlāma made a great impression on the intellectuals in the Jewish communities of Saragossa and elsewhere. Those few friends of learning who rejoiced at any progress whatsoever in the study of Hebrew sang its praise, but in other circles complaints were voiced. Among the Talmud-school students, whose sole concern was the mastery of Jewish law, the argument was put forth that these studies are unnecessary and even harmful, since they at times oppose the interpretations of biblical verses contained in the Talmud and the homiletic commentaries of the Bible. There were also Jewish scholars who opposed Ḥayyūdj's opinions and viewed his theories as an alien element lifted from the Arabs, and admirers of Ḥayyūdj who regarded Abu 'l-Walīd's book as an attack against his memory on the part of a boastful and arrogant savant.[60] A few from among these circles in Saragossa's community wrote and published a small book called *Kitāb al-Istīfā* ("The Book of Completion"), in which they intended to call attention to the defects in Abu 'l-Walīd's work. The authors published it under the name of a man notorious for his ignorance, as if to demonstrate that even he had a greater familiarity with the rules of Hebrew grammar than did Abu 'l-Walīd, who considered himself an authority in this area of knowledge.

Abu 'l-Walīd was very hurt. He was a straightforward person and scrupulous in his scholarship, but far from modest and, in fact, inclined to boast of his achievements.[61] As a typical scholar, he held his field of knowledge to be more important than any other area of learning and considered himself immeasurably superior in his knowledge to any other person engaged in the same pursuit. Although he made no claims to possess ability in other areas of erudition, neither did he refrain from belittling them.[62] After having pursued the study of Hebrew grammar diligently for many years and revealing many errors in the writings of the grammarians who preceded him, he was convinced that whoever refused to recognize him as the greatest of philologists did so only out of envy. Was there any other scholar who drove sleep from his eyelids many nights in order to consider the rules governing Hebrew, while at the selfsame time others were enjoying mundane pleasures? In a passage in one of his books, he notes that on the nights he devoted to study he spent twice as much for illuminating oil as others spent for wine.

At times, in a spirit of arrogance, Abu 'l-Walīd ascribed to himself innovations that were not his own, for in all innocence he believed that no man understood the rules of Hebrew philology in all their scope and depth as did he. Indeed, if someone actually did explain a linguistic phenomenon in a manner similar to his, such a one only *seemed* to plumb its depths. Hence people were suspicious of the veracity of his claim to be the author of many biblical interpretations, and he himself felt encompassed by a wall of hostility. Throughout his lifetime he never wearied of complaining that his innovations were being ascribed to others out of malevolence, and that because of envy he was being denied the place in the firmament of scholarship that was his due.[63]

To reply to his opponents' accusations in *kitāb al-lstīfā,* Abu 'l-Walīd wrote a small book, *Risālat at-tanbīh* ("The Epistle of Information"). In it he clarified, in a thorough manner, some grammatical questions they had discussed in their book; but his tone was mainly one of sarcasm and contempt at their ignorance and lack of understanding of what he had to say.

Shortly thereafter Abu 'l-Walīd wrote another small book. *Kitāb as-Taḳrīb wa 't-tashīl* ("The Book of Approximation and Rectification") is a manual for students of Hebrew grammar written in the form of a commentary upon Ḥayyūdj's writings and designed to facilitate the understanding of Ḥayyūdj's work. In it Abu 'l-Walīd attempted to refute incorrect interpretations of the words of the great Cordovan grammarian. Most of the chapters in this book thus treat of verbs with one weak or gemmate letter.

Abu 'l-Walīd no doubt thought that henceforth he would be able to settle down tranquilly and occupy himself with writing those comprehensive works to which he had, for a long time, given much thought. Through the publication of *The Epistle of Information,* he did, in fact, rid himself of the teasing of his opponents in Saragossa. But meanwhile echoes of the criticism leveled against his first treatise reached him from the Jewish communities of southern Spain. Abu 'l-Walīd's books, *Mustalḥiḳ* in particular, circulated rapidly[64] and were given a reflective reading by scholars of the Hebrew language. Among these, there were former disciples of Ḥayyūdj in Andalusia who viewed Abu 'l-Walīd's book as an insult to their revered master; they claimed that they understood his opinions better than one who had not studied under him.

One day, when Abu 'l-Walīd was at the home of his friend, Abū Sulaimān Ibn Ṭarāḳa, he met a Jew who had come to Saragossa from southern Spain and who transmitted to him some of the arguments that were leveled against him there. A lively discussion promptly ensued, though the visitor tried to avoid it, stressing that he had no concern in the matter and was merely repeating what he had heard. Nevertheless he defended the views of his Andalusian friends on that occasion, and also with other men of learning among Saragossa's Jews when he chanced to meet them, as, for example, in a discussion with one briefly referred to as Samuel the Cantor. After the discussion at Abū Sulaimān Ibn Ṭarāḳa's home, Abu 'l-Walīd put into writing his replies to the arguments the guest had voiced, adding responses he had not made during the discussion, and sent all of them to the Andalusian Jew. But the latter was once again evasive; he wrote that it would be better for him to wait till the Andalusian grammarians published the critique of *The Book of Supplement* they were preparing. However, Abu 'l-Walīd was not to be restrained; he published his replies immediately, giving them the title *Kitāb at-Taswiya* (*Sefer ha-tagmul*—"The Book of Reprisal").[65] In this book he defended himself forcefully against the accusation that he intended, as it were, to lessen the merit of Ḥayyūdj. Provoked by this accusation, he adopted a very sharp tone, protesting that his opponents were involving themselves in a matter that did not pertain to them—that they had no understanding of the rules governing Hebrew.[66]

With the publication of this book, a protracted literary feud began between two factions of Spanish Jewish intellectuals, creating loud reverberations. These debates over the rules of the Hebrew language were not purely theoretical, for the interpretation of the Holy Scriptures, which constitutes the basis of Judaism, depended upon the establishment of the correct grammatical principles. In those remote times, when the natural sciences were at their lowest ebb and all of man's conduct was tied to the commandments of religion and his thinking saturated with religious concepts, every word of the Bible was fraught with great significance: Scripture was the source of both law and thought. For the Jews, therefore, the problems of the national tongue had even greater weight than for the Arabs, who so greatly fostered the science of grammar.

The new literary polemic in which Abu 'l-Walīd became involved was more difficult than the first, as this time one of the greatest scholars of Spanish Jewry stood opposed to him. At the head of the coterie of Ḥayyūdj's admirers in Andalusia, rising to defend his honor against Abu 'l-Walīd's strictures, was Samuel ha-levi, the Nagid, the Jewish vizier of the kingdom of Granada. Since he had, in his youth, been a disciple of Ḥayyūdj, he considered it an obligation to defend his master's writings; and other scholars in Granada and the rest of the cities of Andalusia followed suit. After they had elucidated, through lengthy discussions, the problems raised by Abu 'l-Walīd, the Nagid took it upon himself to frame their responses. Called *Rasā'il ar-rifāḳ* ("The Epistles of the Companions"), these responses were a series of polemic writings published not at once, but one after another.[67] There is no doubt that Abu 'l-Walīd was a greater grammarian than Samuel ha-levi, especially superior in his knowledge of the systems of the Arab philologists. Nevertheless, even the Nagid, in *The Epistles of the Companions,* brought up new viewpoints and made assertions of great weight. He maintained, for example, that in verbs whose last letter is a *hé,* the root actually stems from a *yod,* whereas Abu 'l-Walīd was of the opinion that the root was a *waw.*[68]

Abu 'l-Walīd responded to the arguments of his opponents drawn up by the Nagid with a series of letters later included in a collection called *Kitāb at-Tashwīr* ("The Book of Confounding"). Because these replies, too, were not written at one time, their author returns from time to time to matters he had already discussed; yet this book, which is in four parts, is one of his important treatises.[69] When the first of *The Epistles of the Companions* reached Saragossa, and Abu 'l-Walīd had written the first part of *The Book of Confounding,* he already knew of the existence of additional epistles he had not read.[70] But also in this instance he did not practice restraint and promptly replied to all the arguments in the first epistle.

The Andalusians claimed that Abu 'l-Walīd erred because he relied upon corrupt manuscripts of Ḥayyūdj's writings, whereas they had in their hands the original manuscripts; but this assertion is somewhat dubious and provokes suspicion in the light of quotations from Ḥayyūdj's books cited in other writers' treatises.[71] The language adopted by both groups was venomous: the disputants did not shrink from insulting one another. The Nagid charged the grammarian of Saragossa with ignorance in matters pertaining to Hebrew,[72] while Abu 'l-Walīd, who even accused the defenders of Ḥayyūdj's honor of abandoning his views,[73] did not mention the leader of their faction by name but did speak of his lack of knowledge. As was his habit, he expatiated upon the influence of envy upon his opponents and charged that they were ascribing his innovations to philologists in the Near East.[74] Moreover, he commented on errors in the Arabic style revealed in the *Epistles.*[75] This was, however, the manner of carrying on a scholarly controversy during the Middle Ages, and no one regarded it as being in bad taste.

The contest between the two outstanding scholars and writers of the Spanish Jewish community aroused the attention of intellectuals of every level and even simple people who did not profess to have any say in philological problems. Two factions arose, and a real literary war spread. In behalf of Abu 'l-Walīd were arrayed a number of his friends and devotees in Saragossa and the nearby cities who were attacked in the first of *The Epistles of the Companions* as his "comrades in thought,"[76] whereas Samuel the Nagid was supported by the admirers of Ḥayyūdj and by his own friends in Andalusia. However, even in Saragossa and in the other Jewish communities of northern Spain, not all the scholars sided with Abu 'l-Walīd.

One of the renowned Spanish Jewish writers, Moses b. Samuel Ibn Djiḳaṭilla, who was himself a grammarian of the school of Ḥayyūdj and a biblical exegete, supported the Andalusians.[77] On the other side of the barricade stood a young poet whose name was Abu 'l-Ḥasan Mūsā b. Isḥāḳ Ibn at-Taḳāna. The scion of an esteemed family and an extensively educated person, he dwelt in Saragossa and became known for his poems of praise and scorn. (A Hispano-Jewish writer of that time reports that the poet was killed in an avalanche before he reached his thirtieth birthday—whence his surname, at-Tayyāh, "he who perished on the road.")[78] When the dispute among the grammarians erupted, he wrote a long polemic in verse against Samuel ha-levi, a man who "made books without end," while holding his fellow townsman Jonah Ibn Djanāḥ (Abu 'l-Walīd) to be an exemplary man "who paved the way for the Holy Tongue and opened the gates for its weight and measure."[79]

The literary polemic in which the two camps engaged, each maintaining that it was loyal to Ḥayyūdj, continued even after the publication of *The Epistles of the Companions* and the replies they evoked from Abu 'l-Walīd and his supporters in northern Spain. The Nagid even published a treatise called *Kitāb al-Ḥudjdja* ("The Book of Proof"), wherein he emphatically attached the text of Abu 'l-Walīd's reply to a fourth of his *Epistles.* [80] All these polemic writings were written in the fourth and the first half of the fifth decades of the eleventh century.[81] Thereafter, the last of Ḥayyūdj's disciples in Andalusia having died, the excitement subsided; but even for two generations after that, writers and scholars repeatedly raised and clarified anew the questions over which the disputants had been at issue. Indeed, when Samuel the Nagid died, whoever envied his great achievements but had not dared to utter a word against him during his lifetime now published "epistles" or "treatises" on the grammatical errors in the verse of the distinguished poet from Granada.[82]

At the time that Abu 'l-Walīd was engaged in a dispute with Samuel the Nagid and his faction, he was already a middle-aged man. He felt that the time had come to summarize his life's achievements—to write the comprehensive works he had been preparing for many years. When he approached old age —according to his own words,[83] near the end of the fifth decade of the eleventh century[84]—he made a final redaction of the large amount of material he had gathered and published his magnum opus, whose Arabic title was *at-Tanḳīḥ* ("The Grammar"). It consisted of two parts: The first was named *Kitāb al-Luma'* (*Sefer ha-'arūgōt* or, in Ibn Tibbon's translation, *Sefer ha-riḳma*) and included the grammar in the narrow sense of the term; and the second, *Kitāb al-Uṣūl (Sefer ha-shōrāshīm),* was a lexicon of biblical Hebrew.[85]

In essence, writing a comprehensive account of Hebrew grammar involved an element of novelty, since for the earlier grammarians it sufficed to clarify special problems or to write grammatical surveys as a preface to a Hebrew lexicon. In the manner of the Arab grammarians, whose influence on his research was very great, Abu 'l-Walīd did not present his material in a systematic or clearly constructed way. One can break it down into three principal sections: Chapters 2–9 contain the theory pertaining to letters; chapters 10–24 deal with verb forms and nouns; and chapters 25–34 are concerned with special modes of expression—both as regards the form of words and in respect to syntax, as in the case of word repetition, the use of the singular in place of the plural and vice versa, and the exchange of letters and of words. Apart from the topics he skipped because Ḥayyūdj had already dealt with them in his two Hebrew treatises on verbs, there is practically no problem relating to the rules governing Hebrew that Abu 'l-Walīd did not clarify. The book is based on continuous comparison with biblical Aramaic, with the language of the Mishna, and with Arabic. In his introduction Abu 'l-Walīd justifies his method by arguing that wherever there is no material for comparison in Hebrew, one must depend upon parallel words in Aramaic and Arabic, and he turns for support to the Gaon Rabbi Saadya, who followed this procedure. As sources for his interpretations, Abu 'l-Walīd relied upon the books on the Massora, the *Targumim* (Aramaic versions of the Bible), both Talmuds, the *Tosefta,* the *Sifra,* the *Sifré,* the *Mékhilta,* the *Midrash B'rēshīt Rāba,* and the *Midrash Tanḥūma,* as well as the writings of the Babylonian *geonim,* such as the commentaries of the Gaon Rabbi Sherira on various tractates of the Talmud, the *Ḳitāb al-Ḥāwī* of the Gaon Rabbi Hai, the *Sefer ha-miṣvōt* of Ḥēfeṣ b. Yaṣliaḥ, and, of course, the translations, commentaries, and philological works of the Gaon Rabbi Saadya.[86] Abu 'l-Walīd depended upon all these books primarily to clarify concepts and subjects mentioned in the Bible and not really to explain actual language forms. His dependence on the methods and systems of the Arab grammarians can be felt in almost every chapter; this, at times, leads him into obstacles, since the principles of Arabic grammar are not always similar to those of Hebrew grammar.[87] Nevertheless, the linguistic instinct of Abu 'l-Walīd stood him in good stead, and some chapters of the *Kitāb al-Luma'* match the profound research of recent philologists who are expert in the other Semitic languages and employ modern scientific methods.

Abu 'l-Walīd's lexicon is also a masterwork; it is one of the great achievements of Jewish scholars in the Middle Ages. The *Kitāb al-Uṣūl,* like the *Sefer ha-'ōsher,* written in almost the same period by Samuel the Nagid, was an attempt to gather together the entire store of biblical Hebrew by means of a consistently alphabetical arrangement, extending even to the root's second and third letters and employing the paradigmatic letters *pe, 'ayin,* and *lamed* as indicators of the root letters and as models for the forms of various words. Samuel the Nagid had done a similar thing, but Abu 'l-Walīd's work was more systematic and more crystallized—quantitatively small, as it were, but qualitatively outstanding. Abu 'l-Walīd did indeed aspire to give his lexicon the character of a complete thesaurus of biblical Hebrew. In order not to exceed the bounds of lexicography, however, he did not include the names of personalities, cities, and countries found in the Bible. On the other hand, the *Kitāb al-Uṣūl* does not lack for excursuses on grammatical and exegetical problems. Comparisons of words that are similar in Arabic and Hebrew, for example, take up more space in the *Kitāb al-Uṣūl* than in the *Kitāb al-Luma'.* Although it is clear that it was not Abu 'l-Walīd's intention to exhaust all the linguistic material that lent itself to comparison, nevertheless his comparisons of Hebrew, Aramaic, and Arabic words far exceed in sheer numbers as well as in quality all that had been done in this respect by his predecessors, such as Judah Ibn Kuraish.[88]

During his lifetime Abu 'l-Walīd's works[89] served as textbooks both in Spain and outside, providing the impulse for scholars to carry on their own research and write their own books. For it is the way of geniuses—and Abu 'l-Walīd was one of them—to stir many to productivity and to promote the development of the culture of their age. They are the pioneers who march at the head of the camp, while the multitude follows on their heels. They are the innovators by reason of the divine spark with which they have been endowed, and the many others merely imitate them.

III

While Abu 'l-Walīd Ibn Djanāḥ labored diligently over his grammatical researches at Saragossa, there dwelt in that city one of the greatest Hebrew poets of all the generations. His writings are among the most distinguished Hebrew verse since biblical times. Even in that generation blessed with so many talents, this poet evoked the amazement of everyone familiar with his work, so that he won renown while still a youth. For the Jews of Saragossa, however, he was a completely mysterious person. His fellow townspeople's attitude, a mixture of both admiration and wonder, is reflected in his contemporaries' vague and obscure descriptions of him; and it is also evident from his own verse. Because the life span of this man of many achievements was brief, the riddles connected with his life story are even more numerous: They are like the appearance of a spark, riveting the attention of the onlooker but soon extinguished.

This poet was Solomon b. Judah Ibn Gabirol. The family name, which was pronounced "Ibn Djabīrōl," was a compound of the Arabic word *djabīr* and the Spanish suffix *ol.* The combining of Arabic names and Spanish suffixes to form family names was common in Spain. In a short biography a contemporary Arabic writer devoted to the poet, the author refers to his subject by the commonly accepted name with a slight modification, also customary: Ibn Djabruel. Another version of the same biography uses the name Ibn Djabīr. The poet himself signed his name Gabirol[90] and was known by this name in the literature of later generations. He was also called Solomon ha-Ḳāṭān ("the small"), an appellation which he, at times, used for himself.[91]

Like many writers from the Jewish communities of Saragossa and other towns in the Ebro region, Solomon Ibn Gabirol was an Andalusian Jew who emigrated from southern Spain after the collapse of the Omayyad kingdom. His family dwelt in Cordova at the beginning of the eleventh century, but at the time of the great upheaval in Cordova in the second decade of that century moved from there to the port city of Malaga. There, in 1022, Solomon Ibn Gabirol was born.[92] The change in the family's place of residence no doubt involved many hardships. Ibn Gabirol's family had not even been wealthy in Cordova; they were certainly not numbered among the affluent in Malaga. But the future poet's father was, relatively speaking, an intellectual and held in esteem by his fellow townsmen.[93] When the migratory movement from Andalusia to the banks of the Ebro River increased, Solomon Ibn Gabirol's father decided to test his fortune in Saragossa, the flourishing capital of the Arab rulers of the Tudjībid dynasty. Solomon was still a small child at the time, from which it can be inferred that he received his rearing and education in the city on the Ebro.[94] It was not his father's destiny to supervise his education for long: Solomon Ibn Gabirol was still a young lad when his father died. A short time before his father's death, Solomon's mother had also died, and since he had no brothers or sisters, he remained all alone in the world. Being orphaned at an early age proved to be a hard blow for the delicate and talented youth, but he nevertheless persevered in his studies.

As did other children of his age, he studied the traditional subjects—the threefold curriculum of Bible, Oral Law, and Talmud that was the formal basis of Jewish education throughout the Diaspora. But like the majority of youths in the Jewish communities of Spain who were talented and had a strong desire for broader knowledge, he also acquired a thorough knowledge of Arabic. He steeped himself in Arabic belles lettres, verse, books of diverting tables, and rhetoric. The intellectuals of that era had a vision of general culture that encompassed the fixed transmitted sciences (*al-'ulūm an-naḳliyya,* that is, religion, poetry, philology, and history) and the experimental exact sciences (*al-'ulūm al-'aḳliyya,* that is, knowledge acquired through deductive reasoning, namely, philosophy and the natural sciences). Young Solomon Ibn Gabirol absorbed these subjects both from teachers and from books. He studied logic, philosophy, and mathematics from Greek scientists' and philosophers' books, translated or adapted into Arabic.[95] His very powerful memory and his persistence in his studies benefited him greatly. He became a veritable savant, possessing a deep knowledge of both Jewish wisdom and the secular sciences.

But in spite of all the progress he made in his studies and the pleasure he derived from his achievements, the youth was depressed by his orphanhood. No matter what his age, a person must have—like the air he breathes—the warmth of love and devotion only a family can provide. It is what makes him firm in spirit, strengthening and fortifying him in the face of life's hardships; and the more tender and spiritual a person is, the harder life is without the nest of a family environment. Solomon Ibn Gabirol was such a person. Time and again he was overwhelmed by moments when he loathed life and when it seemed to him that no one's lot was more bitter than his. At such times he would mourn his father, weeping and lamenting his own fate.[96]

Solomon's pride over his accomplishments and the bitterness caused by his loneliness prevented him from making enduring friendships and, as the days went by, even caused troubled relations between him and his fellow townsfolk. While still very young, he composed poems—both secular and religious (for example, *azhārōt*)—that won renown.[97] However, his success made him conceited. In a poem composed when he was seventeen years old, he described his fame as being known in all the lands of the East and West.[98] For other poets he expressed contempt, composing rhymes in which he compared them to ants as against his greatness.[99] At times he would accuse them of stealing rhymes from his poems and preening themselves with them as if they were the product of their own genius.[100] But the very poems in which he denigrated his rivals testify to how avidly he sought recognition: Despite his contempt for other poets he could not conceal his yearning for friendly relationships.

Solomon also wanted to enjoy mundane pleasures, yet even these were denied him. After his father's death he was poverty-stricken and had to rely upon the kindness of patrons. This dependence aggravated his bitterness; he came to feel more and more that he was being humiliated because he was a genius others envied and wanted to crush, and all his days he inclined to irritability and anger. Gripped by these emotions, he attacked his fellow townsmen both by word of mouth and in writing, not sparing even those of high station.[101]

Solomon Ibn Gabirol earned a living by his verse. At times he would be asked to teach a lad, but he was not cut out to be a teacher.[102] As did many Arab poets, he wrote poems extolling rich men and composed rhymed greetings in connection with family events, expecting a proper gift in return. He wrote verse in honor of scholars who were appointed rabbis or presiding officers of the communal court, poems on wedding occasions, and elegies for people who had suffered a loss in their family.[103] Some of the wealthy for whom he wrote poems were not his fellow townspeople but merely men with whom he was acquainted or of whom he had heard, such as a certain Isaac or the wealthy Jacob in whose honor he composed flowery verse, and of course he wrote verse especially for anyone known to be a friend of literature.[104] But most of the men to whom he offered his poems were, like him, inhabitants of Saragossa. In one poem, for example, he addressed himself to three of his companions—Aḥiya, Isaac, and Ḥayyūn—who had set out on a journey, expressing the hope that they would see each other soon.[105]

For a time Ibn Gabirol had a generous supporter in Saragossa who provided for his needs; the benefactor also understood him and appreciated his talents. This man was Yéḳūtiēl Ibn Ḥassān, the dignitary at the royal court of the Tudjībids. Most "patrons" of poets were would-be intellectuals who did not really grasp the character of their verse, but Yéḳūtiēl Ibn Ḥassān was a man of broad knowledge who plumbed the depths of a poet's thinking and understood the allusions embodied in his verse. Consequently, Ibn Gabirol was bound to him by real admiration, which found expression in fervent laudatory verse. The period in which he benefited from Yéḳūtiēl's patronage was the best of his life. When Yéḳūtiēl was killed in the spring of 1039, it nearly broke the heart of the young and highly sensitive poet. He bewailed the death in a number of elegies that show his deep emotions and his great poetical skill; this was a loss he really could not replace.[106]

Yet even after the death of his great patron, Solomon Ibn Gabirol had friends with both understanding and means who gave him assistance. The most important was Samuel ha-levi from Granada. Friendly relations between the poet in Saragossa and the Nagid in Granada had already started during the lifetime of Yéḳūtiēl. When Ibn 'Abbās, the vizier of the kingdom of Almería, who was a bitter foe of Samuel, was vanquished and slain in 1038, Solomon greeted his friend with a fervent poem.[107] Thenceforth the eminent vizier of Granada remembered him with gifts, and ties of friendship based on mutual appreciation bound them together.

The young poet overcame to some degree the pain Yéḳūtiēl's death had caused him and continued with his studies and poetic activity. Some time after Yéḳūtiēl was slain, he wrote a didactic poem entitled " 'Ānāḳ," concerning the rules of Hebrew grammar. Modeled on the didactic poetry of the Arabs, it consisted of 400 verses, and its four sections contained the entire body of Hebrew grammar.[108]

Around that time, however, his weak state of health began to becloud all the poet's ambitions. From his earliest days he was sickly and had to take to his bed periodically.[109] What had seemed at the beginning a passing ailment became a constant illness as time went on, gripping him at frequent intervals and causing him much suffering. It was a skin disease, which expressed itself in swellings and bruises. As he disclosed in his verse, he suffered from sleeplessness during the periods of illness, and it was hard for him to walk even a few steps. In keeping with the custom in those days to exhibit both the beautiful and the ugly, he described with much elaboration the symptoms of his malady in all their loathsome repulsiveness, giving special stress to the pus-filled sores that gnawed at his body.[110] He wrote the poems depicting his illness when he was especially low in spirits because of his suffering. But in any case, his illness, in addition to his loneliness, left its mark upon his emotional makeup. First and foremost, Ibn Gabirol viewed the world as having negative aspects—suffering and ugliness in all their manifold hues.

Ibn Gabirol's approach to human life never changed throughout his lifetime, and its impress is evident in his verse. Hence derives the gloomy spirit of depression and hopeless sadness that overlays so many of his poems and the scorn of possessions and children that he expressed in them.[111]

Aside from this pessimistic outlook, the character of his secular verse was molded particularly through the great influence of Arabic poetry. This influence is readily recognizable in the form of his poems, which have one given rhyme after the fashion of the Arabic *ḳaṣīda,* but particularly in the manner of expression—in the images that are interlaced with biblical allusions and even with words carried over from Arabic. Arabic poets and the Hebrew poets who were influenced by them also found merit in hyperbole; and Solomon Ibn Gabirol waxed eloquent along these lines. Typical of his imitation of Arabic poems is his beginning a poem with a description of night in a garden.[112] Many expressions in Ibn Gabirol's verse indicate concepts taken from Arabic poetry, such as the numerous complaints against treacherous "time"—the vagaries of fate[113] —and "the daughters of the days," the events every day produces.[114] The poet complains of "separation" from his companions, who "have wandered" afar,[115] and at times he actually depicts them as would a Bedouin Arab—mounted on camels as they move further and further away from him.[116] These literary ingredients borrowed from Arabic verse abound in the writings of all the Hebrew poets in Spain, but they are especially abundant in the poems of Ibn Gabirol.

The Arabic influence, however, expresses itself primarily in the poet's choice of subjects. Rural life was even more remote for the Jewish poets of Spain than for their Arab counterparts, but their collections contain many poems describing the grandeur of nature, and there is no lack of them in the *diwan* of Ibn Gabirol. Almost all his nature poems revolve around the Arab poets' themes. He describes the scene of a garden in springtime, the rainfall in the winter months, and the blessings it holds in store.[117] He is moved to wonder by the beauty of the world at sunset[118] and especially by the magic of night, as in a poem in which he depicts a nocturnal storm.[119] In fact, the description of the beauty of nature at night is a prominent element in Hispano-Arabic verse, which, however, describes only sparingly the landscape at sunrise.[120] Ibn Gabirol composed a number of wine songs as well as love songs; there are also poems depicting the desire of a man for a pretty boy, "a graceful gazelle"—a type of verse popular among Arab poets and those Jews who copied them. Solomon's verses dealing with such themes do not appear to reflect true feelings, and it would seem that he wrote them to show that he too could compose these species of verse.[121]

Especially numerous are the poems in which he expresses his longings for friends; this too was a popular theme with the Arabic poets in Spain.[122] The poems in which he addresses himself to those whose friendship, in his opinion, is merely a pretense also display quite plainly the stylistic influence of the Arabs. Indeed, Ibn Gabirol's tendency to praise himself and to stress in biting words his superiority over others did not stem alone from his personal traits; here, too, he imitated many poems written by Arabs. What seemed to people of a later period like boasting seemed to the people of that era decidedly appropriate. Time and again Ibn Gabirol returned to this theme, proclaiming his ability for composing verse[123] while treating his contemporaries with scorn for their utter inferiority, as he does in a long poem addressed to Abu 'l-Ḥasan Ibn Ḥayyūdj.[124] Mordantly sarcastic poems always constituted a significant aspect of Arabic verse, and Solomon Ibn Gabirol in turn directed stinging verses against opponents who seemed envious or anyone he thought had slighted him, at times heaping abuse upon them.[125]

In all these poems, therefore, he did not blaze any trails with respect to style or content. From the verse of Dūnash b. Labraṭ, Isaac Ibn Khalfōn, and Samuel the Nagid, he even copied figures of speech they had invented.[126] Generally speaking, Ibn Gabirol's poems fail to express powerful emotions, and hyperbole is conspicuously prevalent in them. At times opposing tendencies within the poet himself come into conflict with each other in one poem, as he interlaces emotional outflow with cool, rational analysis.

In one aspect, however, Solomon Ibn Gabirol was superior to all the Hebrew poets who had preceded him. He was a master of the language. Although some of his poems are rather slow-moving, most are outstanding for their polish and powerful expression, their elegant style and distinguished manner of utterance, and they contain no unseemly expressions or allusions. By reason of his marvelous command of the storehouse of biblical language, Ibn Gabirol sometimes employed highly uncommon words and coined new ones, such as verbal nouns having the form of *p'īla* on the pattern of the Arabic *maṣdar;* or he gave Aramaic words a Hebrew form. In this manner Ibn Gabirol performed an important function in adapting the archaic biblical language to the needs of the regenerated Hebrew verse.[127]

In his sacred poetry, in contrast to his secular verse, Ibn Gabirol made innovations of his own. To be sure, he sometimes wrote liturgical poetry in the mode of Near Eastern hymnologists, and at times he even imitated them deliberately. But in most of his religious verse, he developed a new style, which came to typify the Hebrew poets in Spain who followed him. The religious poetry of the Oriental Jews was detached from life, all its imagery being taken from the Bible. The hymnal style of the Jews in the Near East was laborious and vague and its language artificial. The hymns of Ibn Gabirol also contain theologico-philosophical elements, as when the poet addresses himself to his "exalted soul"; but their preponderant note lies in their simplicity and in the expression of sincere emotions.

Ibn Gabirol's sacred verse is utterly different from his secular poetry. Anyone reading his sacred poems feels that they emerged from the very depths of the poet's soul. His hymns also surpass those of the Oriental Jews because of their magnificent language, which soars to insurmountable heights. In the "r'shūyōt," which are short proems to prayers, the poet stresses man's insignificance and pleads that he therefore be forgiven by the Creator of heaven and earth. By intensifying his expression, Ibn Gabirol succeeds, in these small hymns, in summoning from his innermost being his intense, latent yearning. Even more, his unadulterated faith in God's mercy emerges from these hymns. In the "tōkhāḥōt," as in the "*r'shūyōt,*" the poet speaks of the troubles that plague man—his material and spiritual poverty—ultimately arriving at an acknowledgment of divine judgment. A considerable number of these hymns are distinguished by a masterly form and some by repetitive imagery patterned on Arabic verse. Many others end in fragments of verses called *mustodjāb* whose last word is always the same. The hymns that are preludes to the daily prayers, such as the *yōṣēr, bār'khū,* and *ḳaddīsh,* are sublime laudatory poems to the Holy One, blessed be He, in which the poet speaks of His essence and His deeds, interlacing his verse with selections from mystical folklore. In hymns intended to precede the reading of the *Sh'ma',* his verse is a paean to the Creator of the universe; and in those designated for the repetition of the *'Amīda* prayer (*ḳ'rōbhōt*), he praises God's deeds on Israel's behalf. Again in the "ahābhōt" the poet dwells on the link between the *Sh'khīna* ("Divine Presence") and the Jewish nation, which it has not forsaken even in its exile. These poems, which pour forth devotion to God, self-sacrifice, and belief in the future, at times become real love songs through use of figures of speech culled from the Song of Songs.[128]

Ibn Gabirol was quite familiar with the ancient kabbalistic lore and in the hymns called "ōfānīm" mentioned the names of the angels in passing. In the hymn "Shin'ānīm Sha'anānīm," which is based on the description of the *Merkābha* ("the Chariot") in the Bible and in the folklore of the literature of mysticism, he introduces hosts of angels who sing sweet melodies as they stand at their guard posts.[129]

Among the most exalted of Ibn Gabirol's poetical creations are the "g'ūlōt" and the other poems wherein he expresses his yearning for the redemption of Israel as God's people. In these hymns he lays his complaints before the Creator in a bitter outcry against the sufferings of his people. He describes in picturesque language the gloom of exile and in most instances ends with an expression of faith and hope. In a quiet, sorrowful voice the poet humbly turns to his God only to ask why such a thing was done. The poems in which Solomon Ibn Gabirol voices the national yearnings of the Jewish people are superior to those resembling them written by the other Hebrew poets in Spain. In these hymns there is no artificiality and no hyperbole. The same Ibn Gabirol who, in his secular verse, is clearly a child of secular eleventh-century Arabic Spain—the poet in the palaces of the "benefactors"—appears here as the spokesman for the Jewish people throughout the generations; a Jew loyal to his people, who hurts with the pain of the Jew wherever he may be and yearns for his redemption.[130] Indeed, a Hispano-Jewish writer who lived two generations later reported that the great poet engaged in eschatological computations.[131]

Solomon Ibn Gabirol produced his numerous and eminent poetical creations when encompassed by many hardships. His poor health and his dependence on the generosity of patrons and wealthy men oppressed him and increasingly embittered his life. As long as he enjoyed the patronage of Yéḳūtiēl Ibn Ḥassān he did not need to worry about the next day, and even his foes refrained from harming him to avoid conflict with the powerful official who protected him. However, after Yéḳūtiēl's death, all this changed. Time and again in poems he inveighed against his benefactors for neglecting him and not keeping their promises; an example is the poem he sent to Ibn Manṣūr b. Manasseh Ibn al-Ḳauṣar. Sometimes he would confess it was his own fault that they kept their distance from him, and he would endeavor to appease them.[132] In any case, relations between him and people in general worsened over the years. During his youth people could more readily forgive the poet his arrogance, as self-praise was, as already indicated, the hallmark of versifiers in those days, and in general during that era people openly stressed their individuality and accomplishments, not attempting to conceal such feelings. This was all the more the case for those who were in the forefront culturally. Even Samuel the Nagid designated himself "unique in his generation," having himself established new interpretations in the sacred law while the learning of the other scholars was barren.[133] But when Solomon reached maturity, no one found any reason to forgive him his pride.

Nevertheless, Ibn Gabirol remained in Saragossa for a long time. It was in that period that his friendship with Samuel the Nagid grew in strength. The Jewish vizier from Granada gave him material assistance and encouraged him to continue following his way of life, and Ibn Gabirol was grateful to the Nagid for his generosity and full of admiration for his wonderful personality. From time to time he would send him a fervently laudatory poem, especially when a new work the Nagid had written would arrive at Saragossa.[134] In accordance with the practice of the poets in that era, who would refer to a person by another appellative resembling his or alluding to him, Ibn Gabirol at times would adorn the Nagid with the title "Ben Solomon," an allusion to the Nagid's writings *Ben Mishlē* and *Ben Ḳōhēlēt.*[135]

But Samuel the Nagid dwelt in faraway Granada, while in Saragossa itself the poet was isolated and alone. The absence of any reference in his poetry to family life implies that he was a bachelor all his life. Also in this aspect of his life, fortune did not shine upon him. He was short and ugly, so women were not attracted to him.[136] Meanwhile his malady attacked him repeatedly, bringing him to the threshold of despair. But he clung to life, being convinced that he was born to be a great creator in the fields of poetry and speculative philosophy. The pen never left his hand. Besides poetry and philosophy, he found much of interest in ethical writings and collected aphorisms on the characteristics of men from Arabic books, such as Ibn Ḳutaiba's *'Uyūn al-akhbār* and Ibn 'Abd Rabbihi's *al-'Iḳd al-farīd.* The product of this preoccupation was his book *Mukhtār al-djawāhir,* which was translated into Hebrew in the twelfth century and called *Mibhḥar ha-p'nīnīm* ("Choice of Pearls").[137] However, for all that he sought to submerge himself in meditation and literary creativity, the circumstances of his life pressed hard upon him, becoming almost unendurable. Sometimes he would make friendly overtures to one of Saragossa's or a nearby Jewish community's eminent men, such as the grammarian Abu 'l-Walīd Ibn Djanāḥ, to whom he addressed, among other things, a poem in Aramaic.[138] However, such attachments were of temporary duration. Relations between the Jews of Saragossa and the poet, whom they regarded as a strange, inordinately arrogant person, grew worse from year to year, and gradually he came to the decision to leave the city.

In 1045, while he still dwelt in Saragossa, Ibn Gabirol wrote an Arabic treatise entitled *Iṣlāḥ al-akhlāk* (in Hebrew, *Tiḳḳūn ha-middōt*—"Improvement of Character"). This is a small compilation of verses from the Bible and sayings of Greek and Arabic sages concerning the good and bad traits of man.[139] But shortly thereafter he left Saragossa in order to seek a more pleasant dwelling place where he would find fellow intellectuals who could understand his inner nature and show him proper esteem. When he departed from Saragossa, he wrote two poems in which he revealed his exasperation and ire at the malign attitude from which he suffered during his many years there. In the poem "My Throat Is Parched with Crying Out," he fulminated against them:

They are a people whose forefathers I despise
Too mean to be dogs for my sheep
Their faces do not turn red

Except they paint them with scarlet
In their own eyes they are giants
In mine—they are but grasshoppers.

And in the poem "What, O My Soul" he speaks, as it were, to his soul, saying:

Return, O my soul, to God
Return and refresh thy heart
Make supplication to Him
And let thy tears also well up before Him
Perchance He will command that thou be sent
From the pit wherein thou liest
Among boorish men
Whom thou dost hate and despise.[140]

In this verse the poet also expresses his intention to leave Spain altogether for the Near East; but in point of fact he never ventured so far away.

His first destination was of course Granada, the "pomegranate city," the home of his benefactor the Nagid. Dwelling in the shadow of the sage and learned vizier, who appreciated him sincerely, afforded him much gratification and actually refreshed his soul. The friendship the Nagid openly showed for the young poet naturally established the attitude of his circle; the Nagid's intimates and subordinates esteemed Ibn Gabirol and did all they could to make his stay in Granada pleasant. Ibn Gabirol, in turn, was filled with admiration when he came to know the Nagid face to face and expressed it in poems he presented to him.[141] From time to time the Nagid was compelled to leave Granada because of a military campaign or to carry out an assignment connected with the management of the government administration. These temporary separations provided the young poet with an opportunity to express anew in verse the greatness of his admiration and love for the Nagid.[142] Nevertheless, after a time Ibn Gabirol himself left Granada. No doubt he felt that he was not constituted to be a courtier and that it was best, therefore, that he not prolong his stay. In any event, he parted from the Nagid with expressions of cordiality and made him a gift of a poem of parting.[143]

The tie between the Nagid and the poet continued; as before the vizier sent Ibn Gabirol gifts together with rhymed letters, to which the poet replied with verses of thanksgiving.[144] But when people find themselves far apart from each other, possibilities develop for misunderstanding and estrangement. After his departure from Granada, Ibn Gabirol did not attain a state of rest and security but continued to search for friends and supporters among the Jewish communities of Spain, meeting instead with much disappointment. At times an anguished cry burst from the heart of the afflicted and sickly poet as he addressed himself to the Nagid, who he thought had forsaken him.[145] In the meantime, in Granada, there was someone who spoke slanderously about him to the Nagid. For even in the Jewish community of Granada, alas, Ibn Gabirol had unintentionally made enemies. There, too, some people thought him an outsider; and such a one will not be liked by the ordinary folk. They brought it to the attention of the Nagid that in the verse Ibn Gabirol wrote in his honor, he never spoke of his greatness as a statesman, as did the poetasters who heaped flattery upon anyone who had achieved greatness. Even more, they charged him with not praising the Nagid's poetry in a fitting manner. At times they even whispered that the poet from Saragossa made disparaging comments on the Nagid's own verse; and indeed in a careless moment Ibn Gabirol had written concerning the Nagid's poems that they were as cold as the "chill of the night." News of this, no doubt, reached the Nagid speedily, and he responded with stinging words. Solomon felt that he had overstepped his bounds—he had repaid his benefactor with evil. Although he was then far from Granada, he undertook the hardship of a long journey to return to the Nagid's residence and present him with a poem expressing his apology.[146] However, the reconciliation was only temporary. Talebearers again made accusations against Ibn Gabirol to the Nagid, who became filled with rage at the ungrateful poet. Ibn Gabirol endeavored to allay his anger; when a new poem by the Nagid reached him, he sent him a short verse, "The song of the psalmists Asaph and Heman/Is like your song which can quicken the dead," wherein he urged him to give no heed to "slanderers."[147] As before, the Nagid showed forbearance and suppressed his anger, so that the ties between the two eminent cultural leaders were not broken.

When Samuel ha-levi decided to have his son Joseph marry the daughter of Rabbi Nissīm, and the great rabbi from Kairawān agreed to his proposal, the Nagid also sent an invitation to Ibn Gabirol to participate in his happiness. Again the poet made the journey to Granada, where he passed the time in company with the Nagid and his family. On this occasion he even attended the learning sessions given by Rabbi Nissīm and afterwards composed a poem in his honor in which he praised the rabbi highly and called himself his disciple.[148]

But soon after the wedding, Ibn Gabirol again left Granada and continued his wanderings. The circumstances of his life were especially hard at that time. He suffered attacks of skin disease at more frequent intervals, and his weakened physique became vulnerable to other maladies. Being a constant wanderer, he was unable to make regular use of a large number of books. This made it necessary for him to rely on his memory, which was indeed remarkable. And it was during these years that Ibn Gabirol was engaged in writing his great philosophical works, revising and completing one book after another.

One of these books, since disappeared, was his essay on the

soul. In this book, which, like his other philosophical works, was written in Arabic, he described the psychological faculties in terms very similar to the psychological tenets of Avicenna.[149] Of another treatise only its name is known: *Maḳālat aḍ-diyā wa'ẓ-ẓalām* ("The Essay concerning Light and Darkness").[150] Yet another of his works can be translated as *The Origin and Cause of Being.* This was a treatise dealing with the divine will, its effect and impress on the created substance. Ibn Gabirol dwelt on the question of where the will of God manifests itself as a visible creative force and where it remains hidden; and he expatiated in particular on the phases of His activity manifest in the creation of the universe.[151]

After having written these treatises, Ibn Gabirol summarized his philosophic views in his book *M'ḳōr ḥayyīm* ("The Fountain of Life"), which was written in the form of a dialogue between a teacher and his disciple. Apparently he did not succeed in giving this great work its finishing touches, for it is replete with wearying repetitions. Nevertheless, it is a profound metaphysical work based on a fundamental acquaintance with the schools of philosophy then widespread throughout the Arab world, including Aristotle's. Ibn Gabirol was familiar with Aristotle's philosophy primarily through the writings of Abū Naṣr al-Fārābī (d. 950), who was called *al-mu'allim ath-thānī*—"the second teacher"—after Aristotle, who was, of course, the first. From this philosphy he derived the great principle that all objects existing in the universe are composed of matter and form, that is, from raw matter and from the element that makes it unique and differentiates it from other substances. From the Alexandrine philosophers, who developed the Neoplatonic system of thought, he carried over the assumption that the contradiction between the undivided, sublime, and infinite divinity and the numerous created beings, base and limited as to time and space, cannot be explained except by the concept of intermediation. Although the Arabs were unfamiliar with the writings or even the name of Plotinus, the greatest of Neoplatonic philosophers, books explaining his doctrine and attributed to ancient Greek philosophers such as Pythagoras, Empedocles, Plato, and Aristotle were circulated among them.

In the tenth century various writings ascribed to Empedocles—thought to be a disciple of King David—were brought from the Near East to Spain by the philosopher Muḥammad b. ʿAbdallāh Ibn Masarra (d. 931). One of these was *The Book on the Five Substances,* which exerted a potent influence on philosophic thought in those generations. Aristotle's *Theology,* which had already been translated into Arabic in the ninth century, had disseminated among the Arabs the doctrine of emanations—the basis of Neoplatonism. The *Treatise on the Causes,* a much-read work, contained a digest of this doctrine as summarized by the Neoplatonist philosopher Proclus. Without accepting all the philosophical principles as he found them in these works, Ibn Gabirol was nevertheless influenced greatly by them: They shaped his approach, giving it a Neoplatonist semblance.

At the time that Ibn Gabirol lived in Saragossa, *Rasāʾil Ikhwān aṣ-Ṣafā* ("The Epistles of the Pure Brethren") was being circulated within the city. This encyclopedia of a society of philosophers in Baṣrah and Baghdad had been brought to Spain by Abu ʾl-Ḥakam ʿUmar al-Kirmānī, who, like Ibn Gabirol, was a native of Malaga who dwelt for a long time in the city on the Ebro, dying there in 1066 at the age of 90.[152] There can be no doubt that Ibn Gabirol had perused the *Epistles;* it was primarily from this work, also written in the Neoplatonic cast of thought, that he received his views on nature.[153]

The difference between Ibn Gabirol's system of thought and that of pure Neoplatonism expresses itself in his understanding of the concept of the Godhead. In his system the concept is not as unified as it is with the Neoplatonists: Ibn Gabirol felt a distinction should be made between mathematical unity, as human beings understand it, and metaphysical unity, which is the unity of God.[154] In contradistinction to the Neoplatonists' concept of the immanence of God, Ibn Gabirol put forth the concept of a transcendental Godhead existing beyond the world of created beings. As a Jew he believed in the creation of the universe as a consequence of a decision of God. In combining Neoplatonic ideas and conceptual elements of ancient Jewish mysticism as expressed in *Sēfer y'ṣīra* ("The Book of Creation"), Ibn Gabirol saw the "Will of God" as a force that creates *ex nihilo.* The "Will," from the aspect of existence, is identical with God, yet apart from Him as concerns His activity. By means of the Will, substances are brought from a potential to an actual state; His Will creates the form and unites it with primordial matter He Himself created directly.[155] Assigning the creative function to the divine Will frees the existence of the universe from the necessity of a process of emanations—a doctrine assumed by Neoplatonism.

The central problem the Neoplatonists sought to solve by their system was, as mentioned before, the creation of the world by the Godhead. In order to explain how substances, highly diversified but finite, were created by the undivided and infinite Godhead, these philosophers assumed the existence of intermediate stages in the creation of the universe. Solomon Ibn Gabirol accepted in its entirety the concept of emanations promulgated by the Alexandrine philosophers, and he diligently applied himself to proving that the creation of the world was achieved by means of spiritual forces, with each one creating the next. Like the idea advanced in the Neoplatonic treatise on the five substances attributed to Empedocles, Ibn Gabirol believed that God had created primordial matter to which His Will had given form until it became the "Intellect." In turn, the Intellect created the "Soul," and the Soul created "Nature." These are the energetic forces that emanate from each other. Our world, the world of the senses, is, as a product of Nature, at the lowest level; for every emanation is lower and inferior to the one that begot it. Ibn Gabirol held, as did Plotinus in his day, that even the simple, spiritual substances that mediate between God and our world are combinations of matter and form, but in his opinion there is no difference between the "matter" of these substances and the matter of the world of the senses. "Matter" is the designation for the ability to receive form—the passive state of the inchoate mass. "Matter" does not become more inferior as it is further removed from the primal source, God, but the "form" of the corporeal makes it into a body. The "form" is therefore something that exists in another thing, completing the existence of its subject.[156] Since the spiritual substances, namely the first emanations, are compounded of matter and form, there is no contradiction at all between the world of the spirit and that of the senses. There is no contradiction in values between them; that is to say, the world of the senses is not originally evil. This unifying conception of the two worlds is the apogee of theological speculation in the Middle Ages.

The goal toward which the philosopher, like every religious person, aspires is the cognition of God, which will cause the soul to return to its source. In the manner of Neoplatonists, Ibn Gabirol held that this end can be achieved by contemplation, meditation, and good deeds, but primarily by freeing the soul from the fetters of materialism through the ecstasy of devotion.

Even though the important elements in the philosophic system of Ibn Gabirol are not his own, their combination and elaboration into an integrated structure based on logical proofs constituted a wonderfully thought-out architectural achievement. In spite of various discrepancies, his system is impressive in its decisive conclusiveness. Despite being influenced by the Neoplatonism that dominated thought in his day, Ibn Gabirol succeeded to some degree in freeing himself from it and in maintaining the theological position of Judaism, basing his work on the concept of a personal God who created the world according to His Will. In contrast to the pessimism that informs his secular poetry, he remains faithful to the optimism that lies at the heart of Judaism.

Nevertheless, the majority of Jewish intellectuals who read *M'ḳōr ḥayyim* were astounded when they contemplated the great differences between it and the other books on philosophy that circulated among them. Most of these had been written in order to bring about harmony between Arabo-Hellenic philosophic thought and the belief in a religion based on God's revelation, and yet Ibn Gabirol had written his work as if there were no rift between them—or so it seemed to Jewish readers. Even more, no references to biblical verses or sayings of the Talmud were to be found in it. It consequently aroused opposition, and in time it was forgotten by the Jewish intellectuals who studied books of philosophy—especially after Aristotelian philosophy thrust aside the Neoplatonic system. On the other hand, Ibn Gabirol's book was translated into Latin at Toledo in the twelfth century; and the system of "Avicebron," as they called him, was much discussed in the scholastic philosophy of the Christian clergy, who considered him to be one of them or else a Moslem. Thus many centuries went by without his identity being known, until a Jewish Orientalist rediscovered it in the nineteenth century.[157] Thus the lot of the poet-philosopher after his death was as it had been in his life—that of a misunderstood man who provoked opposition.

It is somewhat ironic, then, that Ibn Gabirol wrote his book *The Fountain of Life* as a metaphysical study with its own place but devoted other works to the purpose of harmonizing his philosophical system with the Jewish religion. One was a commentary on the Bible (or on sections of it) that was lost except for some quotations in the writings of a later author. Ibn

Gabirol's commentary was written in his own philosophic spirit; by making use of allegorical interpretation, he meant to harmonize his Neoplatonic viewpoint with traditional faith based on Scripture. So, for example, he explained that the river going out of Eden described in Gen. 2:10 is primordial matter. Like most contemporary philosophers, Ibn Gabirol maintained the Aristotelian view of the existence of three spirits on different levels: The simplest is the vegetal; the intermediate one, the animalistic stage; and the highest, the intellectual. Hence he interpreted the serpent (in Gen. 3:1) to be the symbol of the vegetal spirit; Eve, that of the animalistic spirit; and Adam, who gave a name to every object, that of the intellectual spirit. Adam—so goes Ibn Gabirol's explanation—was initially a spiritual substance who did not come down to the corporeal state until he was driven from the world of pure substances, that is, until he was expelled from the Garden of Eden (Gen. 3:24).[158]

In the same spirit Ibn Gabirol composed the poem "The Royal Crown," the greatest and the most distinguished of his poetical creations. It is a depiction of the universe according to the scientific views current at that time. The earth is at the center of the universe and is surrounded by nine moving spheres, one inside the other. Seven of these heavenly spheres, or "wheels," are planets. Above them is the zodiac, but the ninth wheel above it is called the "diurnal" sphere because it completes its round in the course of one day. The poet sets out in spirit on two journeys from the lowest to the highest region of the entire universe, beholding hosts of angels and the places where the sinners and the righteous dwell; but he also depicts the life of man from the day of his birth until his death. The poem also contains a complete confessional prayer,[159] and therefore it was included in the prayerbook for the Day of Atonement, for which it may have been originally designated. This union of scientific scrutiny with lyrical effusion was in accordance with the taste of the intellectuals in the Middle Ages; even the Arabic poets in Spain enjoyed describing journeys through the starry universe.[160] But even later generations, which believed there was no room in a poetical creation for data concerning the measurements of celestial spheres and the speed of their circuits, admired the poem's structure and its magnificent style.[161]

Ibn Gabirol completed all these works by the time he reached his thirties; shortly thereafter he died while still in his prime. When he left Granada the second time, after participating in the celebration of the nuptials of Samuel the Nagid's son Joseph, he set forth for the East, reaching Valencia. Since this port city did not boast many intellectuals, he assumed that he would be welcomed with open arms. But Ibn Gabirol's stay in Valencia did not last long: he died there a short time after arriving. A Hispano-Hebrew poet of the following generation reports that he died in Valencia after he was thirty years old, in the ninth century of the fifth millennium[162]—approximately in the year 1054.[163]

IV

The works of Abu 'l-Walīd, Ibn Gabirol, and other writers testify, as though they were a thousand witnesses, to the great influence Arabic culture exerted upon the cultural life of the Jews in Moslem Spain. These writers and scholars had recourse to the lore of the Arabs in the secular sciences, but in the generation following that of Abu 'l-Walīd and Ibn Gabirol another Jewish writer went far beyond them, daring to carry over ideas from Moslem theology to the religious thought of the Jews. In keeping with Jewish practice in past centuries to foster remembrance of literary works while neglecting the memory of the writers, very little is known about this thinker who gave Jewish literature one of its most original works.

The man was Abū Isḥāḳ Baḥyā b. Joseph Ibn Paḳūda,[164] a member of a family long settled on the banks of the Ebro. The family name, Ibn Paḳūda (or Baḳūda), testifies to this; it is a Spanish name by which even Christians were called in that period.[165] The given name—Baḥyā—was also common, especially among the Jews who dwelt in the Ebro region.[166] Baḥyā Ibn Paḳūda himself lived in Saragossa, the city of Abu 'l-Walīd and Ibn Gabirol, as is expressly stated in manuscripts of the later Middle Ages.[167] He was born apparently in the fourth decade of the eleventh century, and became a scholar of distinction, well versed in all branches of Jewish lore, a man to whom the intricacies of the Talmud and the homiletic interpretations of the Aggada were entirely familiar. In time he was appointed to a judge's bench; consequently the title *ha-dayyān* ("the judge") was usually appended to his name. But like so many of the Jewish scholars in Moslem Spain, he did not neglect the study of the secular sciences. He was interested in mathematics, such as the Greek Euclid's works, which had already been translated at an earlier period into Arabic.[168] He read the books of the Arab philosophers and was, of course, quite familiar with the writings of the Jewish scholars who followed along their paths in an endeavor to erect a structure of Jewish theology based upon rational proofs and rules of logic. But in a very special manner, he was attracted to the books of the Moslem mystics, as well as those by Moslem ascetics—that branch of Arabic literature called *Zuhd.*

These books served as guides to the direction Baḥyā Ibn Paḳūda took in life. They molded his thought and character. On the one hand he became an eminent Arabic stylist, distinguished for his fine sense of language, and on the other he adapted to his purposes the views of Moslem ascetics, who were revolted by the identification of religion with the enactments introduced by Moslem jurisprudence. Baḥyā Ibn Paḳūda was enraged at those zealous rabbis who regarded the strict observance of the religious precepts of the Written and Oral Laws as all important. Their extreme punctiliousness regarding the Written Law was linked, in his view, to neglect of genuine devotion and seemed to him to strangle the wellspring of religious being, turning it into a matter of rote; for without real devotion there is neither rhyme nor reason. But when he expressed his opinion before learned Jews in his city, arguing that it does not suffice for a person to rely on what the ancient rabbis had enacted, he provoked their strong opposition.[169] At times, Baḥyā himself felt that he was being influenced too much by the ideas of the Moslems and would then back away. These recoilings, however, were temporary, while his belief grew ever stronger in his ability to blend Moslem concepts with the Jewish tradition and to make an important contribution toward the refinement of the religious life of his people.

In the third quarter of the eleventh century, when fully aware of this goal, he wrote *al-Hidāya ilā farā'id al-ḳulūb* ("The Guide to the Duties of the Heart").[170] It was Baḥyā Ibn Paḳūda's aim to write a guide to pure religion in which profound feelings would charge the observance of the commandments with rich content. He wanted to rouse within those who read his book the inclination to asceticism as an expression of the worship of God in addition to the fulfillment of the commandments in the Written and the Oral Law. In order to bring them to this stage and to make it a matter of conviction, he endeavored to base the commandments and the supplemental asceticism upon logical reasons.

On the assumption that it is necessary to have a religious consciousness in order to worship God wholeheartedly, Baḥyā placed two chapters at the beginning of his book that serve as a theological preface. Chapter 1 ("The Gate of Unity") contains demonstrations of God's existence. As many of his theologian contemporaries had done, Baḥyā sought to prove that everything that exists in the universe is finite and composite, and that hence there is one Creator Who is truly a unity. Although it is beyond our power to comprehend His essence, we can observe living creatures and draw certain conclusions. This is the theme of chapter 2, in which the author explains the usefulness of the creation of the universe, whose crowning glory and final goal is man. Recognition of this obligates man to obey and worship God.

In chapter 3 Baḥyā predicates that the soul is an alien spiritual essence in the material world. In being combined with the corporeal body, the soul is given a test in which it will be successful if it is reinforced by the worship of God, by the fulfillment of the commandments, and by the acquisition of qualities that will bring it nearer to the Creator of the universe. One of the most important of these qualities is the sense of trust in God (described in chapter 4) which alone can confer tranquillity upon man. Yet another quality, no less important, is sincerity in the worship of God. In the chapter devoted to this theme (chapter 5), Baḥyā explains that our intent in whatever we do must be pleasing to God, whether our action is overt or covert. Baḥyā borrowed this concept of "unity of action" (in Arabic, *ikhlāṣ al-'amal*) from the religious thought of Islam; like the Moslem theologians he depicted the struggle with the impulses, indispensable for anyone desirous of acquiring this quality for himself, as taking on the aspect of a holy war *(djihād)*. The evil impulse within man's heart confuses him and lures him away from the traditional faith to the point where he becomes a heretic. The believer is therefore obliged to struggle with this impulse unremittingly, and Baḥyā supplies him with rules for this struggle.[171] In order to ascend the ladder of devotion, a person must overcome his pride and acquire submissiveness (explained in chapter 6), a step toward the acquisition of added virtues.

Baḥyā also made use of the concepts of Moslem asceticism

to define the quality of submissiveness and to clarify the means to its attainment. Sincerity in the worship of God and submissiveness will, naturally, effect in man a turning away, in penitence, from wrong behavior. In chapter 7, the chapter on repentance, Ibn Paḳūda analyzed the various stages involved in this, such as contrition, forsaking of sin, a plea for forgiveness, and the assurance that there will be no reversion to evil ways. Again in his thinking he followed the Moslem ascetics, though he avoided the Moslem doctrine that the sin was decreed.[172] As an indispensable condition for the prevention of sin and a return to a state of repentance, it is necessary to engage constantly in self-examination. Baḥyā assigned an entire chapter (chapter 8) to this theme, in which he enumerated the matters to be examined. In addition, in order to worship God wholeheartedly, continence is necessary. Quite naturally, Baḥyā, influenced by the Moslem mystics, meted out an excess of praise for asceticism; but he classified ascetics according to the degree to which they coordinated their lives with the Written Law. In his opinion the ascetics closest to God are those who do not withdraw from their fellow men.[173] The goal of the believer who follows the path counseled by Baḥyā is to achieve a love of God that will overwhelm him, so that he becomes oblivious to all else. In the last chapter of his book, in which he dealt with this theme, Baḥyā explained that to achieve this love it is necessary to acquire a double measure of the other qualities—that is, sincerity and submissiveness and the like. As did the Moslem writers, Baḥyā enumerated the signs that distinguish a person who has attained this stage of devotion to God and also conveyed at length the words of the renowned Moslem mystic Dhu-'n-Nūn.[174]

The marked aspect of the book—called in Hebrew *Ḥōbhōt ha-l'bhābhōt* ("The Duties of the Heart"), which is its abbreviated title—is its electic character. In its first chapters it sets before the reader the philosophical views current at the time. The opinion that faith must be based on intellectual cognition is a tenet of the Mu'tazilites. The ideas Ibn Paḳūda needed for his proof of the existence of God he found in the literature of the *Kalām* and its Jewish followers, especially in the books of David al-Muḳammiṣ and the Gaon Saadya. But he did not copy their words without adding a comment of his own, thereby imparting a certain degree of originality to his work.[175] The concept of God and His attributes and the view concerning man and the soul are culled from Neoplatonic philosophy, whose ideas, so widely accepted among the Arabs of Baḥyā's generation, were circulated by means of *The Epistles of the Pure Brethren.*[176]

Aside from being attracted to the views of contemporary philosophers, Baḥyā was especially influenced by Moslem asceticism. The essence of the idea expressed by the very title of the book—namely, that one must differentiate between the commandments that call for action by the body's limbs and the commandments of the heart—is itself a concept of the Moslem devotees of the school of Ḥasan al-Baṣrī.[177] The structure of the book, based on the hierarchy of degrees of one's closeness to God, is so close to the books of the *Zuhd,* such as the *Ḳūt al-ḳulūb* by Abū Ṭālib Muḥammad b. 'Alī al-Makkī (d. 996), that it is sometimes thought to be a translation of that book or of some other Arabic treatise. But a careful comparison of *The Duties of the Heart* with such works also reveals how its author endeavored with all his might not to be too much influenced by the Moslem writers and to preserve the Jewish character of his system of asceticism. Typical of this is his position relating to "trust" (chapter 4): He clearly dissociates himself from all the Moslem writers who, in consonance with the tenets of their faith, treat affirmatively anyone who rejects personal effort to make a living and merely depends upon God.[178] Baḥyā condemns the hermits who withdraw from group living, acclaiming, instead, the middle road. The truly abstemious person in his opinion is one who always acts as if God were before his very eyes and at the same time attempts to discharge the obligations of human society. Baḥyā rejects exaggerated asceticism, such as fasting on a festival day or abstinence from family life, and he is, of course, careful not to carry over from the books of the *Zuhd* ideas that bear a Christian stamp.[179]

Under no circumstance was Baḥyā attracted to the Moslem writers to the point where he would write a book in the true spirit of Moslem mysticism. The author of *The Duties of the Heart* does not, for example, discuss mystic radiance, which a believer would merit by following the path marked out by him; and as for the love of God, to which he devotes the last chapter of his book, he believes it to be not the highest level but rather the totality of the qualities that can be attained. Baḥyā sought not the mystic union with the Godhead toward which the seers aspire but a love derived from reverence for the remote.[180]

Nevertheless, Baḥyā's book bears the stamp of the symbiotic relationship between Jews and Arabs that crystallized in Moslem Spain; and this is felt in it more than in the works of other contemporary Jewish writers. Not only did he borrow ever so many ideas and concepts from Arabic literature and cite many sayings ascribed to Mohammed and the pioneers of Islam[181] and even phrases from the Koran,[182] but also the very views he propounded were not quite in keeping with official Jewish tenets. Thus the idea that observance of the commandments of the Written and Oral Law does not in itself assure attainment of religious perfection but must be augmented for this purpose, and the absence of emphasis on the chosenness of the Jewish people or any expression of their national yearnings, set *The Duties of the Heart* apart from the majority of the books by medieval Jewish philosophers and theologians. Yet Baḥyā Ibn Paḳūda's book is characteristic of the views held by many Spanish Jews in that era; as proof, consider his observations on the value of occupation with the sciences,[183] words which no Jew, writing a similar book in another era, would have uttered.[184] All this notwithstanding, Baḥyā's book won the affection of pious Jews everywhere for many generations.[185]

As was the case with many scholars in Spain, Baḥyā tested his skill at composing religious hymns. He mentions two in his book. One, a "Poem of Rebuke," was accepted into the Yōm Kippūr prayerbook in Spain and Italy; the other is a supplicatory hymn. Both lack a fixed meter and rhyme. The "Rebuke" deals with the themes Baḥyā discusses in chapter 3 of *The Duties of the Heart,* namely, the origin of the soul and its intended purpose within the body.[186] In the "Supplication" he speaks of the Creator of the universe and the soul of man, including within it a confession in the form of an alphabetical acrostic.[187]

2

DIARY OF A JEW IN ELEVENTH-CENTURY SPAIN

I

Among the myriads of Spanish Jews who were not conspicuous for their deeds, who did not become officials at the courts of the kings nor even poets or writers who left behind important works, thereby gaining enduring fame, there lived in that era in Toledo a Jew whose name was Abū Ya'ḳūb Yūsuf.[1] He was forty years old and a man of consequence, a person who earned an ample living and whom people regarded with respect. He was engaged in the business of expensive textiles, especially silks. For some time now he had been in contact with manufacturers in Almería and elsewhere in Andalusia. The merchandise he bought from them he sold through his agents in northern Spain in the principal cities of León and Castile, where the demand for silk clothes was great.[2]

While many of the Jews of Toledo lived in rented houses in the Jewish quarter not a few of which were owned by Moslems and Christians, Abū Ya'ḳūb's dwelling was in his own house.[3] To be sure, the house was old, but it was well built and relatively spacious. The pillars were of ashlar and the walls between them, of clay, bricks and cement, were patterned on the construction method the Spaniards had taken over from the Romans, as it added much strength to their houses.

A long corridor led from the outer gate and made a right-angled turn to an inner door by which one reached a square inner courtyard. The courtyard was paved with slabs of clay, large and small, on which were figures such as small stars of many varieties. On every side of the courtyard was a narrow path made of bricks placed atop the pavement, and in the middle was a small pool two meters long and one-and-a-half meters wide set in a framework of varicolored glazed stones. Almost all the rooms opened on the courtyard—their source of daylight, since they had no windows opening to the street. The rooms, paved with the same slabs of clay—plastered with red paint—as the courtyard, had doors to the courtyard, except for a small annex to the large family room that served as a bedroom. This arrangement, too, had been taken over centuries before by the Spaniards from the Romans.

The ground floor of the house encircled the courtyard on all four sides; on only one of those sides an upper story, reached by wooden stairs from one corner of the courtyard, had been built. Since Abū Ya'ḳūb intended to use the upper story for his own family and the person who rented it had promised to vacate it in the near future, he refrained from following the common practice of building a special staircase leading to it from the street. Abū Ya'ḳūb and his family dwelt on the ground floor, which had four rooms altogether, while the upper story (in Spanish, *al-miṣriyya*), which he had rented to the son of a business acquaintance who had recently married, had only two rooms.

In a corner of the courtyard was the privy, reached by way of a winding corridor separated from it by two doors. This small room was constructed near an outer wall of the house. From the trough in the middle of it, a small trench ran to a pipe attached to the cesspool in his neighbor's house. The privy was, thus, appropriately installed inside the house, but the absence of an underground drainage system and the junction of the sewage pipes at a number of houses led, more than once, to disputes among the neighbors.[4] This was, however, but a minor flaw, and in general Abū Ya'Ḳūb had no reason for dissatisfaction with his house or his neighbors, from whom he was separated by thick walls.

The location of the house, which he had bought some few years before from an aged widow, was, in addition, very convenient. It was in a back street called Darb Walad El'āzār in a neighborhood known as Darb as-Suwaiḳa, which was located in the middle of Toledo's Jewish quarter in the city's western section. A long alley with much traffic, it connected the street emerging from the gate of the "Jews' Fortress" on its northern side with the street that originated from the neighborhood plaza.[5] This site was quite far from the western wall of the city that also served as the Jewish quarter's western boundary; for it was the accepted practice in Spanish cities to fix the location of the Jewish neighborhood near the city wall and the synagogues as far as possible from the neighborhoods of non-Jews. In this way they avoided giving a pretext to the enemies of the Jews who complained because the prayers were recited loudly.

The entire Jewish quarter was most often called *rabaḍ,* the Arabic word denoting a suburb or a large neighborhood inside the city.[6] Sometimes in Moslem Spain the Jewish neighborhood was called *al-djamā'a* (short for *djamā'at al-yahūd*), "the community,"[7] and at times it was even given the same name in Hebrew (*ha-Ḳāhāl).*[8] In Toledo, however, people were not familiar with these expressions. On the other hand, the Jewish quarter in the city was so big that an Arab writer of the eleventh century called it *madīnat al-yahūd*—"the city of the Jews."[9] Inside the Jewish quarter were several neighborhoods called *darb,* of which Abū Ya'ḳūb's Darb as-Suwaiḳa was one of the largest.

These Jewish neighborhoods were blocks of houses surrounding an alley, usually a cul-de-sac whose open end was closed in with a gate that was locked at night. Housing in closed-off neighborhoods gave the inhabitants of the Moslem cities the feeling of security and tranquillity for which they so greatly yearned. Since what separated the one small neighborhood from others on all sides were the utterly inpenetrable outer walls of the houses, the security of the inhabitants depended almost entirely on the attentive watching of the gate. The inhabitants actually hired watchmen, accompanied by dogs and carrying lanterns, who patrolled it throughout the night. In Spain these watchmen were called *darrāb* (from the term *darb*), whereas in the Near East they were called *ṭawwāf.* In times of disturbances and also during civil wars, it was easier to defend closed-off neighborhoods, since only a few were needed to defend the gate of a *darb* even when the number of attackers exceeded by many that of the defenders.

In addition to the advantages regarding security, the residents of these neighborhoods also benefited by seclusion from the noise of the streets and from the customs of other groups within the population who were alien or even repugnant to them. For this reason the Moslem cities, which suffered so much from frequent wars and revolutions, were for the most part composed of closed-off neighborhoods consuming a large segment of their area.[10] The workshops and stores were located in other sectors. In this respect the cities in Moslem lands differed for centuries from the cities of Christian Europe. While the craftsmen's shops and stores in Christian cities were on the bottom floor of the houses in which their owners dwelt, the residence and the shop of a man in a Moslem city were generally in different sectors, far from one another.

The advantages of housing in isolated neighborhoods were especially great for a religio-national minority such as the Jews; consequently, there were many *durūb* (plural of *darb*) in the Jewish quarters of the cities of Moslem Spain. Even after the Christians had reconquered most of Spain and considerably changed the appearance of its cities, the Jews continued to live in the same neighborhoods.[11]

Embedded in the Moslems' character was the desire to keep to themselves within the bosom of the family, without neighbors disturbing them and observing what went on in their homes. They kept a strict watch over the purity of their family life, and the Christians and Jews who lived among them adopted this practice. In fact, for a long time after the cities in the Moslem area of the Iberian Peninsula returned to Christian dominance, their Christian residents fostered this way of life—one they had grown to like. The municipality of Christian Toledo had a city ordinance stating that no one should have a door opening opposite his neighbor's gate, for "this would lead to disclosure of private and secret matters."[12]

The responsa of the rabbis of Spain in that period indicate how much the Jews endeavored to maintain the Moslem-like way of life, and they shed light on the problems that arose from residing in closed-off neighborhoods. A question the Jews of Granada addressed to a great rabbi at Lucena carries the report of people who, after the death of their father, requested of householders in a *darb* permission to pass through their quarter. They made this request on the strength of the argument that the people in the *darb* had never sold this right-of-way to their deceased father. Clearly, they regarded it as worthwhile to bring suit to obtain right-of-passage for this shorter way, thereby saving themselves several times a day the trouble of going around the quarter that intervened between them and the nearby street. However, the rabbi to whom this problem was addressed found in favor of the heirs opposed to this.[13]

Life in the closed-off neighborhoods in the Jewish quarters did not change for several generations after the Christians became the rulers of most of Spain. One of the rabbis of Aragon, who lived for a considerable time after the cities in the Ebro Valley had been reconquered by the Christians, was asked to arbitrate a question involving "a house in an unopen alley which had one window that opened on the alley." One "Simeon, who lived in the alley, had made a window opposite the aforementioned window. . . . Now Jacob was requesting of Simeon that he block up his window since the existing visibility he gained from the window could be damaging to Jacob, and Simeon argued that a person may make a window opening opposite a window in an alley in accordance with the statement in *Baba Batra* 60a, where such a window is only prohibited in a courtyard."

In this case, too, the rabbi rendering the decision found for the person who sued to preserve his right to live protected from the eyes of the curious, handing down the decision that an unopen alley has the same legal status as a courtyard.[14] This was the accepted view of the Spanish rabbis during the eleventh century and the beginning of the twelfth.[15] Sometimes a dispute would be provoked because one of the householders wanted to use his house for other than residential purposes, and the neighbors in the alley were apprehensive about the increased numbers of those coming and going to and from his place. In this connection the selfsame Aragonese rabbi states that "the majority of our rabbis wrote that the argument against 'coming and going' does not apply except for one who does not have at all any passageway in that alley, as, for example, someone from another alley; but whoever has one entrance within the alley can make all the entrances he desires, only taking care that they are not directly opposite other entrances [based on the aforementioned citation in *Baba Batra*]." He therefore concludes, in his responsum, that it is permissible for a householder in an alley to engage in any profession even though this may cause many to come and go.[16]

Abū Ya'ḳūb Yūsuf, the dealer in textiles from Toledo, was a lucky man. Among other favors of fortune bestowed upon him was that of being graced with pleasant neighbors with whom he never had disputes. Business success smiled upon him. His son and daughter grew up strong and healthy, giving him much pleasure; and his wife, who was called by the Spanish name "Dona," treated him as the apple of her eye.[17] On the Sabbath he would cast off from himself the yoke of his business enterprises, and holidays in his house were actually festivals.

One chilly autumn morning when he awoke and saw that his wife was already awake, he asked her to hurry and prepare his breakfast. That day was the eve of the Festival of Sukkot. He was pressed for time, since he intended to arrange various matters on that day—to make certain payments and prepare for the days of the festival. He therefore refrained from attending the synagogue but prayed at home; immediately thereafter his wife set before him bread, butter, milk, and green olives as big as plums, as are eaten in Andalusia. This meager meal sufficed him till noon, for Spanish residents are accustomed not to partake of much food and drink in the morning. Abū Ya'kūb did not linger long, promptly going on his way.

At first he went to the butcher shops, it being his habit to buy meat and fowl himself lest he should, heaven forbid, be led by chance into eating forbidden (nonkosher) food. The butchers were suspected sometimes of selling nonkosher meat to the women, so he and many other affluent men and persons of distinction found it worth taking the trouble to go to the shops themselves. The butcher shops were somewhat far from his house: He had to pass through several streets and lanes. A stranger would have gotten lost quickly in all those blind alleys and crooked lanes, even if he asked for directions. The small alleys were named for people who lived in them, while the wide, long streets had no names. Abū Ya'ḳūb, however, being native to the city, made his way in confidence without looking at the houses, which were familiar to him from his boyhood days.

In truth there was really not much to see there. Most of the houses in the Jewish quarter in Toledo, as well as in the other cities of Moslem Spain, had only one floor—a ground floor. Arabic documents from Toledo frequently mention basement apartments called by a Latin name, *soter,* and often the documents state that this or that house is tiny *(duwaira).* But alongside these small houses where, most often, one family dwelt, there were also large houses containing rented apartments in which many poor families lived. All of these apartments, like the Spanish houses currently known as *mesón,* faced upon a large courtyard. At that time these houses were called *corral,* and some of them were also found in the Jewish quarter.[18]

The characteristic common to all of these houses, the large and the small alike, was the fact that only walls without windows faced the outside, giving the streets a monotonous and gloomy look. From some of the houses projected balconies enclosed by wooden latticework—called *mashrabiyya* in Arabic —and by heavy drapes behind them. In other houses the entire upper story projected outward or was even connected with the house opposite. It was, indeed, the intent of the inhabitants of the Moslem cities to exploit the narrow area between the walls to the fullest possible extent, but in doing so they gave little thought to the need for air or light.[19] Like their facades, the gates of the houses were unadorned, and almost all of them were low and small.

The houses stood next to each other without any space intervening. This crowding was especially great in the Jewish quarter.[20] In other cities in Moslem Spain, there were markets in the Jewish neighborhood, such as the shops of silk merchants or metalsmiths.[21] In Toledo, however, there were only a few stores in the Jewish quarter,[22] excepting a small market *(suwaiḳa)* on a small square where vegetables and other comestibles were sold, as also existed in the Jewish neighborhoods of the other Spanish cities. Apart from this square all the other streets were narrow, especially the lanes, and though they were paved,[23] it was hard to walk on them. The paving was done with small stones, which, when wet, were easy to slip on. In the middle of the lanes were trenches into which streams of water flowed on rainy days. Not infrequently, they would fill up with sewage as well. Much attention and effort was given to this by the *muḥtasib,* the official in charge of keeping the marketplaces and the streets in order. Time and again he would request that the city's inhabitants not throw dung into the streets, that they repair the holes in front of their houses where water collected, and in particular that they not empty the drains into the alleys but make pits inside.[24] But quite often his admonitions were of no avail.

The butcher shops were near the "Jews' Fortress," because this structure had relatively large halls where the animals could be kept before being slaughtered; moreover, the strength of its walls made it suitable for this purpose. Indeed, in the other cities of Moslem Spain, too, these security structures were employed in peacetime as cattle sheds for the slaughterhouses.[25] When Abū Ya'ḳūb reached the butcher shop where he had been a customer for several years, a few other customers were already there. While waiting his turn, he scrutinized closely the actions of the butcher, for one can never be secure against deceitful practices. The butcher might fix the scales at a high starting point and slip a bone or a slice of cheap meat onto one of the balances, then add the slice which had actually been sold, weighing it together with the other. Or he might slice the meat with a large butcher knife that also cut through bones, so that the purchaser also paid for the bones.[26] To his joy Abū Ya'ḳūb saw that the butcher was as trustworthy as he had always been. He quickly bought the amount of meat he needed and brought it home.

Once again he took leave of his wife and went up the hill on which the Church of San Tomé now stands but where a mosque stood then; from thence he turned right, on the road leading eastward to the center of the city. Near there was the edge of the Jewish quarter, which was encircled by a wall separating it from the other quarters. This wall, connected in places with the outer walls of the *durūb,* had gates that were locked at night and well guarded. In other cities of Moslem Spain, as, for example, in Tortosa, the Jewish neighborhood had only one gate for security reasons.[27] But in Toledo the wall had a number of gates.[28] One was in the street in which the edifice of San Tomé stood,[29] somewhat back from the spot at which the street rising out of the "Gate of the Jews" within the city's wall reached it.[30] When Abū Ya'ḳūb arrived at the gate, it was already open, and he was able to continue on to the market area within the center of the city. He passed in the vicinity of the mosque, near the merchants' counters, which were set up in the streets and protected by awnings from the sun's rays, threading his way among the counters with difficulty and being very careful not to be struck by a protruding rod or beam.[31] Eventually he reached the marketplace called al-Ḳanāt, where the majority of the merchants were Jews.[32] There, among the other shops, was his shop.

It was a small store containing no more than one room, somewhat long and quite dark. Light entered it from the street door, which consisted of an upper and a lower shutter. The upper shutter, made fast to the lintel overhead, rested on a strong beam, becoming in effect an awning that protected the merchant and his wares from sun and dust. The wares were placed on the lower shutter, which rested on top of the floor and protruded somewhat from the front of the house. It had the same function display windows perform today. On this big plank Abū Ya'ḳūb put beautiful silk veils adorned with designs such as multicolored flowers, attracting passersby.[33]

Naturally, this small shop did not suffice for a successful merchant who engaged in export; Abū Ya'ḳūb therefore had a warehouse in the upper floor of the house. Such upper stories abounded in the marketplaces of the cities of Moslem Spain and were called—as were the upper stories of the residences—*miṣriyya* or *ghurfa.* They served as workshops for the shopkeepers on the ground floor, as residences for unmarried laborers, or as warehouses. Generally a special gate was set up at the front of the house near the store by which one ascended on stairs to the upper story.[34] Abū Ya'ḳūb had agreed quite willingly, since he needed it very urgently, when the manager of the Moslem religious endowment that owned the house suggested he build an upper story that would be rented to him, though the rent would be quite high.

When he came to his shop, he found there his clerk-assistant, a young man of twenty. They promptly sat down on their mats, examined some accounts, and discussed matters that had to be taken care of, such as letters to be written and merchandise to be prepared for transport. But their discussion was not prolonged, and Abū Ya'ḳūb arose and went on his way.

II

A week earlier two *a'wān* (singular: *'aun*), messengers of the Moslem court, had appeared at his shop and summoned him to come this very morning before the judge, as a claim had been brought against him by a Moslem. Abū Ya'ḳūb was not alarmed, since he knew whom it concerned. The plaintiff was a porter he had engaged to haul merchandise until the man demanded a payment that was not due him. Abū Ya'ḳūb was quite sure that the judge would find in his favor.

But it was not only because he was convinced that he was in the right that Abū Ya'ḳūb went with tranquil heart to the Moslem judge. In other countries a Jew would have reason to be apprehensive of favoritism in a Moslem court; but in Spain, particularly during that period, the judges had begun to exercise impartiality between litigants, whether of their faith or not.

For the principle that was the basis of the juridical position relating to the status of Jews and Christians in the Moslem state, as it was propounded by the Moslem theologians, was not held to be an impracticable rule in Moslem Spain. According to the concepts of Moslem justice, the status of non-Moslems was based on "the covenant of protection" that safeguarded their lives and property in exchange for the payment of a poll tax and obedience to laws limiting freedom of worship and precluding the spreading of religious propaganda. Information in the writings of the Arabic historians indicates that the authorities did indeed take measures against Moslems who harmed Jews. One Arabic writer describes a revered Moslem theologian, a person of consequence, who, in a fit of religious zeal, killed a Jew and immediately fled from the city because he was apprehensive of the reaction by the authorities.[35]

Just as his life was protected, so was the Jew assured of his property's protection. A trustworthy Arabic source reports in detail a dispute between a Jew and an Arab prince in which the Jew won, thanks to the uprightness of the *kadi,* or Moslem judge. The account deals with an incident that occurred in Mérida in the first half of the ninth century. One day, the Arabic writer relates, there came to the city a Jew who dealt in the slave trade. He brought with him maidservants from Galicia—very popular among the Arabs because of their red hair.

Most of the Omayyads, in particular, married such women. Now at that time the ruler of Mérida was Prince Muḥammad, the son of Emir 'Abdarraḥmān II. When the prince learned that there was a fascinating beauty among the maidservants brought by the Jew, he asked him to sell her to him. But the price the Jew demanded seemed to the prince to be too high. He then proceeded to take her by force without paying for her. The Jew turned to the *kadi* for redress, and the latter courageously compelled the prince to return the maidservant. The *kadi* then went to Cordova to explain his action to the emir, who held him to be justified. But in the end—so the Arabic writer's account continues—the *kadi* said to the Jew: You have won that which is coming to you, but it seems to me that now you should send the maidservant to the prince in exchange for the price he is prepared to pay you. The Jew accepted his opinion; and as for the prince, he appreciated the judge's uprightness so much that on mounting the royal throne at Cordova, he appointed him *ḳādi 'al-djamā'a,* chief judge in the capital city.[36]

Of the statutes that limited the rights of the non-Moslem communities, the one that offended them most was the law obliging them to make themselves distinguishable from the Moslems by special signs on their garb. To be sure, the members of the non-Moslem communities tried hard to avoid wearing these marks, but every so often the authorities in the Near East, egged on by zealous theologians, reenacted the requirement that Jews and Christians abide by this law. The Spanish Christians who wrote books in Latin in the middle of the ninth century in which they bitterly lamented the status of their community under Moslem dominance do not mention these distinctive signs. On the other hand, they were instituted in Tunisia during the last third of that century. Interesting data on this matter are given us by an Andalusian theologian who lived most of his life in Tunisia and was a disciple of the renowned Malikite jurist Saḥnūn. That theologian, Yaḥyā b. ʻUmar, reports that the judge of Kairawān, Abu ʼl-ʻAbbās ʻAbdallāh b. Ṭālib (d. 888), required of the Jews and Christians that they distinguish themselves from Moslems by means of thick belts of a different color than their garments' and also prohibited their riding upon any animals.

Yaḥyā b. ʻUmar goes on to relate that he himself was once asked by the police chief of Kairawān *(ṣāhib as-sūḳ,* that is, the *muḥtasib)* what to do with a Jew or Christian found on the street without a patch on his garments and without a thick belt, to which he replied that such a one must be flogged, displayed in the Jewish or Christian neighborhoods, and imprisoned for all to observe—and be struck with fear. Thereafter, Yaḥyā b. ʻUmar's account continues, ʻAbdallāh b. Tālib commanded the Jews and Christians to mark themselves with white patches bearing pictures of apes and pigs and also to mark their houses by means of boards on which monkeys were depicted.[37]

This was the position of the esteemed theologians of North Africa who fashioned the Malikite Islam of the Maghreb (North Africa). In that era the influence of the theologians was also very powerful in Yaḥyā b. ʻUmar's native land of Andalusia, which he visited at frequent intervals. The *fukarah* (jurists—singular: *faḳīh*), who had studied in Kairawān (in Tunisia) and in various cities in the Near East, promulgated the Malikite school's spirit of fanaticism throughout Spain and also introduced there some of the enactments of the "Covenant of Omar" (the document regulating status of non-Moslems within Islamic countries) imposed upon the non-Moslem communities in Near Eastern countries. Then the Christians and Jews of Spain, too, were obliged to wear the thick belt as a distinctive sign. Poems written by Spanish Arabs during the eleventh century, as well as other literary works, mention the thick belt as the Christians' distinctive sign.[38]

In that era, however, a spirit of tolerance prevailed among

most of the Moslem states in Spain, and the non-Moslem communities ceased observing the law obligating them to distinguish themselves from Moslems. The Jews in particular stopped marking themselves by means of the belt. The devout theologian Ibn 'Abdūn, who lived in Seville in the second half of the eleventh century, states in his book on the *ḥisba* merely that it was desirable that Jews and Christians should not dress like notable Moslems but use some unspecified badge.[39] This writer does not mention any particular mark, which can only mean that the old law was no longer observed. He merely expresses a vague aspiration, and he makes no mention at all of the prohibition against horseback riding which had been imposed upon non-Moslems in the Near East and Tunisia.[40]

To be sure, the orthodox Moslem theologians read the books written by their colleagues in other lands, and in the course of their travels beheld with their own eyes how Jews and Christians were belittled in various ways. Prompted by this impression, they would voice demands to introduce the laws of the Covenant of Omar into Spain. They demanded that the authorities prohibit Moslems from serving the "infidels." For example, Moslems should not lead a riding animal upon which a Jew or Christian is mounted nor hold his stirrup; nor should he give him a massage, clean his cesspits, or remove the trash from his house.[41] An Arabic poet writing in the middle of the eleventh century composed a poem expressing scorn and contempt for the Jews of Granada. He also mentioned that they were mounted upon mules employing riding saddles by way of alluding to the laws of the Covenant of Omar which reserve this privilege for Moslems.[42] But all these assertions and demands fell upon deaf ears: The rulers gave them no thought.

Aside from the distinctive signs on their garb imposed upon the Jews and Christians in most Moslem countries, the encroachments on their rights of worship were most stringent. They were not permitted to build new houses of worship or enlarge the old ones. They were forbidden to hold processions in the streets. In this connection, the Arabic chroniclers in the Near East tell of a long list of trials and disputes, persecutions and attacks. In Spain the non-Moslem communities were not hindered over a long period of time from erecting new houses of worship or enlarging the old ones.[43] But in the second half of the ninth century, the fanatic *fukarah* created a stir on this very issue, and the Omayyad government began to act more strictly in the matter. In 871 Emir Muḥammad I permitted a church in Toledo to be converted into a mosque in order to enlarge a Moslem house of worship alongside it, and in like manner churches in the cities of the Ebro region were taken away from the Christians.[44] At the beginning of the tenth century, the question of whether it was permissible for Christians to build new churches was laid before the *fukarah.* They answered that such a thing was forbidden in a Moslem city such as Cordova, though it was allowable in suburbs where Christians constituted the majority.[45] Nevertheless, even after this judgment was made, the Christians and Jews built houses of worship inside Moslem cities—even in Cordova proper.[46]

In the earliest years of Moslem rule in Spain, Christians were permitted to ring church bells, though according to the laws of the Covenant of Omar it was only permissible to use wooden knockers. The Christian writers of the middle of the ninth century speak of the ringing of the bells as an accepted practice in the cities of Andalusia.[47] It is quite true that the Christians often lived in the suburbs, outside the walls of the inner city. But in any event the permission given them to ring the bells constituted a great privilege that was denied their coreligionists in many Moslem countries. To be sure, when Moslem fanaticism waxed stronger at the end of the ninth century the authorities forbade this practice, but before many generations had gone by the Christians received permission to resume the practice.

Yet despite all this the Christians suffered considerable deprivation in their religious life because of the laws of the state. Certainly, because of their practices and institutions, they suffered more hurt than the Jews. The Jews were not accustomed to hold processions in the streets nor did they have monasteries that were obliged to give hospitality to Moslems. Indeed, the Moslem authorities even issued decrees that initially affected the Christians alone. Among other things they insisted the Christians be circumcised, a practice that was contrary to their religion and angered them greatly.[48] They were affected no less by the right the Moslem government arrogated to itself to appoint and dismiss bishops, as the Visigoth government had done formerly.[49] In all these respects, therefore, the status of the Jews was more agreeable than that of the Christians.

On the other hand Christians and Jews suffered equally from the pressure of taxation. The burden of taxes, imposed in particular on these minority groups within the population, was very heavy during the entire period of Moslem rule in Spain. A Latin chronicler relates that the Omayyad emir Hishām I laid such oppressive taxes upon the Jews and Christians that they were compelled to sell their sons and daughters to pay them. But this report is highly dubious.[50] In the days of Emir 'Abdarraḥmān II, the Christians of Mérida sent a letter to the Frankish king Louis the Pious in which they complained bitterly about the taxes.[51]

These taxes were made up of the poll tax collected in Moslem lands from members of the Jewish and Christian faiths[52] as well as contributions exacted from groups and individuals in accordance with the custom of Moslem authorities, who never introduced uniform taxes. The collection of the taxes was farmed out by the authorities to both the secular and religious heads of the non-Moslem communities. These extorted more than was proper from the members of their community, either because they wanted to provide the rulers with inordinately large sums to curry favor with them or because they wanted to enrich themselves. The ninth-century Christian writers never weary of recounting their troubles and hardships because of the burdensome taxes that were exacted every month—even from the clergy.[53]

In this aspect the lot of the Jews was not different; but there was among them a small group of specially privileged men. These were the descendants of Jews who, in the days of Mohammed, had dwelt in the districts of Khaibar, near Medina, and had wandered from there to other lands; thus they had appeared before the Moslem governments in Babylonia, Syria, and Egypt over a period of many generations. Basing themselves on treaties they had made, as it were, with the prophet of Islam, they demanded to be exempt from payment of the poll tax. Sometimes they succeeded, sometimes not. In any event it is clear from a passage in a Hispano-Arabic lexicon written in Spain at the end of the Middle Ages that in this country, too, they were regarded as a Jewish group with a special status.[54] In general, however, the attitude of the authorities toward the Jews was not better than toward the Christians.

There were among the Jews powerful men who entered into negotiations with the government, leasing from it the authority to collect the taxes. Jacob Ibn Djau, a silk manufacturer from Cordova, was one of them.[55] He took it upon himself to collect the Jews' taxes throughout the Omayyad kingdom. In the questions the Spanish Jewish communities directed to the rabbis of Spain or to the heads of the Talmud schools in Babylonia, the collection of taxes by the community or at least communal responsibility in this matter is discussed. Because of this method of collection, disputes erupted between communities when a Jew would move from one city to another and discontinue participating in the payment of the tax in the city he left. Problems arose when his share of the assessment was not subtracted from the sum imposed upon the community.[56]

But an even greater calamity than the communal taxes were the extraordinary contributions exacted from individuals of means. One question addressed to the rabbis speaks of a Jew who left his city to escape paying taxes and who simulated a divorce from his wife so that taxes should not be collected from her.[57] Rabbi Ḥanōkh b. Moses was asked about "Reuben whom the government had dunned for payment and Simeon and Karmī [who] stood surety for the money with the government in his behalf at a fixed time."[58] The terror induced by these compulsory payments hovered over the wealthy like a sword suspended over their heads. If a Jew informed on another Jew, telling the authorities that he was very wealthy, the Jew who was thus designated could expect to have to make a large contribution—referred to by the rabbis of Spain as a "loss."[59]

Even in the Moslem countries of the Near East, the pressure of burdensome taxes was applied against the Jews and Christians. There, moreover, the authorities also laid hands on their inheritances. Sometimes the officials confiscated estates left without heirs or reserved to themselves the right to distribute the inheritances according to Islamic law. And sometimes they were content to collect sizable inheritance taxes.[60] In the kingdom of the Spanish Omayyads, unlike in the Near East, the Jews distributed their inheritances without interference from the Moslem authorities.[61] The Omayyad government did set up an office that dealt with inheritance matters, but in consonance with the principles established by the jurists of the Malikite school, the Moslem government had no claims on the legacies of Jews and Christians.[62]

Moreover, the position of Jews and Christians insofar as it applied to the employment of non-Moslems as government officials was quite favorable. In other Moslem countries there were frequent dismissals of Jewish and Christian officials because of demands by fanatical theologians, and from time to time the rulers would apply pressure upon them to convert to Islam. In Spain, however, during the tenth century, the Omayyads employed non-Moslem officials unhesitatingly, even appointing them to high office.[63]

Thus the Omayyad government, which determined the Moslem patterns of authority, deviated to a marked degree from the rigid attitude most of the Moslem states displayed toward the Jews and Christians; and the status of their communities in Spain did not conform at all to the enactments of the Covenant of Omar. Instead, in agreement with the Moslems' political conception, the Omayyad government recognized the non-Moslem communities as groups with definite rights and set the leaders of those communities at their heads. The organization of the non-Moslem communities suited the needs of the state, for the heads of the communities were responsible to the government for the meeting of various civic obligations on the part of the members of the communities. They also had to arrange for those public utility services within the communities for which members had no claim upon the state because of their different religion. There was scarcely an independent Moslem kingdom that did not follow this course.

When 'Abdarraḥmān I became king of Moslem Spain, he appointed the Visigoth prince Ardabast as head of the Christian community in all the provinces under his dominion. Thenceforth the Omayyad rulers tended to appoint an esteemed Christian to this office following the suggestion of the members of his community or to give the post to a Christian close to the rulers. The successors of Ardabast were also heads of the Christian community throughout the entire state. This head of the Christian community, who bore the Roman title *comes,* represented his coreligionists before the government and was responsible for the payment of taxes; he supervised all the affairs of the community and stood at the head of a judicial administration that dispensed judgments between community members in civil matters following Visigoth law (*Fuero Jusgo*). Local tax collectors and judges functioned under the supervision of the *comes,* while he himself was the supreme judge of the Christians. For its part, the Moslem government helped those in authority within the Christian community in carrying out their functions and in the collection of taxes exacted for the community's own needs. This framework endured throughout the Omayyad rule.[64]

Just as the Omayyad rulers appointed the *comes* to be the head of the Christian community, so they created a post of leader of the Jewish community. The title of the holder of this post was *nāsī,* and the manner of his appointment was similar to that of the *comes:* Sometimes the Moslem king appointed him at the suggestion of the Jews themselves, and sometimes he appointed a Jew who filled an important function at the royal court or was close to him. In such a case the heads of the Jewish community were called upon to give approval to the appointment after the fact. The two tenth-century *n'sīīm* on whom the Jewish historian Abraham b. Dā'ūd reports were appointed by the government at its own initiative. The lack of consistency in the manner of the *nāsī*'s appointment was characteristic of Moslem dominance, which knew no fixed constitution. The function of the *nāsī* was similar to that of the *comes:* he represented the Jews before the Moslem rulers, was responsible for the taxes imposed upon them, and served as the highest judge in his community.[65]

The Hebrew poets who were contemporaries of Ḥasdai Ibn Shaprūt and sang his praise did not forget to mention his characteristics as a judge.[66] A Judaeo-Arabic letter written in southern Spain at a much later period of Moslem rule gives an account of the condemnation of an offender in the presence of a *nāsī* in Seville.[67] It goes without saying that this head of the community used the power given him by the government to choke off in a malicious way every heretical movement and to cast fear upon sectaries who began to propagate their own views and win adherents. When Ḥasdai Ibn Shaprūt, as the victim of a calumny, determined to take measures against his secretary, M'naḥem b. Sārūḳ, he exercised his function as supreme judge and brought an indictment against him, though the defendant was not present.[68]

The Arab and Berber princes who shared in the rule of Moslem Spain after the disintegration of the Omayyad kingdom and sought to imitate their manner of ruling also appointed Jews as heads of the community. In the eleventh century the government-recognized heads of the Jewish settlements in Moslem countries began to be designated by the title *nāgīd.* Samuel Ibn Nagrela and his son were so entitled, as were those holding this post in the provinces of Spain outside of Granada.[69] For some time now this title had become accepted in Babylonia; and the Gaon Rabbi Hai so designated the heads of Jewish communities in other lands. Thenceforth it achieved popularity in various places. Some of the heads of these communities requested that the Exilarchs and heads of the Talmud schools in the Near East bestow their title upon them. They received letters from them couched in ornate rhetoric in which their deeds for the welfare of the community were extravagantly praised and the title *nāgīd* awarded to them.

The title *nāsī,* however, was more deeply rooted in Spain, and after a while the community heads returned to its use.[70] The appointment of these *n'sīīm* was made in the long-accepted manner, and their functions likewise remained unchanged. As in former times they acted as the recognized representatives of their community, made endeavors for the welfare of communities and individuals, were responsible for the payment of taxes, and served as chief justices.[71]

The Jewish communities in Moslem Spain enjoyed autonomous jurisdiction that was quite wide in scope. As was the fashion of Moslem states, the Omayyads and their successors did not prevent the Jews from conducting litigations in their own courts, which exercised judgment in accordance with Jewish law. These courts covered all civil law cases, that is, suits involving buying and selling, marriage and divorce cases, and also accusations relating to insults, libels, and thefts.[72] Those found guilty of serious transgressions were frequently punished by lashing, the traditional Moslem punishment for disobedience. This penalty was meted out for many violations of the law, such as insults, libels, and perjury, and it was somewhat of a novelty in Jewish justice.[73] The use of lashing came partly as a consequence of the abolition of other penalties, such as the fines annulled in the Diaspora, but it also resulted from the influence of the Moslem penal system. The Jewish courts also had jails available to them. In general, accused persons waiting for their cases to be determined or those who refused to submit to the court's authority were placed in jail; in other words, the prisons were used as a means of coercion.[74]

The circumstances in which the various Jewish communities existed compelled them to deviate from biblical law with respect to penalties as it had been interpreted by the ancient rabbis. Innovations had to be introduced, even regarding rules of jurisdiction. The accepted composition of Jewish courts in Spain was a group of three judges;[75] however, the communal leaders would frequently add their signatures to the actions of the court in addition to the three judges.[76] Small communities sometimes had only one judge, though generally the rabbi did not serve as a judge.

In the way they were composed, therefore, the Jewish courts in Moslem Spain were similar to those in the Near East. However, the procedure used to appoint judges in Moslem Spain was completely different from the accepted practice in Babylonia and the lands adjacent to it. Whereas in the latter countries the judges were appointed by the Exilarch or the heads of the Talmud schools, the judges in Spain were elected by the communities. In a book of deeds (writs) compiled at the beginning of the twelfth century in eastern Spain, there is a writ of appointment of a judge which lays down the obligation to obey him, since the entire community elected him. The author of this collection lived in a district of Spain that had been under Christian dominance for many generations, but he affirms that he found the writ "in some old formularies in a book of deeds."[77] Because they were elected, the Jewish judges in Spain were for several generations referred to most often as "the chosen" (elected). In fact, this title is already to be found in the responsa of rabbis from the end of the eleventh century onward.[78]

The election of judges, some of whom were professional jurists, that is, scholars who made their living by holding office as judges, was, therefore, an accepted practice in Spain, an old tradition influenced by the custom of countries that formerly belonged to the Roman Empire. In those countries it was customary to designate officeholders by elections and to set up bodies of officeholders, while in the Near East the officeholders were designated by those in authority, and every function was delegated to one person who was responsible for all his decisions. Roman-Visigothic tradition was very strong in Spain and even influenced the Moslems, who had the habit of attaching advisors *(mushāwar)* to the judge. The *mushāwar* were appointed by the rulers, whereas the *kadi* (plural: *kudah*) in the Near East very definitely rendered judgment by himself.[79]

In other ways, too, the Jews were influenced by the practices current all around them. Moslem courts would appoint permanent witnesses called *'adl* (plural: *'udūl*), *shāhid* (plural: *shuhūd*), and, in Spain in particular, *wathāk* (plural: *wathākūn).* The probity of these witnesses was strictly investigated. They would be signatories to all acts of the court and also served as notaries outside the court. The appointment of such permanent witnesses—called "city's witnesses" or "the community's witnesses"—was already an accepted practice in the courts of the tenth-century Spanish Jewish communities, and any document to which other witnesses were signatories was considered invalid.[80]

Even the procedure in the courts was influenced by that of the Moslems. As was the case with Moslem judges, the Jewish courts endeavored to exclude lawyers, demanding that those involved in the suit appear themselves and put forward their own arguments.[81] Hence trials took less time than they did in other countries and even in Spain itself during Christian rule, where lawyers would appear with lengthy arguments leading to delays in the rendering of decisions.

To compel parties in the suit to appear before it, the court would invoke the *ḥerem* (ban), the accepted weapon of Jewish communities in every country. People were also compelled to come and testify by being threatened with the ban. It was the custom to proclaim in all the synagogues that anyone having some knowledge in the matter being considered by the court should come and testify.[82] If one stubbornly refused to appear before the court, a proclamation of *nidduy* (a lesser ban) would first be issued by writing a *p'tīḥa* (preliminary summons). If, after thirty days, the person still remained intractable, a severe ban would be proclaimed against him.[83] Anyone who came to the courthouse requesting that a document be indited for him —whether a bill of sale or of gift, a document of marriage or divorce, or a will—paid a sum fixed in advance, which went to the judges. The scribes of the court, who were the only ones permitted to write the documents, received a fixed stipend for every month or for the whole year. They had to be expert in Hebrew and also in Arabic, since deeds relating to buying and selling were written in literary Arabic.[84] In point of fact, the scribes made extensive use of formularies comprising the texts of various documents, since these also contained the laws relating to every type of document.[85]

The Jewish courts in Spain were, therefore, powerful and well organized. However, the Jews also had courts in other Moslem countries that rendered judgment in civil and matrimonial cases. The use of the ban against Jews who brought suit against fellow Jews to a non-Jewish court without a justifiable cause, as well as the imposition of a ban against informers, was customary and accepted in Jewish communities in all the other countries.[86] Yet the scope of the jurisdiction of the judges in the Spanish communities was more extensive than that of their colleagues in the other countries under Arab dominion.

Already at the start of Arab rule over Spain, the Jews received permission to try capital offenses. They availed themselves of this permission especially to impose punishment on heretics and slanderers. In a letter he wrote to the head of the Palestinian Talmudic Academy, Rabbi Joseph Ibn Abītūr recounts that one of his forebears ("my great-great-grandfather") carried out in Spain the Jewish law courts' four forms of capital punishment. This testimony thus refers to the beginning of the ninth century—the second or third generation of Omayyad rule in Spain.[87] Samuel the Nagid reports on severe corporal punishments meted out at a much later period. He states that in a remote era ("in the days of our ancestors"), heretics who inclined toward Karaism were flogged, and that "those who were found deserving of such punishment died while being flogged."[88] But as often as the death penalty was exacted in the case of heretics, it was even more often invoked in the case of informers. An early, authoritative source reports that in the first half of the twelfth century the court of Lucena decreed the death penalty on an informer and it was carried out on the Day of Atonement, which fell on the Sabbath, at the hour of the Ne'īla Service (sunset).[89] This time was, of course, chosen intentionally to stress publicly that the offender was no longer considered a Jew; with this in mind, M'naḥēm b. Sarūk was punished on a Sabbath that was also a festival.[90]

According to the testimony of Maimonides, the punishment of unbelievers and heretics with death was a common phenomenon among the Jewish communities of Moslem Spain during the eleventh and twelfth centuries.[91] The privilege of meting out capital punishment that the Jews had in Moslem Spain was later extended to them in Christian Spain as well; but there they needed special permission in each instance, and in general the offender was executed by the gentiles.[92]

The extreme rigor practiced by the courts in the Jewish communities of Spain is, upon first examination, astonishing. In fact, when Rabbi Āshēr b. Y'ḥīēl came from Germany to settle in Toledo, he expressed utter amazement at the imposition of the death sentence,[93] since the ancient rabbis had, in an earlier era, decided to abolish capital punishment after the Sanhedrin was exiled from the Chamber of the Hewn Stone and the Temple was destroyed.[94] In later periods, especially during the time of the *geonim,* an offender was only rarely sentenced to die.[95] But the practice of informing was held an exception. It was a heinous evil that more than once threatened the well-being of the Spanish Jewish communities, both large and small. Anyone who informed against an individual was penalized by being disqualified to act as a witness.[96] However, the leaders of the Jewish communities and the judges had no other recourse than to have executed in self-defense anyone who was held to be an informer and yet remained recalcitrant despite being interdicted and banned, since he endangered the lives and property of many.

The imposition of harsh corporal or capital punishment upon skeptics and heretics resulted from the spirit of fanaticism and the persecution of heretics that prevailed among Moslem and Christians, in whose midst the Jews dwelt. Yet from days of old, the Spaniards had been noted for the zeal with which they adhered to their beliefs and for the extreme severity with which they treated anyone who denied what they deemed sacred. The Jews, who had experienced persecution at the hands of the Visigoths and later beheld with their own eyes how Moslems put to death anyone reared as a Moslem who became estranged from his faith, would have considered it a belittlement and a contemptuous disregard of the Jewish faith if they had shown a more forgiving attitude toward skeptics and heretics in their midst. For this reason the rabbis of those generations maintained that although the imposition of biblical laws by the Sanhedrin had been suspended, the laws were not void when the circumstances of the time required that they be in effect. This was the halakhic basis on which the rabbis depended in acting against informers and skeptics. In addition, the rabbis facilitated the judicial procedure by directing that in cases against informers and skeptics there was no need for the witnesses to testify in the presence of the accused.[97]

The halakhic reasoning was, however, largely a justification of prevailing practice. Just as the rabbis in the Near East decided to abolish the death penalty after the gentile nations had deprived them of the right to try capital cases, the rabbis in Spain proceeded to validate a practice that was rendered possible when the Moslem authorities gave them the right to do so. This was, to be sure, a special privilege granted the Jews in Moslem Spain, not the Jews in the other Moslem countries or the far more numerous Christians who dwelt alongside them in Moslem Spain. Information culled from Christian sources demonstrates that their communal leaders could not impose the death penalty against persons they deemed to be heretics. They had to resort to various devices against them—for example, denigrating them in the eyes of the Moslem rulers and spreading false and libelous charges against them.[98] In these aspects, therefore, the civil and juridic position of the

Spanish Jewish community was better than that of the Christians. This relatively privileged treatment paralleled the Moslem authorities' less exacting requirements regarding the distinctive signs they were supposed to wear and their leniency in not forcing the Jews out of the central neighborhoods of the cities.

The wide scope of jurisdiction enjoyed by their courts proved to be a big advantage for the Jews' legal status, but the Jews did, nevertheless, have much recourse to the judiciary of the Moslems. They applied to the Moslem courts to get the documents required to purchase and sell real estate; and when they turned to these courts for such matters, the heads of the community could not complain, for they recognized the necessity for it.[99] But they did not recognize the transfer of property so long as the deed lacked the signatures of Jewish witnesses. To justify their stand, they found support in the fact, among other things, that Arabic writing lent itself readily to forgery, since the addition of a dot changes the meaning of a word. They also claimed that the witnesses of the Moslems were not trustworthy. As for deeds of gift executed in the Moslem courts, they accorded them no recognition whatsoever, deeming them to be, like bills of divorce and manumission of slaves, not valid except when drawn up in a Jewish court.[100] On the other hand they did permit a lender to have recourse to a Moslem court if the power of the Jewish court did not suffice to compel the borrower to pay his debt.[101] Still, people would sometimes turn to the Moslem courts for adjudication when they knew that according to Moslem laws they would emerge from the lawsuit in the right; they followed this practice in civil suits and also in cases involving insult and libel. The heads of the Jewish community, of course, strenuously opposed this and demanded that the people have recourse in Jewish courts as long as it was not absolutely necessary to make use of non-Jewish courts.[102]

In a lawsuit between a Jew and a Moslem, however, the Jew had no alternative but to come before a Moslem judge, because the Moslems did not regard Jewish courts as having any authority with regard to them. From the very outset Jews had a basis for apprehension concerning such justice, since according to Moslem law a Jew could not give testimony against a Moslem.[103] Yet a good number of the Moslem judges in Spain endeavored to overcome prejudice and not discriminate against Jews. During the days of Omayyad rule, the *kudah* made a special effort to protect members of the lower orders of society from the rulers and princes;[104] and the Jews benefited from this sympathetic attitude. Even in the middle of the eleventh century, many of the *kudah* in Moslem Spain strove to act impartially and to make judicial decisions only in the light of the facts as demonstrated by trustworthy witnesses and in accordance with statutory laws. Consequently, even a Jew could appear before a *kadi* without any particular fear. Naturally, Abū Ya'ḳūb Yūsuf, the Jew from Toledo, knew this; he was after all a merchant, and it is in the manner of merchants to have recourse on occasion to the courts.

When Abū Ya'ḳūb left his shop to go to the Moslem court, there was already much traffic in the streets. The judge *(ḥākim)* before whom he had been summoned held court in his own house, for it was the custom of the Moslem judges to conduct judicial matters in mosques or in their private homes.[105] The judge's house was not far from Abū Ya'ḳūb's shop, but because of the congestion in the streets and the fear that he might get dirty if he was not careful, he moved along at a snail's pace. From the outskirts of the city came groups of peasants with beasts of burden, and near them crowded butchers carrying slaughtered animals on their shoulders and building laborers with boards and other construction materials. Vendors of cooked foods made the rounds, carrying steaming pots on their heads as they bawled out their wares: roast meat, fish, sausages, or cheese pastries. On the street corners stood perfume vendors who, for a small sum, sprayed their customers with perfume and brokers who gave notice of a public sale of slaves, horses, or coal.[106]

Suddenly, Abū Ya'ḳūb heard a noise that came nearer and nearer to him, and all at once the street emptied, the brokers grew silent, and everyone turned aside and pressed close to the walls of the houses. A moment or two later town criers appeared and announced that a certain offender had been found guilty of such and such an offense and, in punishment, was being put to death. As was customary, the police had paraded the accused around the city. (This was known as a *shuhra.*) The sentenced man, who had been stripped, was seated on a donkey, facing the rear of the animal, on whose two flanks were sacks of straw. Policemen walked in front of him and behind him, announcing his offense and blowing on a sort of pipe. Thus his misdeed was exposed to his everlasting shame.[107]

When this procession had passed by, Abū Ya'ḳūb Yūsuf continued on his way. When he reached the courthouse, the Moslem who had brought suit against him was already waiting for him. Luck was with them; the judge was free and opened the legal proceedings promptly. He summoned the two litigants to sit alongside each other on mats spread before him on the ground; in this way he showed impartiality to Moslem and non-Moslem alike, as the judges were enjoined to do by the rules of procedure in their statutes. He also spoke with them in a like manner. First of all he wanted to hear the claim. The Moslem had worked for Abū Ya'ḳūb for two months, bringing merchandise from an inn to his shop and goods from his shop to another inn. Since this work required only one or two hours daily, they had agreed that the Moslem should be given his wages in one payment on completion of all the work. However, at the end of two months, the porter did not appear to receive his wages. A few days later he did come, demanding additional payment for the time that had meanwhile elapsed, and when his request was refused, he had appealed to the judge. In explanation of his suit, the Moslem argued that Abū Ya'ḳūb had requested that he be available those additional days, and that even though Abū Ya'ḳūb had not kept him occupied, he was obliged to pay him in accordance with this agreement.

For his part Abū Ya'ḳūb stated that he was obligated to pay the porter during the two months only, arguing, moreover, that he had not engaged him for a later period and had entered into no agreement with him respecting those days. In accordance with the procedure of Moslem judges, the *ḥākim* called upon the porter to present the evidence for his complaint; and in consonance with the principles of the Malikite school of justice that prevailed in Spain, it was necessary for him to provide at least one witness and, in addition, to swear that he was in the right.

The porter brought his brother as a witness, and although there are differences of opinion among Moslem jurists as to whether a man is fit to act as a witness on behalf of his brother, the judge was at first inclined to accept his testimony. However, because the brother demonstrated a marked eagerness to swear to the justness of his words, he disqualified him. In accordance with the rules of procedure, the judge had to require the defendant to take an oath if the plaintiff demanded it, in which case the judge would have sent Abū Yā'ḳūb to the Jewish court to have the oath administered to him. Such an oath, however, was imposed only if it seemed to the judge that there was a basis for the claim. But since the conduct of the plaintiff's brother had made a very bad impression upon him, he did not impose an oath upon Abū Ya'ḳūb. He acted thus because if Abū Ya'ḳūb and the plaintiff had supported their arguments with an oath, the position of both litigants would have been equal in respect to their evidence or, more precisely, their lack of evidence. It was an important principle of the experts in jurisprudence of the Malikite school that in disputes over lease and hire in which neither of the litigants has presented superior proofs, the one who can cite a more precise date regarding the end of the contract is to be given credence. For this reason the judge pronounced *ta'djīz,* that is, he rejected the suit for lack of evidence.[108]

Abū Ya'ḳūb Yūsuf bowed to the judge, paid the court messenger for his trouble in delivering the summons, and went on his way.

III

Because of the religious and human value of Jewish education, the Jewish scholars of old deprecated the idea of receiving payment for teaching. To be sure, it was impossible to maintain this noble principle for too long a time, and teaching generally became an occupation along with other occupations that provide a livelihood for those engaged in them. Nevertheless, this practice was still disapproved of in the twelfth century, especially by writers and experts on matters concerning education who belonged within the cultural circles of Spanish Jewry. Even those who averred that there should be payment for children's teachers gave special stress to the view that it should be forbidden to teach the Oral Law for remuneration.[109]

But theory and practice are distinctly separate. In that era most teachers made their living from teaching, and they therefore made agreements fixing the exact amount of their remuneration and the times for receiving it. Although he could, of course, include other conditions in the agreements, the teacher most often received a monthly payment, partly in money and partly in commodities, following the accepted practice among the Moslems.[110]

Besides the fixed remuneration, the parents of the pupils—

only boys, for girls did not study at schools—would also bestow gifts upon the teachers, each parent according to the prompting of his heart and his ability.[111] This was the accepted practice especially in the private schools, where the children of the well-to-do studied. Abū Ya'ḳūb Yūsuf's son was a student in such a school, and on the eve of the Festival of Sukkot the father visited the teacher and brought him a gift, as was his annual custom.

To visit the teacher's house, he returned to the Jewish quarter. The children's school where the youngsters learned at the community's expense was usually in the synagogue—in the prayer hall proper or in one of the side rooms—whereas the private school was generally in the teacher's house.[112] The teacher or tutor *(m'lammēd),* as he was called in that period, with whom Abū Ya'ḳūb's son was studying was renowned for his pedagogic skill; because of it the notables of the community and the wealthy sent their sons to him.[113] Naturally Abū Ya'ḳūb was glad for the opportunity to have a quick chat with him and hear about his son's progress in his studies. On the eve of the Sabbath and on the eve of a festival, no classes were held at the school, and he was sure that the tutor, too, would chat with him willingly and pleasantly.

As soon as he had presented his gift to him, Abū Ya'ḳūb started to ask questions: What did his son find difficult and what did he learn easily, how did he get along with his teacher and his fellow pupils, etc., etc. His son, who was nine years old, had been studying at the school for three years, having started, as did most children, when he was six. This was the procedure advocated by the ancient rabbis, although children exhibiting unusual talent were sent to school at an even more tender age.[114]

In accordance with the accepted custom from the earliest times, the lads first learned reading and writing by means of exercises done on small wooden tablets.[115] The method of instruction consisted of first teaching the boy to read and write whole words, on the assumption that it would be easier for him to remember words denoting concepts.[116] After the boy learned to read and write, he went on immediately to study the Bible. In many countries one followed an old tradition by beginning with the Book of Leviticus, but in Spain, in that period, one studied the portion of the Pentateuch recited that week at the Sabbath morning service. The pupils sometimes studied from scrolls of parchment written especially for them or even from Bible scrolls that had become defective. These scrolls, however, were very expensive, and more often the teacher would write a part of the weekly portion on a big tablet that he would later erase, and the pupils would read from that tablet and copy single words on their own tablets. The study of the Pentateuch usually included the teacher's explanation of the words and a cantillation according to the accents.[117] In addition, the boys learned the prayers and the benedictions—all by heart, since this was the traditional method of learning for Jews and Moslems alike in those times. A boy who managed to learn several portions of the Pentateuch by heart won a prize; and in general pupils were encouraged to study by the awarding of prizes.[118]

A girl's education was the function of her mother, who taught her spinning and various other forms of domestic work. Whether to make a living or to supplement the income or to pass the time, women spent many hours spinning, a craft they learned while still very young.[119] In sum, the education of a woman was very meager.

A boy, however, on reaching age ten, moved on to a higher stage of learning—a sort of secondary education. This was the study of the Oral Law. An age-old custom, such study was also the practice in eleventh-century Spain.[120] The accepted teaching method consisted of the pupil's reading the tractate and the teacher's clarification thereof. In this stage of learning, there was need for much oral repetition; hence the practice was to study aloud. It was customary to use a chant in studying, and therefore cantillation signs were sometimes added not only to the books containing the text of the Bible but also to the texts of the Mishna. Much use was made of mnemonic devices, such as combinations of letters, which served to help retain various principles.[121] Sometimes drugs and nostrums were employed to strengthen the memory.[122]

In the course of his conversation with Abū Ya'ḳūb, the teacher heaped inordinate praise on his son, both with respect to his grasp of ideas and to his diligence. He also expressed the opinion that he would do well even in the study of Mishna, which he was to begin shortly. He also advised Abū Ya'ḳūb that it was worthwhile not to postpone his son's study of languages.

While no importance was generally ascribed to the study of Hebrew in the Near Eastern Jewish communities, the Jews of Spain gave it a place of importance, particularly in the education of a talented boy. To be sure, at times the philologists of that age would complain bitterly about the neglect of the study of Hebrew,[123] but these complaints were not justified. No doubt there were some students who made light of the science of language, but these constituted a limited circle, and their view was not accepted by the majority of those who loved learning. The fostering of the Hebrew language was, indeed, one of the characteristic marks of Jewish culture in Spain for many generations, just as the course of studies of Spanish Moslems differed from that of the Arabs in other countries by its special attention to the study of Arabic. Special teachers taught grammar and all aspects of the Hebrew language. The method of instruction included the reading of classical texts, such as the works of Ḥayyūdj, and the reading of poetry in the presence of the teacher, who corrected the pupil wherever necessary and explained to him whatever he found difficult.[124] This method was adopted by the Hebrew grammarians from that customarily used by the teachers of Arabic. Jewish pupils also studied Arabic with teachers expert in pure Arabic—both Jews and Moslems. The repeated reading of Arabic poems was held to be an especially good method of instruction and was begun at an early age. The instructors, however, were particular about selecting poems with ethical content.[125]

The more the teacher saw how much pleasure he was causing Abū Ya'ḳūb in praising his son, the more he exaggerated. He even began to set forth plans for the continued education of the boy at one of the high schools, deliberating as to whether he should begin to learn in Spain or be sent immediately to one of the renowned schools overseas. It is true that for the Spanish Jews the study of the Talmud did not, in that period, occupy the central position in the educational program that it did among the Jewries in other countries. It was the accepted opinion of Jewish educators in Spain that it was better for the young people not to relinquish any branch of knowledge, since all branches complement one another.[126]

However, the educational system was basically religious in orientation, and the study of the Talmud was, no doubt, greatly fostered by the rabbis and the communal leaders. In accordance with the principle laid down by the ancient rabbis in *Abot* 5:24, boys started studying the Talmud at age thirteen; for three years they studied in a cursory manner, in order to become well versed in it, and thereafter they studied problem by problem at greater depth.[127] In the Talmud schools an established order of study prevailed: first the students learned the tractate *B'rākhōt* and next all the tractates dealing with festivals *(Mō'ēd)* to the very end.[128]

The level of the Spanish schools and their ability to attract students varied, of course, with the level of the instructors who taught in them. In the ninth century the Talmud school of Lucena was the best in Moslem Spain, but in the tenth century, after Rabbi Moses b. Ḥanōkh's arrival in Spain, it was replaced in rank by that of Cordova. In the rabbi's time the Talmud schools in the other cities of Spain lost their power to attract students.[129] In the middle of the eleventh century, there were Talmud schools in a number of Spanish cities whose students applied themselves to their studies with diligence and devoted themselves to learning with great zeal, as had Talmud students throughout the generations. A great Hispano-Jewish poet of that era depicted their manner of study—the din of their voices, their movements while studying, and their discussions—somewhat satirically, bringing to mind the words of the poet who wrote of the *matmīd,* the permanent student "who is like a specter moving to and fro incessantly."[130]

However, the studies at the Talmud schools of Spain were nevertheless somewhat different from those of the similar schools in other countries. For the Talmud teachers in Spain were endowed with a sense of the methodical, and rather than becoming submerged in profound discussions and in the study of problems whose conclusions are not always clearly stated, many preferred to learn from the *geonim,* the heads of the schools of Babylonia, who rendered decisions in clear language. In those generations the perusal of geonic responsa constituted a main subject for study in the Talmud schools of Spain, and the responsa of the Gaon Rabbi Hai in particular were held in highest esteem. The writings of Rabbi Ḥananel were also much read. The great rabbis in Spain, the heads of the Talmud schools, were not strongly opposed to this method of learning, for they were sure that a judge who bases himself on the geonic responsa would not err in his decisions. Moreover, they were apprehensive about decisions based on conclusions one would reach oneself from the Talmud.[131]

In any event, the level of learning and knowledge in the Spanish Talmud schools was high—equivalent to that of similar schools in most countries. However, in the Middle Ages it was the custom not to study in one's city but study with renowned teachers in faraway lands. Young Moslem theologians would wear their feet out wandering "in search of knowledge" from city to city and from province to province; in like manner the Talmud students traveled to places abounding in Jewish lore to study with renowned rabbis and hear new interpretations from them, to be close to them, or, in the language of those days, to "serve" them and obtain from them permission to officiate as rabbis. The Jewish educators of the Middle Ages, who were not blind to the consequences of faulty communication, encouraged the youths to undertake their journeys, finding support in sayings of the ancient rabbis, such as: "Wander afar to a place where learning abides" or "Learn from the writers and not from books alone."[132]

The lives of the Jewish scholars were therefore similar to the lives of the Moslem theologians. The Talmud students would absent themselves from their parents' homes for years to study in distant cities and obtain from famous rabbis permission to become rabbis in turn, just as the young *fukarah* took pride in the *idjāza* (permission to render legal decisions) granted them by one of their great teachers. In the manner of the *fukarah,* some of the young men in the Spanish Jewish communities would go to Kairawān and study in its schools. Kairawān's R. Nissīm b. Jacob, who lived in the first half of the eleventh century, makes mention of the students from Spain who came to study under him.[133] But young Jewish scholars from Spain did not go only to the schools at Kairawān. When the fame of Rabbēnū Gershōm, the greatest of all the German rabbis, who was called "Light of the Exile," became known throughout the Jewish Diaspora in the first third of the eleventh century, students from Spain also went to him, for he mentions such students who "served" him.[134]

Young men who had a tendency toward secular learning studied with Jewish or Moslem teachers who were experts in both the literary and the exact sciences. Arabs, even those from the most noble families, accepted Jews as students. In the first third of the eleventh century, Abū ʻĀmir Ibn Shuhaid was one of the greatest Arabic poets and rhetoricians in Spain. He was the scion of an Arabic family that traced its lineage to al-Waddāh b. Razzāḥ, who took part in the famous battle of Mardj Rāhiṭ in 684. This same family provided officers and viziers at the royal court of Cordova for generations. Abū ʻĀmir himself was a physician, but he was known, first and foremost, as a distinguished writer. Consequently, students came to him to study the lore of Arabic rhetoric and the technique of versifying.[135] According to his own account, cited in a history of Arabic writers from the early twelfth century, an esteemed Moslem from Cordova and a Jew, Yūsuf b. Isḥāḳ, sat before him one day, and studied with him the technique of composing poems according to the classical measure of the *ḳaṣīda.* After he had instructed them in various principles, he called upon the esteemed Cordovan to compose a poem following those principles and bring it to him the next day. The Cordovan stated that he had fully grasped Abū ʻĀmir's views, but the Jew remained silent. The following day the former brought a poem of inferior quality whereas the Jew wrote such a marvelous *ḳaṣīda* that the Moslem himself admitted that the Jew's poem was better than his.[136]

To be sure, the number of talented students who continued their studies on a higher level was very small: The greatest majority dropped from the learners' ranks at a young age. No doubt only relatively few passed beyond the middle level—the study of the Mishna. In those generations a youth who wanted to study was faced with far greater and more numerous obstacles than in modern times. One of these was the difficulty in obtaining the books from which he would study. Since books were handwritten, they were very expensive. In questions addressed to the Spanish rabbis in the eleventh century and in their responses to them, mention is made at times of books being given in pledge and also of the theft of books in order to copy from them.[137]

Nevertheless, among Jews education was in no way the occupation or concern of an elite group. There surely were ordinary laymen who made their living from various kinds of non-scholarly occupations who set aside time for studying Jewish lore. Such persons would come together in study circles and would engage a scholar to teach them at regular intervals for a proper remuneration. In one of the questions addressed to the rabbis during that era, there is an account of an agreement five men in a Jewish community in Spain made with a teacher who came from another country and obligated himself to give them a lesson every day of the week, devoting four days to Oral Law, Thursday to the Bible, and Friday to explaining the portion of the Pentateuch to be read in the Sabbath service.[138]

The general level of culture in the Jewish communities of Moslem Spain in that period was much higher than in most Jewries in North Africa and the Near East, just as the cultural level of the entire population of Moslem Spain was higher than that of the inhabitants of the other Moslem lands and the countries north of the Pyrenees.[139] But in addition the educational goals the Jewish educators and heads of the communities established were much higher. The educators in Jewries of other lands envisioned the education of the younger generation as the study of the Jewish law and the observance of the religious commandments, all else being of secondary importance in their eyes. They viewed such matters as learning the language of the people in whose midst they dwelt or the study of the secular sciences in a negative light. In any case they attached no importance whatsoever to these studies. The basic educational goal of the Spanish Jews in that era was also religious; but the educators also desired to rear Jews who possessed a general education. What prevailed there was not the wish to limit education to talmudic law but rather the desire also to make available to the young that which was beautiful and worthwhile in Arabic culture. This goal corresponded with another purpose: the aim to cultivate in all life's areas the external form, a characteristic typical of Spaniards throughout the generations. In this light the words of Samuel the Nagid, urging his son to study Arabic, are edifying: "Depart from those whose tongue and speech are stumbling."[140]

However, it was hard to attain this goal. To educate large communities to be at home in two cultures or, at least, to master two tongues properly required many years of study; but the fact is that in those generations when there was no obligation to send the children to school, only a few finished their required course of study. Consequently, the majority of the Jews of Spain did not have a proper knowledge of Hebrew. Solomon Ibn Gabirol complained that half of them spoke "the Edomite language" (that is, the Romance language) and half "the language of the children of Ḳēdar" (Arabic).[141] Moses Ibn Djiḳaṭilla likewise complained at the lack of knowledge of Hebrew among the Spanish Jews and averred that by contrast the Jews of southern France know Hebrew well and were even "accustomed to speak it."[142] Solomon b. Joseph Ibn Jacob, a physician from Saragossa who translated Maimonides' Commentary on the Mishna from Arabic into Hebrew at the end of the thirteenth century, was vexed at the Hispano-Jewish scholars of the eleventh and the beginning of the twelfth century, "all of whom wrote most of their commentaries and responsa in Arabic to facilitate matters for the questioners and students."[143]

The large Jewry in Moslem Spain apparently assimilated far more to its neighbors than did other Jewries in important Jewish centers. How great is the difference in the degree of assimilation between Spanish Jewry and the culturally independent Jewry of Babylonia in talmudic times—as well as the Jewries in Eastern Europe in modern times, which were so utterly distinct from their neighbors in religion, mode of life, language, and dress! In addition, the Jews of Moslem Spain were set apart from their Moslem neighbors to an even lesser degree than were the Jews in other Arabic lands from the Moslems in whose midst they dwelt.

In all the Arabic-speaking countries where large Jewish settlements existed, special Judaeo-Arabic dialects developed. The tendency of the Jews, who were not schooled in the text of the Koran and the other classical works written in pure Arabic, to make greater use of expressions from the popular language than was done in speech and in writing by Moslem intellectuals; the great number of Hebrew words the Jews shared in common with the Arabs, and the Jews' practice of writing Arabic in Hebrew letters—all these reasons made even the Arabic spoken by the educated Jews a considerably different language from that of their neighbors. But this distinction was also caused by the varied directions and dimensions of the Jewish migration. When migrating Jews from an Arabic-speaking country established large communities in another Arabic country, the immigrants would preserve, for a number of generations, their particular dialect—especially since new immigrants would join them from time to time. The Arabic spoken by the Jews of Egypt throughout the Middle Ages was noted for distinct forms of the Maghrebin dialects, because the migration of the Jews from the Maghreb to Egypt was unbroken for centuries. On the other hand, there was never a Moslem migration from the Maghreb that was large enough to set its mark upon the language spoken by Egyptian Moslems.[144]

The Romance language spoken by the Spanish Christians, which employed Arabic words but applied to them the meaning of Romance words[145] or added Romance suffixes to Arabic words,[146] influenced Spain's Arabic dialects. However, the Arabic dialects in Spain were essentially related to that branch of dialects to which the Maghrebin vernacular Arabic belonged.

Before the migration of the Banū Hilāl (Arab tribes) to the Maghreb, the Arabic used in speech in the cities of northern Morocco was also spoken across the Straits in the cities of Andalusia.[147] The majority of the vowel changes in the Andalusian Arabic, among which the change of the *kāmeṣ (ā)* to a *ṣēra (e)* was especially conspicuous, as well as variations in accents had their parallels in the Arabic dialects of the Maghreb.[148]

Among the many Jewish immigrants who settled in Spain after its conquest by the Arabs and later, the Jews from the countries of the Maghreb were in fact in the majority. Thus, when they came to Spain, they were indistinguishable from their neighbors in their Arabic dialect. A famous rabbi who immigrated to Spain from the Maghreb at the end of the eleventh century had the habit, in his judicial decisions written in Arabic, of preceding the first-person singular of a verb in the future tense with the letter *nun (naf'al).* This phenomenon, characteristic of the dialects of the Maghreb, is also evident in the private letters of the Andalusian Jews from the first half of the twelfth century, but it is, as well, an identifying mark of the Arabic spoken by the Moslems in Spain.[149] Had a Jew of Maghrebin origin spoken such forms of the verb to an Egyptian Moslem, the latter would have recognized immediately that this person had originated elsewhere, whereas in Spain he would merely have been speaking the accepted form of the language.

The Arabic used in the Andalusian Jews' private letters brings into prominence those phenomena characterizing the Arabic spoken by their Moslem neighbors. In the Arabo-Maghrebin dialect it was customary to express an action that had not yet taken place by adding the word *kāna,* which had become solidified with the future tense of the verb; and this use also appears in the Arabic letters of the Spanish Jews from the first half of the twelfth century. Its use was also customary in the speech of the Spanish Moslems.[150] A typical phenomenon of Judaeo-Arabic is the evolution of the suffix "n" of classical Arabic into a separate word denoting an accompaniment of an indefinite article and also a relative clause with an indefinite relative particle; and this usage that occurs in the letters of Andalusian Jews is also characteristic of the Arabic of the Moslems in Spain (whence it follows that it reached the Near East from the Moslem West).[151] In the Judaeo-Arabic of the Jewish communities in all the lands ringing the Mediterranean Sea, the relative pronoun *alladhī* became fixed and was not coordinated with the relative particle in gender, case, and number. This usage of the relative pronoun abounds in letters of Spanish Jews from the beginning of the twelfth century, but it was—again—customary in Spain among the Moslems.[152]

However, not only were the Jews in Spain indistinguishable in their Arabic dialect from their Moslem neighbors, but it even seems that they constituted one of those language groups that had a decided influence on the shaping of the Hispano-Arabic vernacular by propagating the Maghrebin dialect. One of the words unique to the Arabic spoken in Spain was the word *matā'*, which means "possession." *Matā'* became converted into a particle expressing the genitive or possessive, even to the extent of being declined. This usage appears in a letter an Andalusian Jew wrote at the beginning of the twelfth century and in a document, signed by Jewish witnesses, dealing with the sale of the property of two Toledan Jews in 1117. It also occurs in the writings of Maghrebin Jews who settled in the Near East in the tenth century and later. The expression is also found in a Moslem's lament over the tribulations of the city of Valencia composed at the end of the eleventh century and in works written in the Maghreb during the twelfth century.[153]

Notwithstanding the fact that from the aspect of language the Jews in Moslem Spain were more adapted to their milieu than their brethren in the other Arabic-speaking countries, their knowledge of pure Arabic was generally more meager than that of the Moslems. Even the intellectuals wrote in language containing many elements of the vernacular of the masses, although sometimes with the deliberate intent that Jews in other countries could easily understand them. Consequently, all those syntactical forms typical of the Judaeo-Arabic of the Jews in all the Arabic-speaking countries are evident in the Spanish Jews' letters of that era, such as the dual instead of the restricted plural,[154] the suffix "n" in the dual-construct (genitive) and adjunct forms,[155] improper cases,[156] emendations of redundancies,[157] compounded prepositions,[158] the inflexible rendition of the word *laisa,*[159] and others. To be sure, similar syntactical usages also occur in documents written by the Mozarab Christians, who were likewise less skilled than the Moslems in classical Arabic.[160]

Those Jews of that era who could express their ideas in Hebrew and who realized the goals the Jewish educators had set for themselves were, therefore, persons who generally thought in Arabic, though they had no complete mastery even of it. The fact that they thought in Arabic is clearly evident in all their writings, which are full of "Arabisms." They made extensive use of the passive voice, invented new compound "tenses," and imitated Arabic combinations of word forms such as verbs and prepositions.[161] The prepositions, in whose use the influence of Arabic is particularly evident, take on new meanings; and some of them change into conjunctions.[162]

In the area of lexicography, too, the influence of Arabic is great. The Jewish intellectuals who wrote in Hebrew gave Hebrew words the meaning of similar-sounding Arabic words, formed Hebrew words in a meter parallel to the meter of the corresponding Arabic words, and expanded the area of meaning of a Hebrew word to correspond with the meaning of the parallel Arabic word.[163] To be sure, they frequently made these innovations with the intent to enrich the ancient biblical language and to make it meet the needs of their age. The Hebrew language as employed by the Jewish intellectuals in Spain also underwent a change in word order: The demonstrative pronoun would precede a noun or a numeral.[164] Prominent in the syntax are conditional clauses that resemble those in Arabic and disconnected relative clauses like the Arabic *ṣifa* clauses.[165]

The influence of Arabic, in which they spoke and thought, was therefore very strong among the Jewish intellectuals in Spain who engaged in literary activities. The kinship of Hebrew and Arabic facilitated the transfer of phrases, vocabulary, and syntax, whereas the difference between two linguistic families prevented a similar influence of Arabic upon Romance, the Latin-based tongue that was destined to become the Castilian language.[166] On the other hand, many of those innovations introduced by the writers in Spain struck root in the Hebrew language and in time were not regarded as an alien element. This was, of course, one of the results of the writers' important and highly ramified activity. For in spite of limitations, the knowledge of pure Hebrew and its active use were far more widespread in Spain than they were in other centers of the Jewish Diaspora. This could be ascribed to the merit of generations of educators like that teacher and instructor in grammar in eleventh-century Toledo who taught the son of Abū Ya'ḳūb Yūsuf and other youths like him.

IV

As in other countries, Spanish Jewry was, in a manner of speaking, a "state-within-a-state" or a "city-within-a-city," for in the Middle Ages political authority was less centralized than in our own time and based more on the activities of various autonomous groups—diversified elements such as social classes, religious bodies, and local groups. The authority of the Jewish communities and the scope of their activity were, consequently, broad, and they were recognized by the authorities of the Moslem state. By the eleventh century the Jewish communities of Spain already possessed an old tradition: Their ways of life, which had come down from time immemorial, were fixed and strictly preserved.

Aside from its judicial authority, the power of the community was especially great in the area of taxation, and it naturally was most zealously insistent on keeping to all the age-old rules pertaining to it. The *djamā'a* or *djumla,* as the Jewish community in Moslem Spain was called,[167] collected taxes for the government and also imposed various levies for its own needs. It therefore found it necessary strictly to supervise its fiscal operations. Usually two or three officials of the community were designated to collect a specific tax or to carry out an activity linked with communal outlays. Such officials were appointed for a period fixed at the outset, generally one year, and were obliged to hand in an exact accounting to their colleagues. It was an important principle that no one official collected monies alone but only when accompanied by another.[168] On the eve of a festival, it was easier for these officials to free themselves from their other occupations and devote themselves to the needs of the community. Hence, on the eve of this holiday, Abū Ya'ḳūb Yūsuf was making his way to the Great Synagogue, where the communal offices were located,[169] in order to pay a tax.

The officials who engaged in tax collecting were two members of the communal board. The board members were generally referred to in Moslem Spain as *as-Shuyūkh* ("the elders").[170] Following ancient custom, it was the practice of the Jewish communities in Spain in those generations to appoint seven officials—those "seven representatives of the city" of whom the Talmud speaks.[171] This number was set because according to talmudic justice the decisions and actions of seven officials are binding upon the community.[172] While the Jews of Spain fulfilled this principle, they did not, however, appoint officials in the same way as did the Jewish communities of Babylonia. Instead, they had the custom of choosing their leaders through general elections. The elected leaders were given certificates of appointment, which all or some of the electors signed, that spelled out their privileges and obligations.[173]

This routine, which was utterly opposed to the method of making appointments in the Near East,[174] was inherited by the Spanish Jews from the Jewish communities in the Greco-Roman world. In the Jewish communities that flourished in the Mediterranean countries in the days of Greek and Roman rule, the common arrangements for the conduct of communal affairs were similar to those prevailing in the non-Jewish municipalities. As was the case for the entire city, so too in the Jewish community the general assembly had the highest degree of authority in the community, and the heads of the community, or "elders," were chosen in general elections for a period of one year according to the Jewish calendar's reckoning. This municipal arrangement, which was in effect in Spanish cities in the days of the Roman emperors, continued to exist in Spain, as in most former Roman countries, for many generations—at least as far as the management of municipalities was concerned. This was so despite a deterioration in the cities' autonomy that began in the third century throughout the breadth of the Roman Empire when the authority, in effect, passed from the elected heads of the city into the hands of officials appointed by the government who supervised them.

In Spain the municipalities continued to exist even in the days of the Visigothic kings. At a later period of Visigothic rule, the main functions of the municipality did, indeed, pass into the hands of officials appointed by the state—or the function of the municipality changed altogether. On the other hand, a change also took place to give a more popular character to the municipality, for it was precisely in this period that holders of various offices were chosen by the people, when they had previously been appointed by the royal government. In any event, after the kingdom of the Visigoths came to an end, ancient institutions—such as the assembly of the inhabitants that made decisions on matters of public concern and acted as a judicial authority—were revived in the Christian areas of Spain.

The Mozarab communities in Moslem Spain, which enjoyed both communal and juridical autonomy, elected their officeholders or submitted them to the royal government for appointment, whereas the Jewish communities, which had ceased to exist as recognized corporate bodies a long time before the liquidation of the old municipalities in the later period of Visigothic rule, revived the old tradition that had been broken by the persecutions of the later Visigothic rulers, who were Catholic.[175] Typical of the historical continuity of these municipal institutions on the Iberian Peninsula was the fact that, among the Mozarab Christian communities in the ninth century, the various functionaries were still being given titles that were traditional to Roman municipalities.[176] Jewish communities in Spain, for the most part established by immigrants from the Greco-Roman diaspora, were conservative, as were Jewish communities everywhere, maintaining the arrangements for the conduct of the community that had been practiced formerly in those lands.[177]

To be sure, there were wealthy families of property and distinguished lineage who had dealings with the Moslem rulers; and these had a decided influence in communal affairs. It was an accepted principle that in financial matters the majority to be reckoned with was not that of numbers but that of those who paid the largest sums in taxes.[178] The lower classes were docile and did not dare to initiate a struggle for their rights in the community. In fact, a communal class struggle was an almost unknown phenomenon among the Jewish communities of Spain at that time. When they fought over dominance, members of the poor classes, whether Moslems or Jews, and disaffected intellectuals who resisted the affluent gave their support to one of the powerful groups within the community —or they separated from it and attached themselves to a sectarian movement. Consequently, there is almost no mention in the responsa of the Spanish rabbis or in the other literary sources from the era of Moslem rule of any class struggle within the Jewish community.

The authority of the Jewish community to establish the way of life in its neighborhood was regarded as absolute. The rabbis deemed obedience to its decisions to be as significant as the observance of a religious precept. As the rabbis of Spain made clear at frequent intervals during the Middle Ages, the individual was subordinate to his city's community; the community could make decisions according to its will, "every community in its place [had] authority like the geonim," and its decisions with regard to the individual had the same sanction as the judgment of the highest court of all Jewry.[179] Communal decisions were held to be binding as long as they did not expressly contradict Jewish law, and the rabbis permitted the use of any means to implement them—even if it required the assistance of the non-Jewish authorities.[180]

In the language of that time, the decisions of the community were called *taḳḳānōt* ("regulations"), and in keeping with the democratic system prevailing in the Jewish communities of Spain, they were reached by a majority vote.[181] Sometimes these regulations were enacted for a limited time; sometimes they were accepted as fixed statutes that would continue over a longer period. Because of their great importance, it was customary to give them added authority through the imposition of the ban on whomever violated them, as well as by the establishment of other penalties, such as fines.[182] The language of the regulations was Arabic, though they were interlaced with many Hebrew expressions[183] so that everyone, even the uneducated, would understand them properly. For the same reason, it was also customary to announce them, after the communal heads had signed them, by means of a solemn proclamation made by the cantor in the synagogue in the presence of the entire congregation.[184]

One of the important duties of the leaders and judges was the imposition of religious discipline on the members of the community. Many regulations were enacted for this purpose. At times the judges were unable to punish offenders, either because they were powerful or because no witnesses were to be found to give evidence in the matter; and at times it was necessary to employ preventive measures, the enactment of which was well within the scope of their functions as leaders. It was their habit to adjure a person not to transgress anymore,[185] and, in addition, they naturally had to make considerable use of the ban both for a limited time and as a permanent instrument.[186] It was customary to appoint officials to supervise the morals and the keeping of religious precepts.[187] These would separate a man and a woman who lived together without being married,[188] and they would likewise intervene in the economic activities of members of the community and establish rules to prevent troubles from besetting the public because of the actions of individuals. The rabbis justified these regulations as measures that fell within the spirit of the talmudic law.[189]

A very important function, and frequently the most difficult, was the collection of the various taxes. Managing tax collecting for the Jewish communities' own activities was, at times, harder and more complicated for their heads than was the collection of the taxes imposed upon the Jews by the non-

Jewish authorities. The reason for this was the fact that the incomes of the community were compounded of various taxes that were initially designated for specific expenditures. The absence of a general fund caused many difficulties and great complications, lawsuits and altercations, and could even frequently paralyze the activities of the community. This method of taxation was inherited from the Greco-Roman cities and was carried over to the Jewish communities and preserved by them during the Middle Ages in the Moslem countries of the Orient and also in Spain.[190]

Among the community's sources of income, the leading one was the tax called *ma'ūna,* collected mainly from the slaughter of meat and the sale of wine and sometimes from business transactions. This tax was the most important source of income for the Jewish communities of Spain throughout the generations; and it was, therefore, always designated to provide a livelihood for the rabbis and teachers who engaged in education under the authority of the community and at its expense. Payment to those "who disseminate knowledge," already a fixed practice in the tenth century, was regarded as the very highest obligation of the community; accordingly, the leaders gave this matter much attention.[191] The remuneration of the cantor was provided from the income of the same tax, from the budget of the synagogue, or from communal funds. Sometimes a special tax was levied for this purpose.[192] A special tax was also assessed for the remuneration of those judges who made their livings from their judgeships, for the court scribe, and for the scribe's messengers. A Hispano-Jewish writer who lived toward the end of the eleventh century reported that in most communities there was a "court fund" for which a tax was collected at the beginning or at the end of the year.[193] These levies varied in different generations and locations, but every community had an "alms box," in accordance with the regulations established by the ancient rabbis. The monies from this source paid for the needs of the poor; among other things they were used to provide support for orphans without means and with no kin.[194] From time to time the officials of the community would also be called upon to redeem captives, and to implement this obligation a special levy would also be imposed. As was done among Jewries everywhere, the community officials often, in such cases, turned to other communities, appealing to them to share the burden.[195]

Besides the various taxes, the community had fixed incomes from communal religious endowment funds *(heḳdēshōt)*, of which there were many in every generation. The Moslem government actually gave de facto recognition to these funds of the non-Moslems for the good of their religious institutions and for the benefit of the eleemosynary objectives of their communities—even though this was contrary to Moslem law. In other words, such property was recognized as belonging to these communities or to their institutions, having been deeded to them from legacies. It was therefore obligatory for the authorities to respect these funds and not impose taxes upon them. Like the Moslems, the affluent Jews often dedicated property for sacred purposes to prevent their inept heirs from squandering the wealth they had accumulated through great effort and toil. Some dedicated all their possessions, movable property as well as real estate, whereas others dedicated only a part of it, leaving some for the heirs.[196] The heirs frequently attempted to protest against the dedication of the property to religious endowments and would resort to all kinds of arguments and schemes to pry the property loose from the community.[197]

Sometimes those dedicating the trust would not assign any purpose for which the incomes drawn from the estate were to be used, but merely stated that it was to be an endowment; and sometimes they defined the purpose with exactitude. In responsa of the eleventh century, the synagogue, including all the necessities pertaining to it, is especially mentioned as the beneficiary of endowments,[198] and even a collection of decisions by a Moslem jurist of that century includes a question that was brought to the attention of Moslem jurisconsults at Cordova concerning the endowment of a synagogue.[199]

The accepted procedures followed by the Jews of Spain with regard to endowments were influenced quite patently by the rules of the Moslem *wakf*. The man dedicating the fund would make out a deed in which he stated the amount of property being dedicated and the purpose of the fund and how it was to be managed, just as Moslems did in writing out a *wakfiyya*.[200] At times the dedicator would reserve for himself the privilege of making changes in the dedicated property—he might, for example, substitute other properties for it—and at times he would make it a condition that one of the members of his family be appointed to administer the property. Even these stipulations were characteristic of *wakf* arrangements.[201] Because of the importance of the sacred endowments as a source of income, many communities appointed special "treasurers" or "collectors" who managed them in accordance with their own judgment. If anyone left a sum of money to an endowment, the "treasurers of the endowment" could use it as they saw fit—they could acquire real estate, or invest it in trade, or lend it at interest.[202]

These methods of taxation and management procedures resulted in the communal heads' never knowing the extent of the sums available to them to cover the various expenditures. To be sure, any budget based on taxes is merely an estimate, but the absence of a general fund into which all incomes could be funneled intensified uncertainty, since it was impossible to balance a deficit in one income by a surplus from another. In order to surmount this difficulty and ensure an orderly disbursement of the community's obligatory payments, such as salaries, its leaders adopted the method that was prevalent among public bodies in ancient and medieval times: They farmed out the collection of especially important taxes. This was, for example, a customary practice with respect to the *ma'ūna.* [203]

The farming out of the tax collecting was, however, only a partial solution to the fiscal problems that burdened the leaders of the communities. Although this method assured them of providing for the coverage of ongoing expenditures, they found themselves in great difficulty when confronted with the need to make relatively large outlays for unexpected matters. Unforeseen expenditures were not uncommon. The most frequent among them were undoubtedly sudden demands made by the Moslem authorities, but often enough the leaders would need large sums of money for altogether separate reasons. In such cases they would use money designated for another purpose that became available to them from taxes or from an endowment. But such actions frequently encountered vigorous opposition from those paying the taxes or from relatives of the family that had provided the endowment. The rabbis who were called upon to arbitrate such questions tended to permit the use of funds for other than designated purposes, since these too involved the performance of a religious commandment.[204]

While the administration of tax funds was complicated, methods of collection were very efficient. Scholars and the indigent, who were supported through charity, were exempt from paying taxes, but no concessions whatsoever were made for the other members of the community. The leaders had available to them tested means of coercion to which they resorted without too much hesitation. Whenever they were confronted by recalcitrance, they would punish the one who objected to paying taxes by putting him in the communal jail, placing him under the ban, and—especially—confiscating either part or all of his property.[205]

At no time did Abū Ya'ḳūb Yūsuf show any inclination to avoid paying taxes. He was accustomed to paying his assessment at the appointed time and was, therefore, given a cordial welcome when he came to the community office. The officials promptly recorded the amount of money he paid in their ledger, or *al-bitāḳa,* [206] and, to the accompaniment of manifold blessings, he went on his way.

V

The sun was already straight overhead—the time set for the funeral of a merchant whose shop had been near that of Abū Ya'ḳūb Yūsuf. The deceased had also been a very learned man. It therefore was a matter of course for Abū Ya'ḳūb to accompany the dead on his last journey, thereby fulfilling a commandment. This merchant, who had been his friend for many years, had died the day before, but, unlike the frequent custom in the Spanish communities,[207] he had not been buried on the day of his death.

By the time Abū Ya'ḳūb reached the home of the deceased, a large gathering had congregated before the gate while members of the family were engaged in the ritual purification and dressing of the corpse.[208] Funeral and burial arrangements had been set by the ancient rabbis; and in a community as large and old and with as many learned men as that of Toledo, they were carried out punctiliously. Moreover, the customs that had come into being over the generations of Spanish Jews were enveloped in a halo of sanctity. When someone passed away, vessels were shattered, and sometimes the relatives and friends who came to the house of the deceased would kiss him as he lay on his bier.[209] In the Jewish communities of Spain a man would occasionally be buried in his house, just as Moslems sometimes did. The rabbis complained about this practice because later, during the seven days of mourning, prayers were recited within the proximity of the grave and without setting up a partition, an act prohibited by Jewish law. But there were men who were not worried about defilement ensuing from a corpse and even deemed themselves to be honoring the dead person by reciting prayers near his grave. They found support for their views in a passage in *Baba Kama* (16b) where one reads that "they held scholars' meetings" at the grave of King Hezekiah.[210]

Frequently a man would not be buried at the place where he died but would be removed to another city; sometimes, for example, the deceased would be taken back to the city of his birth in order to be buried near his forebears. The transfer of corpses from one city to another—sometimes over considerable distances—involved great effort because of the speed required to bring the dead to burial before decomposition and unpleasant odors set in. The relatives and friends of the dead person would, at times, carry him on their shoulders, giving themselves no rest, day or night, until they reached their destination.[211] Despite the difficulty involved in the transportation of corpses, Jews in all the lands ringing the Mediterranean transferred the dead from city to city and from one province to another, as did the Moslems.[212]

Generally, however, the dead person was buried in his city's cemetery; and such was the case with the merchant in whose funeral Abū Ya'ḳūb took part: He was to be buried in the cemetery of the Jews of Toledo. For a short time Abū Ya'ḳūb waited with the other men in attendance before the house until the funeral cortège left for the cemetery. He listened to the men who spoke in praise of the deceased, but even as he did, he was wrapped in his thoughts about the life of man—as fleeting as a shadow or a dream that fades away.

The Jewish cemeteries in the Spanish cities were located mainly near the city gate that was close to the Jewish neighborhood.[213] In some cities, however, they were at some distance from the city wall, as in Calatayud, where the Jewish cemetery was two kilometers away from the city.[214] In not a few cities the cemeteries of the various religious groups lay alongside one another, as in Huesca.[215] In addition, Jewish cemeteries located at a distant site were sometimes moved at a later time to a city's center, because of changes in the plan of the city. Something like this occurred in Granada where, in the eleventh century, the Jewish cemetery was near the main gate of the city—a site where there was much traffic.[216] In Cordova the graveyard was first near the gate close to the Jewish neighborhood in the southwestern part of the city, in other words outside the wall, between the Almodóvar and Seville Gates. However, since many neighborhoods were built in the area west of the wall, the site became too circumscribed. Moreover, near the Jewish graves were buried criminals who had been executed by crucifixion or some other method. Thereupon the Jews of Cordova bought a plot of land north of the city outside the León Gate, near the area many of them had lived in at the time of the city's growth in the tenth century. In the eleventh century Jews were still burying their dead at that site. There were at the time big Moslem cemeteries near Cordova's Jewish cemeteries, making it necessary for the Jews to pass through a long stretch of road before reaching them.[217] The graveyard of Toledo's Jewish community was north of the city, not far from the Shaḳra Gate, between the San Roque Monastery and the slopes of the Palomarejos Hills.[218] Near it was the Moslems' cemetery, where their dead were buried during the eleventh century.[219]

For many generations non-Moslem funeral processions through the streets of a Moslem city were fraught with much unpleasantness. The Moslem rabble would mock the "infidels" and even mistreat them. A ninth-century Christian writer from Cordova describes with bitterness how the Moslems of his city insulted the Christians during funerals, throwing stones and filth upon them.[220] The Jews of Toledo were able to avoid any harm because they did not have to pass through Moslem neighborhoods with their dead. Those taking part in the procession could go out of the city by way of the "Jews' Gate," which was within the confines of their own quarter, continuing on their way outside the walls, where there were no dense settlements.

As prayers and psalms were recited, the procession moved along the Jewish quarter's main thoroughfare, which ran parallel to the western wall of the city. After leaving the city by way of the "Jews' Gate," the procession turned right until it reached the cemetery. The grave was already dug, and while all those who were in the procession assembled, Abū Ya'ḳūb cast a quick glance at the grave, as if he wanted to ascertain that it had been properly prepared. Like all graves in the cemeteries of Spanish Jews, it was directed toward the east so that the dead person would face eastward.

In the early generations of Moslem rule, the Jews of Spain tended to bury the dead as the ancient rabbis had ordained. They would dig a cave and, in its side, hollow out a chamber in which they buried the dead. At a much later period the grave actually was conformed to the shape of the human body. In other words, a hollow was dug that broadened out from the middle into two depressions, one for the head and one for the feet. Coffins were not used except when the corpse had been brought from another city and was already in an advanced state of decomposition. Generally the corpse was laid on the earth itself, but the grave was protected from above and from the sides with stones and bricks. If the grave was not roofed over entirely, stones at least were placed over the head and stomach as a protection.

After the dead person was lowered into the grave, one of his relatives would descend into it to straighten out his hands—

in repose on his chest—and would place near him objects that had been dear to him. It was, indeed, the custom of the Spanish Jews at that time to put precious objects such as gold and silver rings into the grave; this was particularly so in the graves of women, who sometimes were also buried with their headgear of gilded embroidery. The rabbis protested in vain against this custom, which was contrary to the views of the ancient rabbis. Writers were often buried with the books they had written, since they were especially precious to them.[221]

After the grave was closed, pebbles were thrown upon it from all sides (in accordance with the old saying that man originated from the four corners of the universe), and the oldest son of the deceased had recited the mourner's prayer *(ḳaddīsh)* in a voice choking with sobs, the people at the graveyard would arrange themselves in rows to comfort the mourners. This was the established procedure for a funeral and the course of conduct at the funeral on the eve of the Festival of Sukkot in which Abū Ya'ḳūb participated. Immediately after the ceremony was concluded, he left in order to visit the graves of his forebears.

Although Abū Ya'ḳūb knew the cemetery very well, he moved slowly through it, tarrying here and there near the graves of people he had known or near those of revered rabbis, usually surrounded by fences. It was deemed a great honor to be interred close to the rabbis. Such graves abounded in nearly all the cemeteries, and one of them, the grave of Rabbi Saadya Abū Hārūn in the cemetery of Granada, is mentioned in a Jewish chronicle of the later Middle Ages.[222]

Most of the monuments over the graves were very large blocks of granite. Their size allowed them to cover the entire grave and protect the interred person from wild animals. The length of those monuments preserved in the archaeological museum at Toledo is between 2 and over 2.70 meters, and their breadth varies between 70 and 90 centimeters, but in height they range from 30 to 40 centimeters. They are made in the form of truncated pyramids atop rectangular blocks. Most monuments in the cemeteries of other Jewish communities in Spain were neither properly smoothed nor polished. Sometimes Roman monuments or fragments of monuments were used, and Hebrew inscriptions would be engraved on the back.[223]

However, in the Jewish community of Toledo's cemetery, which was a very important one, the monuments were well made and the inscriptions upon them testified to the community's high cultural level. Many of the inscriptions, in particular those engraved upon the monuments of notables (officeholders in the royal service and eminent scholars), were long, and they usually were rhymed. In ornate and pointed language, the traits and achievements of the deceased were described, and, in words charged with sincere feeling, the grief of their kin over their deaths was expressed. The authors of the inscriptions demonstrated great skill in their use of verses from the Bible to allude to the names of the deceased and the dates of their deaths. No doubt the majority of these inscriptions were the product of the genius of poets, from whom they were solicited by the kin of the deceased.[224] Only rarely was a jargonlike Hebrew used in an inscription; this might occur when a poor family requested an inscription from an artisan who was not well versed in Hebrew or even from a non-Jew, who merely copied the letters someone had marked down for him without understanding what he was writing.[225]

With a hasty glance at the inscriptions by which he passed, Abū Ya'ḳūb finally reached the plot containing the graves of his family members. It was the custom of the Spanish Jews to bury members of a family near one other.[226] Caught up in memories, he murmured the *ḳaddīsh.* Since he was pressed for time, he did not, however, tarry long but rejoined the group of men returning from the funeral.

They made their way somewhat hurriedly without speaking. Some were engrossed in their sorrow, and others, as it was the eve of the festival, wished to reach their homes quickly. This was difficult for the kin of the deceased because they had taken off their shoes in accordance with the custom that those returning from the funeral of a member of the family should replace their shoes with wooden sandals.[227] Before Abū Ya'ḳūb parted from them, one of the relatives of the deceased turned to him, requesting him to attend an *ashkābha* (mourning ceremony) that had been set for the tenth day after the festival. Since according to an old custom the mourning period could not be in effect until nine days after the Festival of Sukkot for anyone buried on the eve of the festival, the service for the dead was set precisely at the conclusion of the "thirty days of mourning." In the Near East it was the custom to arrange the *ashkābha* for a scholar six months after the memorial service *(hespēd),* but in Spain it was combined with it or even conducted earlier.[228]

Just as burial practices did not all conform to the regulations set forth by the ancient rabbis, observance of the *ashkābha* was one of the customs connected with mourning that was somewhat different among Spanish Jews from what it was among other Jewries. After the interment of the deceased, garments would be rent,[229] and clothes that were either entirely black or had black spots were worn.[230] Throughout the seven days of mourning, the bereaved family sat at home and did not leave even to perform a meritorious deed, such as participation in a circumcision. At times, however, the pain was too great, and, on the day after the burial, the mourners would go to the cemetery and prostrate themselves in prayers at the grave.[231] On the first Sabbath after the *shibh'a* (seven days of mourning), they would attend the synagogue but would not sit in their customary places.[232]

VI

When the procession had entered the city and each man had gone his own way, Abū Ya'ḳūb turned into the street leading from the "Jews' Gate" to the commercial quarter. Before closing his shop for eight days—so he speculated—it would be a good idea to see whether his assistant had done all that was required of him. He had therefore already told his wife that morning that he would not come home for lunch but would take his repast in his store. Consequently, it would have been better for him to enter the city by way of the Shaḳra Gate, which led to the "al-Ḳanāt" quarter by a more direct route. But as a matter of good manners, he wanted to accompany the relatives of the deceased as they returned from the burial, even though walking at noon was wearying. So he ascended the precipitous street from the "Jews' Gate" to the center of the city, time and again mopping the perspiration from his brow, and, after walking about a quarter of an hour, he reached his shop.

Having examined the accounts and the other documents his assistant had prepared and having found that everything had been done properly, Abū Ya'ḳūb sent the man off with many good wishes for the holiday. He then turned his attention to his repast. In the al-Ḳanāt quarter a Jewish cook daily made the rounds, offering various cooked dishes that were strongly presumed to be reliable in their ritual fitness. Abū Ya'ḳūb called out to the cook and bought sausages from him that were then called *mirkās* in Spain and are now known in North Africa as *mergāz.* This sausage was made from lean meat mixed with many spices and with garlic, vinegar, and much salt.[233] After his hurried meal he hoped to stretch out on mats, place a small pillow beneath his head, and rest a short while during the hour set aside for the noontime rest, then known in Spain by the Arabic name *ḳiyāla* but currently called "siesta." At that very moment, however, a Moslem owner of a shop in the perfume bazaar appeared. He had come to pay Abū Ya'ḳūb a noontime visit, as was his habit from time to time during the hours when the marketplaces were emptied of their customers and most of the merchants had closed the shutters of their establishments in order to go home or rest inside their shops.

Abū Ya'ḳūb was accustomed to accepting these visits, since neighborly relations between Jews and Moslems in all of Spain and in Toledo in particular were good in those days. As long as the passions of the masses were not inflamed and daily life continued on its normal course, the Moslems did not evince marked hostility toward the Jews. To be sure, Moslem fanatics endeavored to stir up religious hatred and disapproved of any ties of friendship between the Moslems and the "infidels." A Moslem theologian who lived in Seville in the second half of the eleventh century demanded that his coreligionists keep themselves apart from Jews and Christians, not show them any affection, and not greet them.[234] But such matters were not regarded with approval in those days.

In Toledo, relations among the members of the three faiths were especially close. In other cities, such as Cordova, Seville, and Calatayud, the Mozarab Christians were expelled by the Moslems from the inner city, which was encompassed by a wall. However, in the Spanish capital Moslems, Christians, and Jews had long dwelt alongside one another, and labor and trade relations among them were strong. At the outset of the period of Moslem dominance, the natives of Spain—Christians and Jews alike—viewed the conquerors as ignorant barbarians and took pride in their own culture. It is true that most of the Moslems who arrived in Spain in the eighth century were coarse, uneducated soldiers or peasants. But much time had passed since those days: The intellectual level of the Moslems had risen steadily, and by the tenth century Moslem Spain was already one of the Mediterranean countries distinguished for their level of civilization and the culture of their inhabitants. By the eleventh century there was no longer room for the feeling of superiority toward the Moslems that had formerly nestled within the hearts and minds of the Jews. On the contrary, an ordinary Jew such as the merchant Abū Ya'ḳūb Yūsuf, who was not a person of eminence, thought it something of an honor when a Moslem came to visit him. According to the biography of the abbot John of Gorze, the Mozarab bishop of Cordova told the abbot that the Moslems treated the Christians with respect and displayed contempt toward the Jews.[235] This account, which is included in the work of a Christian cleric of the tenth century, is somewhat dubious. However, after the Christian kingdoms of northern Spain grew in strength and after most of the Moslem kingdoms in the Iberian Peninsula became subject to them, the esteem for the Christians greatly increased. The victories of the kings of León and Castile were not without results: Wherever they took place, the victories exalted the importance of the kings' coreligionists. One cannot put the esteem the Jewish officials enjoyed at the courts of the Moslem kings on the same level with the might of the powerful Christian rulers, who protected their fellow Christians and imparted to them something of their aura of success.

In Arab fashion, the Moslem merchant who came that day to see Abū Ya'ḳūb began the visit with many inquiries into his welfare and that of his family. He asked about the state of his health and, in a vague manner, about his business, replying gently in turn to similar questions put to him, in accordance with custom, by his host. He then mentioned rumors of a coming war between two Moslem rulers—a report being circulated by people in town. Having touched upon matters of politics, he began to express his vexation over the oppression of the Moslems by the Christian rulers in the central and southern sections of the peninsula. It was evident that this subject preoccupied and worried him, causing him to expatiate upon it; but he was even more inclined to discuss yet another matter, about which he spoke during almost every visit with Abū Ya'ḳūb—the nature of the relations among the members of the various faiths within the sphere of Moslem rule in Spain. He revealed a particularly great interest in debates between Moslems and non-Moslems.

The Arabs had a strong impulse toward polemics, and there was apparently nothing that interested them as much as discussions about the superior merits of their religion as against any other. The Moslem theologians in Spain debated with Christian intellectuals[236] and, of course, also with Jews. In general the Moslems in Spain loved disputations on religious questions relating to such things as the doctrines of the Godhead and the systems of various Moslem sects. They also staged public debates between representatives of different faiths and even held disputations with Jews before large gatherings.[237] The Christians and Jews were also caught up in the urge to debate, and there were even occasions when Christians would go to Moslems in particular in order to debate with them.[238] The debaters were mainly distinguished scholars. In his books, the greatest of the Moslem theologians in the eleventh century notes in a few phrases that the Jews with whom he debated were men of much knowledge.[239] These disputations were conducted with the great ardor that is so singularly characteristic of Spaniards: Frequently, before one of the debaters had ended his talk, his opponent would stop him and break into his remarks.[240] Abū Ya'ḳūb's visitor told him with much gusto about a debate between a *faḳīh* and a Christian cleric that had taken place the previous week in his presence. In it, the Moslem had refuted his opponent's arguments quite brilliantly.

Having finished this story, the Moslem merchant moved on to another topic that had been a commonplace subject for conversation among the people of Toledo for a long time. This was an episode enveloped in mystery. According to assertions put forth by many people, a princess of the royal house of Toledo named 'Āisha had shown a liking for Christianity, and was devoting herself to aiding Christians captured by Moslem armies. Ultimately a miracle occurred: The food offered her turned to roses. When the king of Toledo saw this, he permitted the princess to live openly as a Christian. 'Āisha became Casilda, but she was not content with this alone. The princess could no longer be reconciled to the way of life in the court of a Moslem king; she therefore asked permission to go to a spa and then left Toledo for Castile. There she lived in the vicinity of Burgos until her death in 1047, after which she was canonized by the Church as Saint Casilda.[241] The Christians of Castile extolled the courage of the princess of the Dhu 'n-Nūn dynasty. However, the Mozarabs of Toledo itself refrained from talking about this episode, because they were accused of persuading her to desert her faith, and making propaganda for another faith was regarded by the Moslems as a breach of the Covenant of Omar.

Abū Ya'ḳūb's visitor did not, however, want to offend him and thus did not expatiate on the baseness of the Mozarabs, lest his host surmise that he really intended his remarks for the Jews. In all truth his host knew full well that when the opportunity offered itself, Moslems inveighed against the Jews, claiming that although they behaved submissively toward Moslems, they were in point of fact enemies and were crafty and treacherous.[242] In order to get around this problem, the visitor stressed that in general, Christians and Jews in Moslem Spain were faithful subjects, fulfilling their obligations to the state as did the Moslems. In fact, he gave inordinate praise to the monks who cordially welcomed Moslems coming to stay with them. In making this last observation, he spoke rather vaguely. His words hinted at a matter about which it was best to remain silent. It was, after all, customary for Moslems—nobles in particular—to visit monasteries in order to drink wine. This practice also prevailed in Spain.[243] The zealous Moslem theologians fulminated against this way of life, which was altogether contrary to the laws of their faith. In their opinion, drinking wine was a great sin, and in every generation they cried out against the Jews and Christians who caused Moslems to transgress against their faith. A Hispano-Moslem writer of that era demanded that his coreligionists not allow Jews to sit near the gates of their houses, since Jews were suspected of selling wine.[244] But the zealots accomplished nothing by their admonitions; the Moslems drank copiously and were grateful to the "infidels" who provided them with the drink that gladdens the heart of man.

After Abū Ya'ḳūb's visitor reached this topic, his flowing conversation touched on more delicate episodes in the complex of relationships among the members of the various faiths. He told about a certain Moslem who wanted to marry a Christian woman, and of another who was having a love affair with a Jewess. To be sure, incidents like these did happen from time to time. The notorious episode of the Arab chieftain in the province of Granada, Sa'īd b. Sulaimān b. Djūdī, who was a most handsome but licentious person all his days until he was slain in the house of a Jewess, was not completely exceptional.[245] It was not only Moslems and Jewesses who were involved in love affairs. A species of homosexuality (dalliance with youths) that was very prevalent in Spain recognized no boundaries of national or religious affiliation. An Arab poet, a native of Alcira in the vicinity of Valencia, Abu-'l-Ḥasan Ibn az-Zaḳāḳ (d. 1035), who composed poems in praise of the beauty of his native city and of women who fascinated him, also poetized about the lad of his delight, with whom he whiled away the Sabbaths to a point where that day became his favorite, though he was a Moslem.[246] To be sure, the Moslem who had come to visit Abū Ya'ḳūb did not speak of matters such as these; in fact, when he noticed that his host was growing weary, he slackened his conversation, and when he was convinced that Abū Ya'ḳūb was no longer encouraging him to continue, he rose to take his leave. He gave his host greetings on the occasion of the Jewish festival and expressed the hope that "it would come each year while peace abode with him and his family"—and then he departed.

VII

Abū Ya'ḳūb, who had done much walking that day, still wanted to bathe before the start of the holiday. To determine whether it was now time for this, he went out to the nearby square, which had a large sundial. It consisted of a horizontal slab of marble on which the hours were marked, and at its center was an iron rod whose shadow served as a clock hand. These sundials, which were named for the marble of which they were made *(rukhāma)* or for the flat slab that formed their shape *(basīṭa),* were employed in ancient times by most nations with a high degree of culture. Even the prophet Isaiah speaks of "the shadow of the dial, which is gone down on the sundial of Ahaz" (Isa. 38:8), that is, the clock of King Ahaz.[247]

The Moslems also made other clocks—more developed models of the Greek water clock, or clepsydra. They consisted of a receptacle into which water from a duct continually dripped; a needle floating on the water was sometimes fastened to a device that made known each hour. For instance, balls—as many as the number of hours—could be discharged from a magazine, knocking upon taborets and thus indicating the hour. An Arabic treatise written in Andalusia at the end of the eleventh century makes mention of the tiles protecting the hammers that knock against the clock's tablet.[248] In Toledo itself, in the second half of the eleventh century, the noted astronomer Zarḳēl constructed a water clock that was considered one of the world's wonders and prompted a Hebrew poet to compose a poem about its maker beginning: "The marble work of Zarḳēl. . . ." This clock was set up in a palace outside the city.[249] In general, the water clocks, which were truly masterpieces, were few in number, whereas the sundials could be found in many Spanish cities' plazas and in other locations where traffic was heavy. Although it is true that they were not completely accurate, since the shadow of the vertical rod divided both the long summer days and the short days of winter into twelve hours,[250] the sundial satisfied the needs of the artisans and merchants in the Moslem cities who were not very hard pressed for time.

When Abū Ya'ḳūb saw that three hours of the afternoon had gone by, he closed his shop and went to the bathhouse.

For the inhabitants of the Moslem countries, a visit to the *ḥammām* (bathhouse) was one of the greatest of delights. First and foremost, of course, there was the benefit derived from the bath itself, which was essential in the crowded and filthy cities of the Middle Ages. Masseurs, barbers, perfumers, and even bloodletters were also available in the bathhouse. It was thus an establishment where all manner of attention was given to a person's body, where it was treated for whatever was necessary. But the time spent in the bathhouse also resulted in other pleasures. The walls were decorated with designs; and ornaments and statuary, which evoked the admiration of the onlookers, were placed inside. The Arabic writers mention that the statue of a beautiful woman, holding in her arms a baby who was being menaced by a serpent, was once brought into the bathhouse in Seville. They related that the inhabitants were so charmed by this statue that many neglected their work, spending many hours looking at this consummate work of art. The poets of the eleventh century even composed poems about it.[251]

Although one must take into account that there is much hyperbole in the writings of the Arabic authors, it is nevertheless a fact that the Spaniards were accustomed to linger for many hours in bathhouses, which were also convenient places for friends to meet and spend time in a relaxed environment near basins of cooling waters. Consequently, bathhouses were abundant in number. According to one account, there were 300 in Cordova in the days of the Calips 'Abdarraḥmān III, and in the days of al-Manṣūr there were as many as 600.[252] The nobles and the wealthy installed private baths in their houses, but the majority of people resorted to public bathhouses. In most of these, both men and women bathed—usually on different days or else during different hours of each day. But individual bathhouses for men and for women also existed.

As in all the quarters of the cities of Moslem Spain, there were public bathhouses in the Jewish neighborhoods that also served as ritual baths. Because of their close adaptation to Moslem manners, the Spanish Jews practiced ritual immersion more than the Jews in Christian countries. The ancient rabbis had, of course, abolished Ezra's regulation requiring that one who has experienced a nocturnal pollution be prohibited from studying religious texts until he immerses himself. But the Jews who dwelt among the Moslems, who were especially exacting about ritual purity before prayer, continued to practice immersion in such cases. The Jews in Spain were punctilious about this matter for many generations. One of the great Jewish scholars of the Middle Ages, a man who himself originated in Moslem Spain, reported that rabbis coming to Spain from beyond the Pyrenees who witnessed the performance of this custom derided it.[253]

The Jews of Spain built themselves ritual baths in the same style as that employed by the Moslems in building their public bathhouses, apart from some changes in the arrangements and installations customarily found in a *ḥammām.* In the first place, they deepened the bathtub so that a person could immerse his entire body. (In some Moslem bathhouses, the baths were also deep.)[254] In addition, the Jews were particular that the water should not be drawn, because on this rule the rabbis in Spain, as in the Ashkenazic communities, vigorously held their ground.[255] It also need hardly be said that statues and images, which abounded in the Moslem bathhouses in Spain, were absent from those built by the Jews.

Nevertheless, the ritual baths were similar to those of the Moslems, and could be used in a similar manner. Just as the *ḥammāmāt* were mostly in the vicinity of the mosques, so were the Jews' ritual baths close to the main synagogue or in central locations within the Jewish quarters. The ritual bath on del Angel Street in Toledo's Jewish quarter was some thirty meters from the synagogue now called Santa Maria la Blanca.[256] For the Jews as well as the Moslems, these bathhouses in the Spanish cities filled the function of a meeting place; hence they always contained a relatively large lounge. In as small a city as Baza, the lounge was 8.45 meters long and 6.8 meters wide,[257] and in the ritual bath built in Saragossa during the period of Christian rule, it was 8.9 meters long and 7.15 meters wide.[258] In a city with a large community, there were a number of bathhouses in the Jewish quarter. From a document dating from the beginning of Christian rule in Toledo, we know that besides the bathhouse in del Angel Street, there was another Jewish bathhouse located in the "high neighborhood."[259] In the old Jewish quarter of Barcelona, one of the streets is called to this day "The Street of the New Bathhouses."[260] And in the former Jewish quarter of Calatayud, the central street is still called Calle del Barñuelo—"The Street of the Small Bathhouse."[261] These appellations show, of course, the great importance of the bathhouses in the lives of the Jews and their gentile neighbors during the Middle Ages.

The Jews in the cities of Moslem Spain, however, also made

much use of the public bathhouses in the Moslem quarters, to which members of all communities and all classes were admitted. The Moslem intellectuals who were able to express their thinking in ornate poetry found fault with the intermingling of people from completely different classes. They complained that in bathhouses, where people undress and push up close to one another, there is no discernible distinction between a master and his servant or between an educated person and an ignoramus. They were especially disturbed since in Spain people customarily entered the bath altogether naked—a practice that was uncommon in the Orient and evoked astonishment from its inhabitants who visited Spain.[262] The devout theologians condemned the custom that prevailed in the bathhouses for another reason: They complained about the intermixing of Moslems and unbelievers, a practice that was contrary to the Covenant of Omar, whose whole purpose was to separate the non-Moslems from those who believed in the religion of Mohammed. A Moslem theologian who was born in Tortosa in the middle of the eleventh century and studied at Saragossa and Seville discusses this subject in a book on the disgraceful "innovations," that is, the practices contrary to the spirit of Islam that were accepted by the Moslems as a consequence of the influence of people with other faiths. Among these harmful practices the theologian believed should be extirpated was the admission of nonbelievers to the bathhouses. He particularly stressed the fact that the non-Moslem women disrobe there and, when they do so, look altogether like Moslem women.[263] This Moslem writer consequently demanded that Jews and Christians be forbidden to bathe with Moslems. This demand is to be inferred from the fact that he wrote his book after he settled in Egypt[264] where, as early as the beginning of the eleventh century, the caliph al-Ḥākim had imposed upon the Jews and Christians the requirement that they mark themselves with special badges in the public bathhouses. Later, he provided them with their own bathhouses.[265] But the rulers of Moslem Spain in those generations did not bar Jews and Christians from coming into the bathhouses and bathing with the Moslems and, naturally, it was Moslem youths who waited on the "infidels."[266] Another Spanish *faḳīh* who wrote a book at the end of the eleventh century containing rules for the chief of the municipal police did not demand that non-Moslems be prohibited from coming into public bathhouses; he only required that Moslems not give massages to Jews and Christians, because in his opinion such acts would imply contempt for the Arabs' religion.[267] But there is no doubt that even this requirement did not gain much approval and, in point of fact, did not materialize.

That day Abū Ya'ḳūb went to a Moslem bathhouse not far from his shop. Like all bathhouses it was a vaulted structure that stood by itself and consisted essentially of three halls. The bathing visitor would first enter by way of a small corridor into a long and narrow hall—called, in Spain, "the cold hall" because it was never heated. Here the bathers disrobed in compartments that had been set up on both sides; the hall was therefore also called *bēt al-maslakh.* The bather handed his clothes and other articles to an attendant, from whom he got a dressing gown, towel, and wooden shoes, and he then entered the middle hall. This was a handsome chamber that served as a waiting room. In the eleventh-century bathhouse that is still preserved on the right bank of the Darro in Granada, this room is 11 meters long and 7.25 meters wide. In the center of this chamber, there was usually a pool and water fountain over which was suspended a lofty dome. (In the aforementioned bathhouse in Granada, it is 8 meters high.) Around it were balconies separated by arches and columns. The floor was made of varicolored marble slabs, and light entered the chamber by way of roof windows, whose panes were also of colored glass. In every bathhouse this middle hall was the biggest chamber, and, since it was heated, it was sometimes the practice to undress in it on winter days. From there the visitor proceeded to the "hot chamber" (in Spain, *al-bēt as-sakhūn*), which had its name because it was located near the large kettle and because hot water was poured on its floor. The floor was also heated by hot-air pipes in the wall and beneath the floor; the middle chamber was heated in this fashion as well. Because of the heat and the humid air and especially because the door was shut, a person entering the last chamber would begin to perspire. When drops of perspiration covered him, an attendant would start massaging him with gloved hands, particularly on his joints, and then splash soapy water on him. The man would then wash in a tub of water whose degree of heat he himself could control by using two taps near the bathtub—one for hot and one for cold water. The tub was large enough for a man to be able to climb in and lie in it;[268] and this is what Abū Ya'ḳūb did. Usually the bather shampooed his hair with ointment and powder, and, having finished all these cleansing activities, wrapped himself in a clean gown and went out to the middle chamber to relax and spend time in the company of the other bathers as long as he found it pleasant.[269]

But on the eve of the festival, Abū Ya'ḳūb could not sit for a long time like the other bathers. Instead, having rested only for a while, he left the bathhouse.

VIII

Again Abū Ya'ḳūb returned to his house to change into clothes for the holiday. When he arrived, he donned new linen trousers, fastening them with a woolen belt. He then put on a *djubba,* a linen coat that was shorter in front than behind, and over this a wide, long cloak, and promptly left for the synagogue.[270]

In those days in Toledo, as in the other large Jewish communities of Spain, there were marked differences among the city's synagogues. There were relatively large synagogues that were intended for the entire public, and there were small synagogues established by the affluent so that they could pray in them with their intimates and their extensive families. In general, these synagogues were named for those who had established them. In addition, there were synagogues for those who came from a particular city, and schools that served as synagogues. As was the case in the Near East, there were also synagogues in Spain intended for a specific group of artisans—a sort of community within the community.[271] Altogether, there were in Toledo at that time some twelve synagogues.[272] Abū Ya'ḳūb prayed in the synagogue that had been called for a long time the "Great Synagogue," one of the oldest synagogues in the city.[273]

Like the other big synagogues in the cities of Moslem Spain, this was a very ornate one. The Jewish communities in Spain took pains to embellish their synagogues and give them a beautiful appearance. From their exteriors the structures of the synagogues were not very distinguished, lest they provoke the ire of the non-Jews. But frequently a garden would be planted in front of the building, as we learn from various cities and from different epochs.[274] Inside this garden were a well and a basin that served for the lustrations of the worshipers.

Under the influence of the Moslems, who bathed their limbs before their prayers, the Jews in Moslem countries also began to indulge in washing before their prayers. To be sure, there were some who scoffed at this "exterior purification." Judah Ḥayyūdj, the grammarian who lived in Cordova in the tenth century, inveighs against the Moslems, reproaching them with the words of the prophet Isaiah (66:17): "They that sanctify themselves and purify themselves one after another in the gardens,"[275] that is to say, what is the value of their lustrations if, at the same time, they eat unclean foods. Nevertheless, the tendency to adapt to the Moslem environment won out, and, in point of fact, the practice of washing the feet before the morning service was established at an early period. The great teachers, like Saadya, supported this innovation, which had no basis whatsoever in the teachings of the ancient rabbis.[276] Even without the innovations introduced under Moslem influence, the worshipers were enjoined to wash their hands before the service. Hence the basin in front of the synagogue was one of its important accessories. It was customary to engrave an inscription, such as a verse or fragments of verses dealing with fountains and wells, over the well. This practice existed even before the conquest of Spain by the Arabs, and it remained the custom of the Spanish Jews throughout the generations.[277]

It was also common to engrave an inscription with an appropriate text over the door of the synagogue. In this, too, the Jews of Spain were no doubt influenced considerably by the customs of the Moslems, who embellished their buildings extensively by means of inscriptions, since the principles of their faith did not permit them to make designs and images of human beings and animals—particularly in houses of worship. Yet just as the Moslems gave strict heed to the prohibition against placing designs of human beings on the walls of their mosques or placing statues of human beings in them but on the other hand did not refrain from decorating them with carvings of animals, so too did the Jews. An inscription over the door of a synagogue in Toledo, probably engraved in the twelfth century, appeared in both Hebrew and Arabic, the latter being set down in Arabic letters; but in between the lines were carvings of fir-tree branches, among which a serpent was wriggling, while above them were clusters, stars, a young lion symbolizing the tribe of Judah, and four walruses with arms like serpents' tails.[278] These carvings were not made in defiance of the opinion of the rabbis, but with their express consent, as was the case in the Jewish communities of Germany, where the walls of the synagogues bore designs of trees, birds, and other animals.[279]

The synagogue Abū Ya'ḳūb attended was considered a big synagogue by Toledo's inhabitants. Its bigness was, of course, merely relative to the limited area of the cities and neighborhoods in Moslem Spain and to the size of other synagogues. In a small synagogue the sanctuary (the hall where prayers were conducted) was about 7 meters long and about 6 meters wide.[280] This was the approximate size of the synagogue at Cordova that was built in 1315 and has been preserved to our own time. The big synagogue in Toledo, which later was converted into a church known to this day by the name of Santa Maria la Blanca, is about 27 meters long and about 22 meters wide. For a Jewish community as large as that of Toledo, such dimensions—for a central synagogue—are rather scant; but the buildings in the cities of Moslem Spain, and the public buildings in general, were, for the most part, not large. The chief mosque that the Berber kings built in the middle of the eleventh century in Granada, after they made it their capital, was about three times as big as Toledo's main synagogue.[281] Nor were the synagogues in the cities of Spain particularly tall. The central portico of Santa Maria la Blanca is 12.5 meters high, whereas the outer porticos are only 7 meters.[282]

The Jewish houses of worship in Moslem Spain were built in accordance with the style that prevailed at that time among their Moslem neighbors. It is true that this adaptation to the way of life of the non-Jews was not greater than that of the Jewish communities at that time in Christian Europe beyond the Pyrenees. In that epoch the synagogues were also constructed there following the style of building of the non-Jews.[283] A special style in synagogues is evident only in the structures erected in Poland in the sixteenth and seventeenth centuries.

In most cases the synagogues were built in the shape of a rectangle, at whose eastern wall stood the sacred ark. At times the ark's place was marked by a bulge in the outer wall, as in the aforementioned synagogue in Cordova. The ark indicated the side to which one must face during prayer, but, despite its great importance, the "reader's desk" *(bīma)*—or, as it was termed in Arabic, *al-minbar*—apparently remained the center of the synagogue, both in the eyes of the worshipers and from an architectural standpoint. The platform on which the Bible scrolls were placed to be read and from which sermons were preached was set in the middle of the hall. Some drawings in Spanish manuscripts in which synagogue worship is depicted show only the reader's desk, as if it were the main object and all else in the synagogue were of secondary importance. The desk consisted of a wooden platform on four posts topped by other posts carrying connecting beams, thus forming an open canopy. From this aspect there was, of course, no difference between the synagogues in Moslem and Christian Spain, nor between them and the synagogues erected during the Middle Ages by the Jews in Central Europe. There, too, the *bīma* was the focal point of the synagogue.[284]

The great similarity between the synagogues of Moslem Spain and the Moslem houses of worship is apparent from the magnificent synagogue the wealthy Joseph Ibn Shōshan built in Toledo at the end of the twelfth century. It was called for a short time the "New Synagogue," and later it was converted into a church—Santa Maria la Blanca.[285] It is a hall divided by four rows of eight columns into five porticos. The middle portico is wider than the two on its right and left. In the middle of the eleventh century, the Great Mosque of Granada was constructed in accordance with this model. In the second half of that century, the large mosques of North Africa were built along similar lines, but in these structures the outer porticos were wider than those closer to the central portico. This came to be the pattern for the magnificent mosques built in North Africa and Spain in the twelfth century.

The numerous columns in the old synagogue of Toledo give the impression that its area is more spacious than it really is. In addition to its many columns, Santa Maria la Blanca's handsome embellishments impress its visitors. The column capitals are made of plaster carvings whose unusual coloring evokes wonder. They consist mainly of latticework into which scrolls and spirals are interwoven. Above the columns are sculptured work and carved rosettes, and above them and above the arches that join them are frames in which there formerly were inscriptions, apparently not engraved but drawn. These were separated by ornaments or by small, ribbed, perpendicular domes, after the fashion that had prevailed in the Moslem West since the eleventh century. Above these frames bows with lobes are hidden. In the central portico another band of decoration has been added between the frames of inscriptions. The plaster carvings, the combination of lobed and horseshoe bows, the tendency to allocate wider space for geometrical embellishments near carvings of plants—all of these elements are characteristic of the mosques built in the eleventh and twelfth centuries in Moslem Spain and in the western regions of North Africa. The roof of the Ibn Shōshan synagogue was made like the pointed, sloping roofs that were designated as ridged roofs and were customary on Moslem houses of worship in Spain from the beginning of the tenth century onward.[286] It is then no wonder that the edifice built by Joseph Ibn Shōshan appeared like a mosque to people of later generations who were interested in tracing the development of Moslem art in Spain.

The facade of the current building is restored. At its western edge, which once had been wider, was a balcony that held the women's section.[287] Unlike in a mosque, the Jewish women of Spain participated in prayer in the synagogue; but, in allotting them a special location within it, the Spanish Jews were influenced by the Moslems. In the synagogues of the German countries, on the other hand, for a long period during the Middle Ages men and women prayed in the same hall.[288]

One of the particularly conspicuous elements of the synagogues in Moslem Spain was the large number of inscriptions. This paralleled a development in the later Middle Ages in the Moslem houses of worship, where inscriptions also became a most important decorative element. In the small synagogue at Cordova that survives to this day, a band of inscriptions ran along all four walls. Above it were bands of decorations and, above them, additional inscriptions running the length of the walls. These inscriptions were written in red letters on a blue background.[289] For the most part they contained verses and fragments of verses from the Bible. Some, however, such as inscriptions that perpetuated the name of the donor who had erected the synagogue or that had some connection with the festivals—such as the poem about the planets and the year's cycles engraved in a synagogue in Toledo[290]— were different in content. The poem was engraved on a marble tablet and not on the wall itself; sometimes, in fact, the inscriptions would be carved into wooden beams. The Jews in Moslem countries were especially outstanding in this skill.[291]

In the embellishment of the synagogue, great importance was attached to the inscription on the sacred ark. The composition of this inscription was assigned to a famous poet.[292] Nevertheless, the tendency to adapt to the non-Jewish milieu is conspicuous even in the inscriptions themselves. In that very synagogue at Cordova, for example, there are some inscriptions written in the Arabic language using Arabic letters.[293]

In the synagogues of the Middle Ages, the worshipers sat along the length of the four walls. In a Moslem country like Spain, there were no benches and chairs; instead, they sat on mats and cushions. Each man had his fixed location, whether he had it by right of possession, whether it was assigned to him by the leaders of the community or whether he had purchased it from them for a good sum of money. The right to sit in a certain place was very important to a person; to ensure it, he often wrote his name on the wall above the site or on the floor. Nevertheless, quarrels broke out often over the location of a seat in the synagogue.[294]

When Abū Yā'ḳūb Yūsuf entered the Great Synagogue on that eve of Sukkot, the majority of the congregation were seated in their places, waiting for the service to begin. Each man sat quietly on his mat with feet outstretched, and there was hardly any small talk to be heard. The cantor, too, waited for a sign from one of the synagogue leaders. The cantor was a respected person, for great care was exercised in selecting as the leader in prayer one who was worthy in deed and exemplary in his way of life. Anyone of whom people spoke unfavorably—for example, one who was known to seek the company of women—was dismissed. One of the questions addressed to a noted Spanish rabbi in the tenth century concerned a cantor who frequented brothels and, according to testimony, also had homosexual relations with a youth. The rabbi's decision was, of course, that he should be removed and that even after he repented, he was not to be restored to his post.[295] Sometimes the dismissal of a cantor was sought because of reports about the way he had misbehaved in his youth, even though nothing bad had been heard about him thereafter.[296] Moreover, the rabbis were exacting in requiring that no man should serve as a cantor who used improper language or sang "Arabic songs" —the popular songs the public in Andalusia enjoyed.[297] On the other hand, the cantor was also required to be an educated person and, first and foremost, a man with a pleasant voice. Quite naturally, whoever met all these requirements earned the esteem of the congregation.

A few moments after Abū Ya'ḳūb entered the synagogue,

the cantor ascended the platform before the reader's desk, which he occupied during the service following the accepted practice of the Spanish Jewish communities,[298] and started chanting the prayers. He began the *Minḥa* (afternoon service) with *Ashrē yosh'bhē bhētkhā* ("Happy are they that dwell in Thy house"), went on to recite the eighteen benedictions in a whisper, and concluded with *'Ālēnū* ("It is incumbent upon us"). After that he paused briefly and then began the *Ma'arībh* (evening service) with *V'hū Rāḥūm* ("And He is merciful"). The cantor and most of the worshipers knew the prayers by heart, their order having been fixed for many generations, though there were some who could not read Hebrew. This was the order of service that the Gaon Rabbi 'Amrām, the head of the school of Sura, had sent to the Jews of Spain in the second half of the ninth century, and they had made almost no change in it up to Abū Ya'ḳūb's time.[299]

It was customary for the congregation to rely upon the cantor to pronounce the benedictions preceding and following the recitation of the *Sh'ma'* ("Hear O Israel"), while it merely responded with "Amen." However, the prayers recited in a whisper were said by each man for himself, provided he was well acquainted with them.[300] The cantor gave the letters *ṭet, 'ayin, ṣade,* and *ḳof* the same pronunciation as did the Arabs, and he was meticulous about properly articulating the letters *bēt, gimel, dalet, kaf, pe,* and *tav* in every word in which they occurred. He made almost no distinction between the sound of the vowels *ṣēre* and *segol* nor between the long *ḳāmeṣ* and the *pataḥ.* He also pronounced the *ḥōlam* and the *shūruḳ* almost as if they were identical. A mobile *sh'va* was pronounced as if it were a short *pataḥ.*[301] At the evening service attended by Abū Ya'ḳūb, the cantor did not add any new hymns, but after the congregation had read the *Sh'ma'* with him loudly and in a body, he extended a benediction to a man who had been married during that week.[302] But of course this did not greatly prolong the service.

When the service ended, each man wished his neighbor a "joyous festival," to which the latter responded with a "happy holiday." Afterwards they entered the large *sukkah* (tabernacle) that had been put up adjacent to the synagogue. It was an ancient custom among the Jewish communities in Spain to build a tabernacle not in one's home but rather next to the synagogue. Nor did one eat therein: One merely entered it for a short while. Yet in the middle of the ninth century, a question had been addressed to the Gaon R. Natronai concerning this matter, and reference was made to the practice prevailing in antiquity following the account in Nehemiah 8. The gaon's response was that a tabernacle should be built at the synagogue for noninhabitants of the city, namely, for strangers who have come to it in connection with their business; however, the city's inhabitants should be obliged to build tabernacles for themselves in their own homes.[303]

Nevertheless, though it was contrary to the ruling, the Jews of Spain did not alter their practice. At the beginning of the eleventh century, this matter was again referred to a rabbi, this time the Gaon R. Hai, and he responded similarly, to wit: Whoever did not build himself a tabernacle in his house to eat and sojourn therein had not fulfilled his obligation. Yet, notwithstanding both rulings, the Jewish communities of Spain held fast to their practice, as is borne out by the testimony of a Jewish scholar who came to Spain from southern France in the beginning of the thirteenth century. As before, according to the scholar, the Spanish Jews were content merely to enter the tabernacle, to pronounce the blessing, recite the *kiddush* (blessing over wine), and sit within for a short time.[304] Abū Yā'ḳūb also entered the tabernacle, stayed there for a few moments, and then went on his way.

IX

When Abū Ya'ḳūb Yūsuf left the synagogue for his house, it was already dark, and without a lamp to illuminate the narrow and winding streets, the sense of darkness and mystery was even stronger. It seemed as if heaven and earth had become united into one solemn and gloomy essence—basically the way Spaniards had always perceived the world. The air of this ancient city of kings is fraught with heavy melancholy, and when a pall of darkness shrouds everything, the depression grows stronger—every wall and every mute stone combining to bring to mind a remote past of fanaticism and stubbornness, of cruelty and suffering. Abū Ya'ḳūb Yūsuf, nevertheless, went on his way confidently; he was not frightened, nor did he stray. This was, after all, his birthplace, whose air he had breathed all his life.

When he arrived at home, all the members of his family, dressed in holiday attire, were waiting for him. His wife Dona wore a *siḳlāṭūn,* a dress of red silk interwoven with golden threads that gave forth a fragrance of delicate perfume. Abū Ya'ḳūb extended the festival greeting to his family; they responded loudly, and the children kissed his hands. The circular and very low table, around which the members of the family sat on even lower seats, was already set. The head of the house and his wife sat on a couch bedecked with a silken coverlet; the many cushions on the couch were also inside coverlets of silk, which were embroidered with a variety of designs. The children sat on pillows on top of rugs that covered the entire floor. Aside from the couch and table, the room also contained a rather short chest made of wood, set in a framework of iron, and locked with a wooden key. On this chest stood a silver flask, and, in a corner of the room, there was also a tall copper flask. The first had been placed on the chest as a decoration, while the other held a piece of Indian wood that dispersed a pleasant fragrance. Two copper-and-wood candelabra, dull brown in color but polished, hung from the ceiling. Outside of these few pieces of furniture, the room was empty; however, thick mats hanging from the walls filled the void to some degree.[305]

Abū Ya'ḳūb approached the low table without delay and began to chant the *ḳiddush* (blessing over wine) with the verse: "These are the appointed seasons of the Lord, even holy convocations which you shall proclaim in their holy season" (Lev. 23:4). Afterwards, he drank a quarter of the cup of wine and gave some to all around the table to taste. The repast his wife had prepared for that evening was substantial and varied, befitting the night of the festival. As was customary with a festive meal, the family first partook of grapes and dried fruits. Next they ate fish with lettuce and carrots, and the third course consisted of spiced chicken. The very fact that the meal was eaten by everyone together put the children into an exalted frame of mind, since usually the members of the family did not dine together. It was customary to serve the meals separately to the father of the family, to the wife, and to the children; only on the Sabbath and the festivals did they all dine together. Each item of food was put into one big dish on which verses were inscribed, often in gilded letters. Only wooden spoons, not knives or forks, were used, and those around the table took for themselves helpings from the big dish. Abū Ya'ḳūb's wife took good care that the children should not be carried away by their enthusiasm and transgress against the rules of good manners by, for example, poking their heads into the bowl; and she did indeed succeed in restraining them. The last course consisted of soft doughnuts baked in oil that were eaten with honey; in Spain they were called *isfandj*. This course caused special concern to the wife, since she was apprehensive that the children would soil their clothes. Hence it was a great relief to her when Abū Ya'ḳūb signaled that it was time to remove the remains of the food and proceeded to recite the grace.[306]

Having completed the benediction, Abū Ya'ḳūb began to chat with his children. He turned to his son, calling him by his Arabic cognomen, which was combined with the term "Abū" by which he was usually called. These surnames were almost a fixture; thus a boy whose name was Ya'ḳūb could be called "Abū Isḥāḳ," and Yaḥyā could be called "Abū Zakkariyā."[307] In other words, though generally speaking every boy had a Hebrew name, most of them were referred to by Arabic names. This accommodation to the Arabic environment was not exclusive to the Jews: While the Mozarab Christians had Latin names assigned by the church, their secular names were Arabic. Many of the Jewish girls, on the other hand, did not have Hebrew names at all but names that were altogether or partly Arabic or Romance, such as Amīra, Djamīla, Palomba, or Sitbōra.[308]

Abū Ya'ḳūb's son, who was 9 years old, related how he went to the market with the maidservant to buy fish. The fishmarket was northeast of the Great Mosque, between it and the cattle market *(suk ad-dawwāb,* currently called *Zocodover),*[309] which is not a short distance from the Jewish quarter. On his way there the lad passed by other markets, such as those in the neighborhood of the dyers and the neighborhood of the sellers of herbs for medicinal purposes. He encountered the *muḥtasib,* the supervisor of markets, who, together with his assistants, was making the rounds, scales in hand, to examine the merchants' scales and weights, to test the weight of loaves of bread sold in bakeries, and to remove hucksters who had seated themselves in narrow streets. But the lad was particularly impressed by the tellers of tales and the clowns he saw in the marketplaces, and he expatiated on those who bedecked themselves with eagles' heads and played with snakes and scorpions as well as those who wrote incantations on amulets and interpreted dreams, around whom were gathered groups of simpletons, peasants, maidservants, and idlers.[310] The mother enjoyed the flowing and ebullient account given by her son, which testified to his alertness and ability to observe; however, since she did not want to lessen the significance of her daughter, she remarked to her husband that the girl was making good progress in her spinning instruction.[311] A considerable time was thus spent until at last the children were sent to bed and Abū Ya'ḳūb and his wife Dona remained alone to chat by themselves.

Abū Ya'ḳūb loved Dona very much; and he respected her even more than he loved her—so much so that he had never taken another wife. Although monogamy was the accepted custom among the Jews of Spain in those generations, it was not at all unusual for a man to marry two women, especially if the first had not borne a child for many years[312] or if she became ill with a malady that prevented marital relations—particularly since in such a case it was customary in Andalusia to refrain from any contact whatsoever.[313] Polygamy was more common in overwhelmingly Moslem areas, where even the Mozarab Christians were influenced by this practice.[314]

On the other hand, in Toledo, where the Christians were in the majority, polygamy was not a customary phenomenon. Dona, the wife of Abū Ya'ḳūb, had already borne him a son and a daughter, and he was attached to her with all his heart and soul. Even before the eve of Sukkot he had remembered to buy her a gift, which he presented to her with appropriate words of greeting after the children had left. It was a bracelet that he had bought on the suggestion of a metalsmith with whom he had dealt for many years. The Jewish metalsmiths in Spain had acquired renown; they constituted the majority in this craft both in the north and the south of the Iberian Peninsula.[315] The bracelet Abū Ya'ḳūb gave her was really a work of art. Dona was quite excited over it and could not find words to thank her husband.

As if she desired to prove anew that she deserved the affection her husband so abundantly bestowed upon her, Dona began to tell him about the preparations she had made for the winter. In Toledo the winter was indeed very cold and it was necessary to prepare for it early. Dona reported that she had bought firewood and also three bags of charcoal.[316] She added that she had already taken from the chest the winter garments, such as woolen coats, her husband's fur coat,[317] and a waterproof coat for the days when the heavy rains fall. This last was made of a cloth called *barrakān.*[318] She had also taken out the woolen blankets.[319] She then returned once more to a discussion of the children, who she said, thanking God, were developing to her satisfaction. She mentioned incidentally the misfortune that had befallen their neighbors, whose small son had died. Child mortality was indeed very frequent in Spain,[320] and whoever had children who had overcome all the ailments of childhood blessed his good fortune. Having been reminded of the neighbors, Dona told of an incident that occurred in the back street. A magician who roamed the neighborhood offering to tell women the future was invited to enter a house, and took advantage of the opportunity to steal, even attacking a woman.[321] In another house—so she related—some scoundrels perpetrated a theft with the help of trained pigeons.[322] The hour was late, but Dona continued to chat about many matters until Abū Ya'ḳūb casually remarked that he was tired.

X

The next day Abū Ya'ḳūb woke early and immediately rose to prepare himself for prayer. He washed his hands and bathed his feet, reciting the appropriate blessings for these ablutions. He then went on to the morning benedictions until he reached the portion describing the *Tāmīd*—the daily offering in the Temple. Next he studied the portion of Leviticus that is read from the Pentateuch on the first two days of the holiday, reading the Hebrew text twice and the Aramaic translation once. After spending considerable time over these matters, he took up the palm branch and citron—first reciting the proper benediction connected with this act—and went on to the synagogue, accompanied by his son.

Such was the custom in the Jewish communities of Spain on the Sabbath and the festival days. To be sure, some rabbis inveighed against it, claiming that individuals tarry too long at home and that meanwhile the time passes for reciting the *Sh'ma'* and the prayers. R. Judah al-Barcelōnī called attention to the small towns in which it was the practice to go to the synagogue promptly on arising; there the psalms of praise would open the service, the *Sh'ma'* would be recited at the proper time, and the Pentateuch portion would be studied after the service.[323] However, in the large communities the old custom remained.

Anyone present that morning in the Great Synagogue of Toledo when the psalms of praise were recited, particularly when the entire community, word by word and with great devotion, read in unison *Nishmat kol ḥai* ("The Souls of All the Living"), would readily be convinced of the great devoutness of the majority of the congregation. It was evident that old and young were directing their thoughts to their Creator with a perfect and pure faith, and anyone with an eye to see could tell that the worshipers were not merely mouthing words by rote but expressing the feelings of their hearts. No doubt these sentiments were stronger than usual during the month of Tishrē, and the climax of that period came during the Festival of Sukkot when more than the customary prayers were recited. And in the Jewish communities of Spain, more prayers were recited than was customary in other lands. Thus, it was the practice in Babylonia to read supplicatory prayers only during the Ten Days of Penitence, whereas in Spain such prayers were already read on the first day of the month of Ellūl.[324] Many members of the congregation, even during the other days of the year, had the habit of rising at night to recite voluntary prayers. By way of the Arabic word *nāfila,* they called this practice *l'hitnappēl* ("to prostrate oneself") in Hebrew.[325] There were also pious men who fasted on a given day of the week[326] and performed other, similar acts of devotion.

However, not all the community was so zealous in its religious practices. It goes without saying that not everyone was educated or knowledgeable in the Hebrew language, and this naturally had a diminishing effect on their devotion in prayer. The number of uneducated people was not small, and the spiritual leaders of that generation were therefore preoccupied with this problem. R. Isaac Ibn Gayyāt was asked what the law was concerning the Jews who did not understand what the prayers meant; he replied that they nevertheless must pray.[327]

On festivals the service lasted a long time. Before the *kaddish* doxology preceding the prayer *Yōṣēr,* the cantor would chant a supplementary composition called *r'shūt.* After the benediction he would add other supplementary prayers. It was the custom of the cantors in the Jewish communities of Spain to compose liturgical poems and to chant them before the congregation. Of course, it was not permissible to alter the basic order of the service; but in this respect the cantors had complete freedom as long as they met certain specified conditions. For example, there had to be a connection between their poem and the obligatory benediction, and they had to revert to the benediction's theme at the close of their hymn to prevent a break in the continuity of the service.[328] The cantors wrought wonders in their compositions. They resorted to most uncommon words, employing appellatives and unusual names for the

Jewish people and its heroes, all following the taste of the times. Most of the poems rhymed, and many of them had a biblical verse at the end of each stanza. Naturally, there were many in the congregation who could not grasp the thoughts of the cantor poets but knew and loved the melodies in which the hymns were sung. These were Arabic melodies that circulated widely at that time.

Because of their characteristics described above, the majority of liturgical poems were repugnant to the rabbis, who complained bitterly about the great amount of license that prevailed in this matter. One was especially vexed over the names that the hymn writers applied to God, which he regarded as bordering upon profanation. He summed up his opinion by saying that the hymns are "words of folly and ignorance far beyond what our forebears could conjecture; and it is all the more incumbent upon us to refrain from even their mention."[329] A Judaeo-Spanish grammarian fulminated against the many uncommon words the hymn writers toyed with—words that were not understood by the congregation, such as the riddles and parables in the hymns composed by ha-Ḳalīr. He also censured the grammatical errors in the hymns that hinted at homiletic and folkloristic explanations of the Bible, saying that a person should quote in his prayers the verses of the Bible according to their original sense.[330] In addition, a great rabbi who taught in Lucena at the end of the eleventh century denounced, in particular, the use of Arabic melodies.[331] But all these rebukes by the rabbis were in vain. It was precisely the Arabic melodies that attracted the public, especially those which were less devout. Many would join the cantor in singing them joyfully,[332] and poems a cantor had composed that found favor in the eyes of the public would shortly be sung in other synagogues.

Such was the custom among the Jewish congregations of Andalusia in the tenth century,[333] and such also was the custom in Toledo and the other Jewish communities in central Spain in the days when Abū Ya'ḳūb worshiped in the Great Synagogue, especially during the Festival of Sukkot. Hence, with all its imaginative additions, the service grew more and extended.

As the service became longer, the worshipers' decorum deteriorated. The children who started out by sitting with their parents ended up seating themselves in the empty space before the row of seats. The adults leaned against the walls, turning this way and that, without directing themselves eastward or even toward the pulpit.[334] In anticipation of the long holiday service, some had even brought prayer rugs, which they stretched out on the cold stone floor. These rugs were made like the prayer rugs of the Moslems, so the rabbis prohibited their use. A great rabbi from Toledo who lived in a later period was asked about "those rugs which are called sadjdjāda" and have the "design of a black cube upon them." He responded that it had been explained to him that "in Toledo it was customarily forbidden to place such a rug in the synagogue in order to sit on it or, all the more, to hang it by the side of the sanctuary, since it is held that the black shape designed upon it is the shape of the site where they go to celebrate in their land, and some say it has on it the design of Mercury and it is their wont to pray upon it and prostrate themselves upon it."[335] As can be deduced from the words of this rabbinical authority, the use of prayer rugs was an early custom stemming from the days of Moslem rule, and even then the rabbis had opposed it very vigorously. However, in this matter, too, the words of the rabbis were disregarded; the assimilation of Moslem customs was too strong. The use of prayer rugs took root among the Jewish communities in Spain and was still common many generations after the end of Moslem rule—as is evidenced by a prayer rug from Spain preserved in a museum in Berlin.[336] Such rugs were also hung on the walls of the synagogues for decoration; even those that the entire congregation stood on when they rose to their feet would be hung up after the service.

The service for the Festival of Sukkot involved many occasions for rising. After the main body of prayers was recited, the ritual palm branch *(lūlābh)* would be blessed, the "Praise" (Psalms 113–18) would be recited, and the Bible scrolls would be removed from the ark while the entire congregation stood on their feet until the reader's desk was reached and the scrolls were placed upon it.[337] Later the desk would be encircled while the prayer *Hoshana* was chanted. In the Jewish communities of Spain, it was the custom to circle the desk only once on the first six days of Sukkot, whereas in Babylonia and also in many communities of North Africa it was encircled three times on those same days. The *geonim* R. Sherīra and R. Hai responded to questions on this matter put to them by persons in North Africa and Spain by stating that the accepted custom should be to encircle the desk three times. Nevertheless, the Spanish Jews clung to their practice.[338] The Jewish communities of Spain also differed from the practice in Babylonia on the day of "Hoshana Rabba," for they would encircle the desk on that day with the willow branch alone.[339] Special hymns were sung on the occasion of these circuits. The number of these hymns was already large in the days of the *geonim,* and in Spain the hymns composed by R. Joseph Ibn Abītūr were especially popular.[340]

An order of precedence was strictly observed in granting the honors for reciting a portion of the Bible *(aliyōt).* The first to be called up would be a man of priestly lineage *(kōhēn),* despite the fact that he might be an ignoramus. This decision was in accordance with the teaching of R. Moses b. Ḥanōkh.[341] The rabbi also would be called up on every festival, and a bridegroom would also merit this honor. When the latter was called, the entire congregation would chant the verses describing how Rebekah was brought to Isaac (Genesis 24).[342]

To be sure, as had been the custom in former times, most men only went up to the reader's desk but did not themselves read from the Bible. Since many were unable to read from the Bible scrolls, the cantor read in their stead. This provoked the angry comment of R. Judah al-Barcelōnī, a contemporary of that age, that though they pronounce the blessing they do not fulfill the commandment of reading the Bible. On the other hand, the rabbi did not object to the cantor's assisting the person called to the reader's desk by whispering to him while he read aloud.[343] The *Targum of Onkelos* was in desuetude in Spain a long time before the eleventh century, but it would be read on a Sabbath to impart a specially festive air to the service, as, for example, when the congregation wished to honor a man who had taken a wife during that very week. The Aramaic translation of the *Hafṭāra* would be read on the festivals as well.[344]

XI

On returning home after the service, Abū Ya'ḳūb ate a light repast, which was served to him in the parlor where the entire family had dined the night of the festival. He then adjourned to another room to read a book one of his friends had lent him. He was, of course, disturbed time and again by the children, who were playing in the courtyard. The windows and doors of all the rooms of his house faced the courtyard, and there was no place where their shouting went unheard. The children played with toys called *kuradj*—horses made of wood that looked like the war horses of the cavalry. These toys were popular at that time even among adults—especially among the female dancers who hung them over their waists when they appeared at parties. The children would dash forward and then backward as if they were riders mounted upon horses, attacking each other amid excited shouts and running to and fro.[345] Dona, who that morning wore a thin, bright *ghilāla* and over it a *miṭraf* (a cloak for the upper part of the body),[346] tried to quiet the children so that Abū Ya'ḳūb could go on reading. She knew that he derived much pleasure from it. But her efforts were in vain.

The book Abū Ya'ḳūb was perusing was a collection of stories written in the Arabic language, though in Hebrew letters. To be sure, Abū Ya'ḳūb, like most Spanish Jews, had acquired in his youth a proper knowledge of the Hebrew language and understood the meaning of the words in the prayers. Nevertheless, he had difficulty reading a Hebrew book.[347] The stories in this collection were similar to the Arabic tales called *al-Faradj ba'd ash-shidda* ("deliverance after hardship"), whose themes were miraculous deliverance, help for a poor man wasting away in need, or the rewards of a pious, God-fearing man.

Jewish writers in Arabic countries imitated this branch of literature. They collected tales from the wealth of narrative material in the homiletic commentaries of the Bible, opened with a preface in the style of these homilies, and added, as a conclusion, a moral lesson based on biblical verses. These tales were intended to encourage God-fearing men. Most of them dealt with simple folk who fulfilled the commandments wholeheartedly, thus meriting a reward; the inclination to evil and its suppression; the performance of good deeds, such as the giving of charity; and tales about good and evil women. Frequently, explanations of passages in the Talmud that had no connection with the theme would be inserted into the tales; but the people of those generations enjoyed such insertions. The language of these stories was not literary Arabic but an Arabic that was somewhat intermingled with the vernacular spoken by the people. This, too, gave the readers pleasure.

One such collection of tales was written by R. Nissīm b. Jacob of Kairawān in the first half of the eleventh century. But this was one of many. Semieducated people were voracious readers of these stories, and a merchant like Abū Ya'ḳūb was no doubt one of them.[348]

That morning, however, Abū Ya'ḳūb was not destined to do much reading. Shortly after he picked up his book, one of his neighbors came in. To all appearances this was a holiday visit, but Abū Ya'ḳūb well knew that what his acquaintance really had in mind was a game of chess.

Among the games with which people diverted themselves in Moslem Spain in their free time, such as backgammon and checkers, chess was the most popular.[349] For the people of those generations it had symbolic significance, since it reflected the struggle on the battlefield and, moreover, called for a keen mind. In this way, chess was a simulated war on a higher level. It was played a lot especially in the epoch of the "provincial kings." Abū Dja'far Aḥmad b. Abbas, the foe of Samuel the Nagid, was an enthusiastic chess player,[350] and the Cordovan poet Abū 'Umar Yūsuf b. Hārūn ar-Ramādī composed a long *ḳaṣīda* about chess.[351] Even the crowned rulers of Spain delighted in the game. Kings and nobles had chessmen that were works of art; there were, for example, some that were gilded or made of ivory. Some even had the form of a woman in front and that of a soldier in back.[352] The game of chess and the splendor of the chessmen also spread into Christian Spain in the eleventh century, for in the wills of Christian princes they are described as if they were precious treasures.[353]

A famous tale in Hispano-Arabic literature makes apparent how the contemporaneous rulers of Spain esteemed the artistic appurtenances of this game. In the second half of the eleventh century, the king of Castile penetrated the kingdom of Seville. The vizier of the king of Seville then went forth to hold a parley with him. He spread a report throughout the king of

Castile's camp that he had in his saddlebag a wondrously beautiful chessboard. Thus the vizier prompted the king to play with him, stipulating that if the king lost he would fulfill any request of the vizier's, whereas if the king triumphed over the vizier the latter would give him all the appurtenances of the game. The vizier, who was an outstanding chess player, defeated the king and declared that his request of the king was that he turn back from the borders of the dominion of the king of Seville. The Castilian ruler kept his word.[354]

Like Moslems and Christians, the Jews too were greatly interested in chess, and there were Jewish players who acquired a reputation for themselves. An Arabic source from the twelfth century mentions *al-yahūdī* (without naming him) as one of the three outstanding players of his generation. The author of this source adds that all of these great players could play without looking at the board.[355] Even Hebrew poets in Spain wrote verse about the game of chess. One of them wrote "a song of a war in progress" depicting "kings and their camps arrayed for battle. . . . They do not draw their swords, for their war is a matching of skills."[356]

A Jew like Abū Ya'ḳūb would also not look askance at this pastime, and when his acquaintance, who was known to be fond of chess, came over, he promptly invited him to a game. The latter, of course, responded willingly. Abū Ya'ḳūb brought out a beautiful wooden box inlaid with other kinds of varicolored wood, such as sandalwood, and also with tiny pieces of ivory. Inlaying was a masterly skill in which the Spanish Moslems excelled especially, and there was scarcely a living room of a wealthy man that did not contain a chest embellished to some degree in this fashion. But the greatest achievement of these artisans lay in the work they did on various kinds of boxes, such as the one in which Abū Ya'ḳūb kept his chess pieces.[357]

In that era it was customary to classify those who played

chess, or *shiṭrandj,* as it was called. In other words, the ability of each person as a player was considered, and the player of lesser ability was accordingly allowed some advantage at the start of the game.[358] Thus Abū Ya'ḳūb allowed his guest an advantage, knowing that he was not an outstanding player. But this time the visitor planned his moves cautiously, and the game lasted a long time. *Shiṭrandj,* in fact, was generally a slower game than the newer version of chess.[359]

The guest left, and the members of the family assembled to eat the noontime meal together, as was customary on a festival day. This meal, too, consisted of especially tasty foods. First they ate a kind of pie spiced with vinegar and wine called *bawārid.* The second course consisted of *harīsa,* a gruel made from flour; chopped meat greased with fat; and then, as a concluding dish, another pie with pieces of chicken *(thurda)* and mushrooms.[360]

XII

Abū Ya'ḳūb reached the synagogue in time for the afternoon service, which was recited shortly before the evening service.[361] The dinner his wife had prepared for the second night of the festival was no less rich than that of the first night. As he had then, he spent some time after the meal engaged in small talk with his family. However, he did not prolong it this time, having been invited that evening by one of the rich men of the congregation to a party he held annually on the second night of the festival. This rich man was well endowed with property and of a good family whose members were intimates of the kings of Toledo. He was therefore held in esteem by the community, and whoever was invited to come to his home considered it an honor and a distinction.

Most of the guests were wealthy merchants and men of property, middle-aged men whose mien attested to their social status and their successful lives. They gave the impression of men who paid much attention to their outward appearance, all of them having grown beards after the Moslem fashion.[362] Anyone observing them closely would marvel at their flawless teeth. Generally speaking, their faces were somewhat long, quite handsome, and marked by straight jawbones. But particularly prominent in them were their large eyes and their narrow, protruding noses.[363]

A stranger chancing upon this group of Toledan Jews would have observed no singular differences in their outward appearance or in their speech. The majority spoke the Arabic vernacular current among the people in the city on the Tagus and its environs, but some spoke Romance. Occasionally, those gathered around the table would change from one language to the other. Moslem Spain was truly a bilingual country. The number of Arabs who came to the Iberian Peninsula at the time of the conquest was not large, and they and their offspring married Spanish women who spoke Romance within the bosom of the family. Consequently, members of all classes of society spoke both languages; the ring of Romance could even be heard in the royal court of Cordova. There were Moslem officers and judges in the capital of the Spanish caliphate who preferred speaking Romance, and some did not know Arabic at all. There was no change in this situation until the end of the eleventh century,[364] and in this respect the Jews were no different from their neighbors.[365]

In addressing one another, those present generally did not use surnames, and only rarely did they call someone by his full name—that is, his family name. The surnames were largely compounds of Abū ("the father of") and biblical names, which were common among Arab-speaking Jews, or else they were names that had been attached to a person because of some incident, like Al-Masmūm ("the poisoned one")[366] or Pollo ("rooster").[367] At times an entire family would receive such an appellation—for example, Abū Dirham.[368] Some of the surnames had to do with a person's appearance, as with Royo or Royuelo, "the ruddy one."[369] These were Romance surnames, whereas others were Arabic with a Romance suffix such as -ol, -el, -elo, or -ayr.[370] The proper names of Spanish Jews of that epoch were mostly biblical with an Arabic cast; yet even names that were clearly Arabic were customary—except the names Aḥmad and Muḥammad, by which non-Moslems were forbidden to be called.[371] Sometimes a man was called by the name of his father, although his father might still be alive. Consequently, people had names such as Isaac b. Isaac.[372] Family names were, for the most part, compounded with Ibn, which was frequently pronounced "Aben."[373]

At an occasion like the festival gathering of the community's notables attended by Abū Ya'ḳūb, everyone was especially fastidious in observing the rules of politesse in the manner of addressing one another. Each person sought to treat his friend with deference, and the host made a special effort. As was customary for such gatherings, the host had engaged a particular cook who was well known for his skill and ample experience.[374] The latter first served fruits to the guests and followed this with squabs stewed in vinegar, an especially tasty and elegant treat.[375] The meal was concluded with a dessert, and servants then heaped choice fruits on the low, round tables.[376]

The flow of friendly conversation was audible from every corner of the salon. After speaking of various matters and inquiring extensively into each other's welfare and the welfare of each other's families, they turned to the vexing problems that were disturbing the Jewish community very much. Most of those gathered were leaders of the community, who made its concerns their own. It was their exalted purpose to preserve the solidarity of the community and its religious discipline. In their view, any measure was deemed appropriate to attain this goal. Consequently, they regarded every attempt at innovation in matters of faith and law as an unforgiveable sin, and they were prepared to fight against heretics to the bitter end.

To their great chagrin, however, Karaism became widespread in Spain, particularly in the north, and in Toledo and the nearby cities as well.[377] The spiritual leaders of the Jewish community felt a need to wage war against its influence. Samuel the Nagid himself voiced a complaint in a poem in which he explained how he came to the decision to write his *Hilkh'ta gabhrāta:* "For the heretics have opened their mouths and spoken in derision . . . blackening piety which is pure and calling black wickedness white."[378] A scholar who lived in the generation following that of Samuel the Nagid inveighs against the Karaites who state that a woman can become ritually clean by means of drawn water. The vigorous style in which he expresses himself testifies to the apprehensions felt by the leaders of Spanish Jewry concerning the inroads of Karaite influence.[379] At that time heretical views had also spread among the philosophizing intellectuals, such as the Zoroastrian belief in two forces—good and evil—that struggle against each other, a belief against which Ibn Ḥazm wrote a special treatise.[380] The leaders of the Jewish communities employed the weapon of the ban against such seductive views.[381] In the course of the discussions that took place at the gathering attended by Abū Ya'ḳūb, a proposal was made to employ this stringent weapon.

Another problem that occupied the leaders of the community was that of gentile maidservants, who sometimes constituted an impediment to normal family life. In every well-to-do house there were men servants and especially maidservants who did the heavy work. It was customary for a bride to bring a maidservant with her when she married.[382] In a formulary for deeds and documents written at Lucena in 1021, a deed for the sale of male or female servants is included;[383] and in the formulary of Judah al-Barcelōnī, there are a number of texts of deeds concerning menservants.[384] A collection of responsa from a great rabbi who lived in Spain at the end of the eleventh century contains judicial decisions regarding male and female servants who had been given away as gifts, had been sold, or had been given as a pledge. The rabbi was also asked to whom the child of a maidservant would belong if she had been presented as a gift to a bride but had given birth before the bride actually was married.[385] The Moslem authorities did not prevent Jews from acquiring male and female servants who were non-Moslems. A *ḥisba* book dating from that epoch merely asserts that Jews must be prevented from acquiring a minor unless his mother is sold along with him.[386] Most of the maidservants in Moslem Spain were Christians who remained loyal to their faith. The aforementioned rabbi was once queried regarding an "Edomite" maidservant who sought permission from her master to join the Christian merchants who came to his home. He replied that if she had informed her master of her intent to retain her religious belief at the time she was purchased, then by right he should grant her request.[387]

In any case, both male and female servants aggravated the difficulties of their masters. They would, for example, threaten to become converted to Islam if their demands were not granted, for by conversion they could achieve manumission. However, the greatest obstacle involved in having male and female servants was provided by the "handsome girls" whose masters took them for concubines. Already in the ninth century El'azār b. Samuel, a Spanish rabbi, had addressed a question to Palṭoi, the head of the school of Pumbedita, concerning the status of a child born of a maidservant. The question particularly concerned whether her master thereby became exempt from the obligation of a levirate marriage.[388] Such relations with the female servants undermined the peace of the household so much that the leaders of the Jewish community continually sought a remedy. There was thus good reason for this subject to be broached whenever the notables of the community met, as they did at the party on that Sukkot night.

But the host had not invited his guests to take counsel with them on community problems. He did, however, prepare diversions for them. His attendants served them excellent wines and once again brought in fruits to counteract the taste of the wine, as well as bowls of incense and various woods that gave forth fragrant odors. In the meantime, a screen was set up behind which singing girls chanted their songs.[389] At the soirées of the nobles, the singing girls appeared openly, but at the parties of middle-class persons, this was not the case. These songstresses were specially trained for this function, singing tender melodies to the accompaniment of a harp, in solo or in chorus.

None of these girls were Jewish, but there were many Jews among the male singers in Moslem Spain. In the eleventh century a Jewish singer in Toledo acquired renown because of his great talent. His fame spread everywhere, and it was declared that he even surpassed in talent Ibrāhīm al-Mauṣilī, the famous singer in Baghdad during the resplendent days of the Abbasid caliphs. When al-Ma'mūn, the king of Toledo, once arranged a grand soirée at which the renowned Jewish singer performed, accompanied by a band of musicians, the singer overwhelmed the guests.[390] These singers were notoriously corrupt. They cut their hair after the fashion of women so that their locks hung down from their temples, and they even imitated the women with their voices.[391] But their singing was pleasing to the ear, and there was scarcely a party at the home of a wealthy person from which they were absent.

On that Sukkot night the men sang and played on instruments after the songstresses had left, evoking enthusiasm among the guests. When their performance was over, halvah of exceptionally fine quality, containing almonds, was served to the guests, as well as nuts and sesame seeds.[392] Next, there appeared one of the Jewish magicians who had acquired fame in Moslem Spain. This magician could make articles materialize where they had not been previously. He could even make horns attach themselves to the head of a person and then cause him to disappear, while the spellbound guests were unable to explain to themselves what had happened.[393]

The guests praised wholeheartedly the artists who had given them pleasure that evening with their diverting talents. Full of satisfaction and pride, they asked themselves if there were another community that had such talents as their singers and especially their highly capable liturgical poets. It was evident that they saw in this an additional indication that the Jewish nation constitutes the people of the Bible, the chosen people. Once more the conversation went from one topic to another. As the guests' mood became more cheerful, they began to heap inordinate praise on their entire community, comparing it to their Christian neighbors and in particular to the Jews of other countries.

The Jews of Spain indeed thought themselves to be indubitably superior to other Jewries. All Spanish Jews regarded themselves as having descended from the inhabitants of Jerusalem—the most important and most highly esteemed of the Jewish people of old—finding support for their view in the words of the prophet Obadiah (Obad. 1:20).[394] Some Spanish Jewish families even traced their lineages directly to the House of David.[395] Since the Arabs also ascribed much importance to family origins and prided themselves on their ancient ancestral progenitors, the tracing of lineage and the awareness of noble descent became matters of basic value to Spanish Jewry in general, and to families and individuals in particular. With the passage of time and particularly after the forced conversions during the later Middle Ages, the Jews bequeathed this attitude to the Christians. As a result the matter of *linaje,* as it was called in Spanish, became one of the important values in the

Christians' consciousness as well.[396] The contemporary Spaniard's belief that his is a distinguished people that brought culture to vast continents, that is loyal to its God and to its tradition, and that lives by its faith and is therefore misunderstood and hated by other nations—this conviction is only another aspect and a continuation of the Marranos' belief in their chosenness.

The Spanish Jews' sense of superiority, however, did not rest only on the tracing of their lineage to the ancient nobles of Judah. From the time in the tenth century when throughout the Iberian Peninsula there was an increase in the number of Jewish intellectuals who became writers, and when schools that maintained a high level of learning were established, the Jews of Spain decided that their cultural capacity was immeasurably superior to that of other Jewries. It seemed to them that they were endowed with talents that the Jews of other lands did not possess. They gave full expression to this view, and their writers recorded it in their works. A Hispano-Jewish historian who wrote about the migration of a scholar from Spain to Babylonia, where he was appointed head of a school, adds a note to his account concerning the intellectual decay in the birthplace of the Talmud contrasted with the superior intellectual achievements of the Jews in Spain.[397] In his poems Solomon Ibn Gabirol not infrequently stressed his ties to Spain, "his country," and also contrasted the achievements of its Jewish scholars with those of the scholars of Babylonia.[398] In a book on the theories relating to Hebrew poetry, another poet included a chapter on the theme of why the Jews in the Spanish diaspora excelled in the composition of poetry, rhetoric, and the epistolary art in Hebrew more than all other Jewries.[399]

A notable Jewish intellectual who was born and raised in Moslem Spain commented in one of his responsa that the Jews of France and the other Christian countries were not well versed in the laws, because the rulers of those countries did not permit them to exercise juridical authority.[400] In a letter written by this great man to his son, he warned the latter about the writings of Jewish scholars in France, because in his opinion they did not have a proper concept of the Creator: "While they eat boiled beef, dipped in vinegar and garlic—a snack known in their tongue as sauce—and as the fumes of the vinegar and garlic permeate their minds, they then imagine that by these they will attain a concept of the Creator . . . Who will be near them in their prayers and cries." This intellectual also protested against the Jews of Germany, "who have no fixed ideas except on intercourse, eating, and drinking." He therefore urged his son: "Stay clear of them and do not come within their embrace, and as for you, my son, let not your pleasant companionship be with any other than our beloved Spanish brethren who are called Andalusians, for they have intellectual capacity, understanding, and clarity of mind." In the course of his remarks, he expresses an extremely negative opinion concerning the Jews of the Maghreb.[401]

Such was the attitude of the great Jews in Spain toward the other Jewries. Even ordinary Jews, such as our friend Abū Ya'ḳūb Yūsuf and the other guests at the festive gathering, believed in all sincerity that they were the elite among the Congregation of Jeshurun.

3

THE TWILIGHT OF AN EPOCH

I

The death of al-Mu'taḍid occurred at the end of March 1069. The day after he died, Abu 'l-Ḳāsim was crowned king of Seville.[1] Abu'l-Ḳāsim, who was surnamed al-Mu'tamid, was a young man of about 29 years when he began to rule. But ever since he had been designated as the crown prince, his father had prepared him for his lofty role. He had appointed him commander of his armies during military campaigns, and had bestowed upon him the office of governor of important provinces. Thus, the young prince became skilled and experienced in matters of government. His father bequeathed to him not only his rich experience in statecraft but also his great ambition. Indeed, throughout his lifetime al-Mu'tamid endeavored to enlarge his kingdom by annexing those small princedoms that sprang up like mushrooms all across Spain after the disintegration of the Omayyad caliphate.

However, though he received his political vision from his father, al-Mu'tamid nevertheless differed from him in his methods—first and foremost in his relations to his subjects. His father had been a cruel tyrant, whereas he behaved graciously toward his people and was interested in acquiring a good name. He was revolted by contemptible means of governing, and instead of casting fear on his subjects, he won their loyalty with acts of kindness. He brought back many whom his father had exiled and endeavored to reach all elements of the population.

Al-Mu'tamid's strong impulse to enjoy all the delights of life to the full was a conspicuous aspect of his character. He devoted days and nights to the endless parties at the courts of the Moslem kings in Spain, and in the course of them he would drink the excellent wines of Andalusia until he was intoxicated. The Arab writers reported that, during the years he held office, 800 women were in his harem and that on their account he neglected the fulfillment of his duties. But he was also an intellectual, well versed in all the branches of the substantive Arabic literature, and a master of rhetoric. He was able to employ all the literary conceits—allusions and comparisons—that were so popular with the Arab intellectuals and that drew abundantly upon the treasures of the Arab poets' figurative language. He himself composed poems on the spur of the moment, and when anyone addressed him by means of verse, he would answer with a poem in like meter and rhyme. His verses were collected by the learned writer Ibn Bassām in a special collection. Al-Mu'tamid demonstrated great affection toward poets, showering abundant gifts upon them and appointing them as his viziers. He was always surrounded by writers and poets who came to him from afar. In fact, his court became famous in his time as the forge in which Arabic literature was fashioned.

Even more than the other inhabitants of Seville, the non-Moslems benefited from the change of rulers. Al-Mu'tamid was less observant than his father and his attitude toward his Christian and Jewish subjects was more easygoing, though his impulses sometimes beclouded his judgment, provoking him to devise evil against them. To be sure, the change in attitude toward non-Moslems resulted not only from the character of the new king of Seville but also from the political situation in Moslem Spain in his day. As a consequence of the Christian kings' resurgence of strength and their pressure upon the Moslem states after the decline of the Omayyad caliphate, the Moslem rulers were increasingly compelled to alter their attitude toward their Christian subjects and to grant them certain concessions. Since they depended upon the aid of the Christian kings or had to take their power into consideration, they no longer observed, or observed to a lesser degree than ever before, the Moslem jurists' age-old regulations designed to fix the status of the non-Moslem communities. One of these regulations was a law included in the Covenant of Omar that prohibited Christians from ringing their church bells, permitting them only to knock upon wooden clappers—provided these did not make a loud noise. However, Arabic poets of the first half of the eleventh century reported that in their days this regulation was not enforced, even in Cordova itself.[2] In Seville, the seat of the sanctimonious Arab kings of the Abbadid dynasty, the ringing of church bells was heard as in a Christian city. A Moslem theologian who lived in Seville at the end of that century complained bitterly because of this breach of the laws of Islam.[3] Even the old law requiring that Christians be circumcised was no longer observed, to the great distress of the Moslem theologians.[4]

As an incidental result of the improvement in the condition of the Christian Mozarabs, a change for the good also occurred in the status of the Jews. At the beginning of al-Mu'tamid's reign, an incident took place in Seville involving harm to a Jew, and the measures taken by the officers in charge of security aroused great excitement among the populace. A Moslem claimed that a Jew had uttered slanderous remarks about the Islamic religion and began to beat him in the marketplace, injuring him severely. The Moslem then incited the people against the Jews. The governor of the city, 'Abdallāh Ibn Sallām, imprisoned the Moslem—an act that increased the unrest of the populace. Al-Mu'tamid was not in Seville at the time, and the governor therefore sent a messenger to him in haste to ask for his instructions. When he heard of the tension prevailing in Seville, al-Mu'tamid sent his son, Sirādj ad-daula, there with a troop of his best cavalry, commanding him to go at full speed to quell the disturbances. He also ordered his vizier, Abu 'l-Walīd Ibn Zaidūn, to proceed posthaste to Seville, even though he was ill.[5]

Just as al-Mu'tamid protected the rights of his non-Moslem subjects, he also readily welcomed them into the service of his government, without regard for the laws of Islam that forbid such a thing. There were Christian mercenaries in the army of the kingdom of Seville during his reign. One of the high-ranking officers was Muḥammad b. Martin, a Christian who had become a Moslem.[6] Christian intellectuals frequented al-Mu'tamid's royal court, one being the poet Ibn al-Margharī, who excelled at composing girdle poems.[7] As the friend of writers and the patron of men of culture, as a man who was liberal in his views and in his way of life, al-Mu'tamid also befriended Jewish intellectuals, made use of their talents in the performance of important functions, and appointed them to various posts.

Immediately after ascending the throne, he invited the Cordovan scholar R. Isaac Ibn Albalia to Seville and appointed him as his astrologer. In accordance with the practice of the Moslem kings to appoint a Jew who was close to them as head of the Jewish community, he also gave him this post. Over a period of many years, R. Isaac Ibn Albalia performed his duty faithfully, defending Jewish interests before the nobles and officials in the kingdom of Seville and acting as their champion. Every Jew knew that in a time of trouble he could seek aid from the *nāsī* at the royal court. The rabbi was also chief rabbi of the Jewish communities in that large kingdom, serving as a teacher and replying to questions addressed to him. Al-Mu'tamid remunerated him generously for his services, bestowing many gifts upon him, so that he soon became extremely wealthy. R. Isaac Ibn Albalia was then able to perform a last act of grace on behalf of his former benefactors, the two *nagiddim* of Granada. He endeavored to collect anew the huge library that they had acquired over a period of many years but whose books had been scattered after the murder of Joseph. His agents and subordinates made every effort to discover the books, which had been sold by the rioters in various cities, and to persuade their owners to sell them to him, as a friend of the *nagiddim,* so that they could again be collected together and thus serve as a fitting memorial to them.[8] R. Isaac Ibn Albalia also did much to elevate the status of religious learning among the Jews of Seville. He encouraged talented young men by granting them material aid. Jewish students and scholars from the other Andalusian cities began coming to Seville to seek his support, so that their number in the city increased greatly.

To be sure, the flourishing of Seville's Jewish community and the development of its cultural life were not due solely to the influence of Isaac Ibn Albalia. At that time there were other men of means among the Jews of the city who gave assistance to many members of the community. In general the economic condition of Seville's Jews was good, and they acquired property—particularly vineyards—in the city's environs.[9] A number of Jews holding important positions frequented the royal court of al-Mu'tamid. Most of them were members of distinguished Jewish families in Andalusia who had long since established ties with the Arab rulers and served them as their agents.

A question addressed to one of Spain's rabbis at the end of that century demonstrates the great economic and social importance of the wealthy Jews' ties with the royal court. In this query, made after a change in the policy of the rulers toward non-Moslems, it was stated, with some exaggeration, that the Jews of Seville formerly had no other means of livelihood but the work they did for the government. Those making the inquiry went on to recount all the tribulations that beset the community when the Jews lost these positions.[10] However, when Moslem fanaticism waned in the middle and the end of the eleventh century, the kings did not hesitate in appointing non-Moslems to official posts, and the wealthy Jews and officeholders in the government began conducting themselves like nobles. One of these affluent families, Kamniel, was close to the rulers of Seville for a long time.[11] Another highly esteemed family was that of Ibn Muhādjir, which produced many nobles and men of culture in that era. In the days of King al-Mu'tamid, a very high post in the government of Seville was occupied by Abū Isḥāḳ Abraham b. Meïr Ibn Muhādjir; he was awarded the title of vizier along with other resounding titles. Contemporary Hebrew poets extolled him as the savior of his people who patronized the Jewish communities in the kingdom of Seville as well as those in remote lands. He was both a scholar well versed in Jewish lore and an expert in astronomy.[12] After the manner of wealthy Spanish Jews, he employed his power within the community by imposing religious discipline on Seville's Jews.[13] Another family that also held a place of esteem among the Jews of Seville at the end of the eleventh century was that of Ibn Yātōm.[14] This family, however, was not numbered among those who were intimates of the royal court.

Among the many intellectuals in the community of Seville at that time, a kinsman of Abraham Ibn Muhādjir called Abū Sulaimān Ibn Muhādjir was especially prominent. He was a renowned poet and also a scholar in various branches of science.[15] The poet Abu 'l-Fatḥ El'āzār b. Naḥman Ibn Azhar, the scion of a family close to the Moslem rulers, was given the appellative "prince" by a contemporary Hebrew poet who petitioned him to intercede on his behalf before the *nāsī* because he had fallen into ill repute.[16] The number of scholars who were preoccupied with talmudical studies within the community of Seville was also not insignificant. One of them was Meir Ibn Migash, the son of the Joseph Ibn Migash who had come from Granada and served King al-Muʻtaḍid. A prominent person, he was also a bosom friend of Isaac Ibn Albalia.[17]

Nearly all of these intellectuals and writers and the members of their coteries were from wealthy and distinguished Andelusian Jewish families, the sons or kin of those viziers and nobles in whose honor the poets wrote fervently laudatory poems. Of course, the major and minor works these writers have left us represent the views that were current in this social class. Their attitude toward the traditional religious values was somewhat reserved or even skeptical. Their opinions concerning the Bible were realistic and critical. However, the members of the lower class of Spanish Jews were all fervent in their adherence to the faith of their fathers; they believed wholeheartedly whatever was written in the Holy Scriptures, accepting them quite literally and as the ancient rabbis had interpreted them over the course of many generations. Scholars of that class expressed their class's religious attitude with much vigor, in the manner of Spaniards, who were inclined to fight for their opinions energetically.

One of these scholars was called Judah or, in Arabic, Abū Zakariyyā Yaḥyā b. Samuel Ibn Balʻām.[18] He was born in Toledo in the middle of the eleventh century and grew up and was educated there as a member of a poor family.[19] In his youth he delved into all the branches of the ancient Jewish literature, studying much of the Talmud and reading the homiletic commentaries of the Bible and books on all the problems of religion, such as *The Book of Beliefs and Opinions* by

Saadya; but first and foremost he was interested in biblical commentaries and studies dealing with the lore of the Hebrew language. He was attracted in particular to Abu 'l-Walīd and meditated on his writing day and night. He had an excellent memory for all that he learned; yet he was also noted for his critical attitude toward the writings he perused, and he began to blaze his own trail in biblical exegesis. At this early stage in his life, he was sometimes influenced by the secular mood of the Spanish intellectuals in those generations. Like them he composed girdle poems, such as a song of desire written to a "graceful gazelle," a 15-year-old youth.[20] Just as his parents had been, Judah Ibn Bal'ām was poor and had to work hard throughout his life to earn his bread.[21] He eventually moved to Seville, hoping that in this affluent city he would be able to earn his living more easily. Serving as a teacher, he remained there until his death.[22] But his status in life was not altered, as is reflected in his writings that stress the conservative piety that was generally characteristic of the lower classes in those generations. In addition, his work reflected an embitterment that resulted in aggressiveness.

Judah Ibn Bal'ām became one of the most important biblical exegetes in Jewish Spain. He wrote commentaries in Arabic on most of the books of the Bible, a task that occupied him for many years. He first wrote on the Prophets and Hagiographa; these commentaries are called *Nukat al-Miḳrā* ("Pointed Comment on the Bible"). Later he wrote a commentary on the Pentateuch entitled *Kitāb at-Tardjīḥ* ("The Book of Reconciliation"),[23] and finally he again went over his work on the Prophets and Hagiographa, made emendations, and added supplements.[24] In his commentaries, written generally very succinctly, he was content to explain passages and difficult words, placing the emphasis on the philological exposition. He sought to explain the Scriptures in terms of their literal meaning, rarely changing his course in order to clarify a theological problem connected with some passage. In his philological commentary he was a faithful disciple of Abu 'l-Walīd. Like him, he found support for his opinions, mainly on the meaning of words, by comparisons with Aramaic and Arabic. In fact, in some of Ibn Bal'ām's commentaries, Abu 'l-Walīd provided the chief source.[25] But although the influence of the great scholar of Saragossa is evident everywhere, Ibn Bal'ām's commentaries nevertheless emphasized with great clarity his independence of thought.

Aside from Abu 'l-Walīd's writings, which he frequently quoted from without mentioning their author's name, Ibn Bal'ām cited many other commentators in order to reconcile their opinions—a purpose indicated by the name of his commentary on the Pentateuch. He cited the words of Judah Ibn Ḳuraish, M'naḥem Ben Sārūḳ, Dūnash b. Labraṭ, and Ḥayyūdj,[26] as well as the writings of the *geonim,* such as R. M'bhassēr and R. Ḥēfeṣ, Aaron Ibn Sardjadu and Samuel b. Ḥofnī.[27] But in particular he expatiated on the commentaries of Saadya, with whose writings he was perfectly familiar. In many passages of his work, Ibn Bal'ām criticized the gaon severely and charged him with failing to understand the literal meaning of words in the Bible.[28] As did all the Jewish scholars of Spain, he greatly esteemed the opinions of the Gaon R. Hai, and he quoted from his lexicon, *Kitāb al-Ḥāwī,* rather copiously.[29] Occasionally, he cited his responsa and those of his father, the Gaon R. Sh'rīra, that deal with theological questions.[30] Using a fine critical scalpel, he probed the methods of all these writers, having no regard for their eminence if he did not find them correct. At times he even criticized the commentaries of Abu 'l-Walīd mercilessly[31] and wrote in the same caustic vein against the commentaries of Samuel the Nagid. In the dispute that developed between Abu 'l-Walīd and Samuel the Nagid, Ibn Bal'ām sided almost unhesitatingly with Abu 'l-Walīd, attacking his opponent sharply, especially in reference to his treatise *Rasāʾil ar-rifāḳ.*[32] Only on rare occasions did he agree with the views expressed by the Nagid of Granada in matters of Hebrew grammar.[33] In common with the other Jewish scholars in Spain, Judah Ibn Balʿām had also acquired a considerable knowledge of Arabic literature and did not flinch from citing from the Koran, from the writings of Arabic poets and from the works of Arabic philologists and historians.[34] Sometimes he even polemicized about the interpretations the Christians gave to various verses in the Bible.[35]

However, Ibn Balʿām was a consistent conservative, keeping faith with traditional Judaism and neither swerving to the right or to the left. Consequently, he endeavored to refute the arguments of the Karaites contained in their exegetical literature, though he was prepared to accept some of their interpretations.[36] Because of his conservative approach, Judah Ibn Balʿām was especially opposed to the rational type of religious interpretation so characteristic of many upper-class Spanish Jews in that era. He knew Moses Ibn Djiḳaṭilla, one of the prominent representatives of such views, and he debated with him over his approach to exegesis. He found repugnant biblical criticism as it was fostered by Moses Ibn Djiḳaṭilla and those who had the same ideas, for in his opinion it emptied Judaism of its original content. He suspected that their real purpose was to erase the contradictions among the religions and to bring them all to a common level, somewhat similar to what had been done by the upper-class Mozarabs in the days of the Omayyads. And indeed, they did endeavor to harmonize their religious beliefs with the dominant faith. This was the basis of Ibn Balʿām's anger whenever he mentioned the commentaries of Moses Ibn Djiḳaṭilla.

Judah Ibn Balʿām condemned him sharply for giving a rational interpretation to the miracle of the sun standing still as related in the Book of Joshua (10:12).[37] He wrote a special treatise on the miracles mentioned in the Bible and on the phenomenon of prophecy, expressing without reservation his belief that God would again alter the natural course of existence when the time was appropriate for it.[38] When he wanted to contradict Ibn Djiḳaṭilla's interpretation of a verse that refers to the end of the world, he charged him with revealing his propensity toward the views of the philosophers who negate the doctrine of *creatio ex nihilo* but believe in the eternity of the world.[39] In other words, he attacked the commentator from Saragossa as one who denied the basic principle of the Jewish religion. But he particularly denounced him because he explained various verses in the books of the Prophets as applying not to the Messianic Era but to the time of King Hezekiah or that of Nehemiah. In Ibn Bal'ām's opinion, such rational interpretation was utterly opposed to the spirit of Judaism and deprived the Jewish people of its hopes. He therefore labeled his opponent with derogatory epithets and denounced the spread of ideas that lead many to error, noting, albeit with sorrow, that a whole faction sided with the views of Moses Ibn Djiḳaṭilla.[40] Ibn Bal'ām also opposed his philological interpretations, though at times he was compelled to agree with his explanations.[41]

In addition to his commentaries on books of the Bible, Judah Ibn Bal'ām wrote treatises on the lore of the Hebrew language; of these not all have been preserved. In these treatises, which were also written in Arabic, he very consistently followed the path of Abu 'l-Walīd, though he added some of his own conclusions. The small book *Ḥurūf al-ma'ānī* contains a list of biblical particles. The book *al-Af'āl al-mushtaḳḳa min al-asmā* ("The Verbs Derived from Nouns") was, in fact, a supplement to the first book; and the book called *Tadjnīs,* whose full name is *Ta'lif fi 'l-muṭābiḳ wa'l-mudjānis,* deals with biblical words that have various meanings.[42] As in his commentaries, Ibn Bal'ām took advantage in these treatises of his manifold knowledge, quoting various writers—even Arabic poets.[43] He wrote still another book, entitled, in Arabic, *Kitāb al-Irshād* ("The Book of Guidance"), which was a general grammar of the Hebrew language.[44]

In his old age Ibn Bal'ām's piety increased, and a change occurred in the subjects that interested him. To be sure, even in the days of his youth, he had been well versed in the Talmud. When he reached old age, however, he devoted himself completely to its study—to the neglect of practically everything else.[45] Whereas in his younger years he had composed secular poems, when he was old he wrote penitential hymns, which were incorporated into the Festival Prayerbook of many Jewish communities in Spain and North Africa.[46]

II

In that period the communities in Granada and the other cities of the Ṣinhādja kingdom occupied a more modest position within Spanish Jewry. Whereas the Jewish communities in the kingdom of Seville grew and became wealthy, producing officials and dignitaries who had great influence in the government as well as scholars and writers who enjoyed their assistance, the Jewish communities in the kingdom of Granada shrank somewhat, and their economic, social, and cultural levels were much lower. This relative decline was tied to the condition of the entire Berber kingdom as well as to the turnover of rulers in Granada after the murder of Joseph the Nagid.

The kingdom of the Ṣinhādja then grew very weak; the king of Granada's authority was undermined, and he was unable to defend himself against his enemies within and without the state, unless a ruler stronger than himself helped him.

To be sure, for a period of time after the murder of Joseph, Bādīs overcame his helplessness and regained his strength.

Under the strong incentives of rioting in the capital city and the slaying of his vizier inside his own palace, the inner strength that marked him as a young man, the energy and resoluteness that had once been so well known throughout the breadth of Andalusia, again asserted itself. After securing the aid of al-Ma'mūn, the Berber king of Toledo, he began a campaign against the king of Almería, who had conquered the eastern districts of Granada. This war ended successfully: The areas the Granadans had lost earlier were reconquered.

However, in exchange for his help, Bādīs had to turn over to al-Ma'mūn the district of Baza. Yet the dominance of the Ṣinhādja in Granada proper was speedily shaken. After the murder of Joseph, the Slav an-Nāya exercised the real authority. Bādīs handed over to him command of the army and appointed him grand vizier. But he was hated by the Ṣinhādja, and relations between him and the officers of the army grew increasingly bad. They charged that it was his intention to mount the royal throne and reign with the help of the Berbers of the tribe of Birzāl. Many of the army's men left Granada, some for Jaén, where an officer called Musakkan governed in the name of Prince Māksen. There, a faction of Berber nationalists had assembled who opposed the appointment of Jews and Christians to high posts. An-Nāya succeeded in stirring up a rebellion within the fortress of his foes, forcing Musakkan and Māksen to flee and restoring the city and its region to Bādīs. Ultimately, however, an-Nāya was slain by his enemies. Bādīs then invited the Christian Abu'r-Rabī', who had served his government in the time of Joseph and fled from Granada after his murder, to return to conduct the administration. Abu'r-Rabī' willingly accepted his invitation and was appointed as a vizier.[47]

In 1073 King Bādīs died, and his kingdom was divided between two of his grandsons, 'Abdallāh and Tamīm, the sons of Bollugīn. 'Abdallāh took Granada and all the districts in the east as well as the western districts north of the Sierra de Alhama and Sierra de Abdalajis mountains. Tamīm received the princedom of Malaga, which stretched along the seacoast until the environs of the Almuñecar within the kingdom of Granada. The city of Alhama proper was annexed to Malaga. From the beginning of 'Abdallāh's reign, the nobles and governors raised the banner of revolt and entered into negotiations with the rulers of the neighboring provinces, so that the young king was faced with a difficult struggle. When the rule of the Berbers was weakened as a result of dissension among themselves, the Arabs and the other natives began to defy them. Naturally, the Berbers retaliated, displaying their enmity toward the intellectuals in particular, since these last regarded the African soldiery with contempt and did not always curb their tongues.[48]

Under these circumstances the rulers of Granada again had to show favor to the Jews and turn over to them important functions in the service of the government. Upon the return of Abu 'r-Rabī', who was accustomed to cooperating with the Jews, and afterwards when many of the intellectuals fled to nearby Almería to escape the Berbers, who were taking revenge upon them on account of their hostile attitude, many of the Jews were restored to the royal service.[49] Precisely at that time the king needed huge sums, and who was better suited than the Jews to supply his needs and properly collect the taxes?

One of those officeholders in the service of the king of Granada was Abū Ibrāhīm Isaac, a scion of the esteemed Ibn Ezra family. An intellectual steeped in the various branches of Arabic and Hebrew literature, he was, like his father Jacob, given an important function in the government administration. He was his father's oldest son and had educated his brothers.[50] His wife, too, came from a noble family; she was the daughter of a wealthy man surnamed "Nagid."[51] In addition to being a practical man, Isaac Ibn Ezra composed poetry.[52]

As in former generations, there were also in Granada during that period Jewish scholars who devoted most of their time to the study of the Talmud and the teaching of Jewish lore. To this circle belonged two rabbis, Abūn and Joseph Ibn Madjanīn, to whom a contemporary poet dedicated many poems. Like Isaac Ibn Ezra, Abūn was a famous scholar who was able to boast of worthy forebears. He was the scion of a family of wealthy men who had exercised power. Joseph Ibn Madjanīn was also descended from an esteemed family.[53]

III

In those days the political struggle among the kings in Spain considerably worsened. To be sure, ever since the Omayyad caliphate had disintegrated, conflicts and wars among the rulers of the various princedoms of Moslem Spain had been a common phenomenon, and there was almost no year in which war did not spread through one of its regions. These wars were mainly limited in scope. But in the last third of the eleventh century, there came into being in Moslem Spain states that imposed their authority over wide regions and wielded much power. These states swallowed up the small princedoms, and their kings aspired unremittingly to enlarge their areas. At that time the strength of the Christians in northern Spain greatly increased, and the threat to the dominance of the Moslems in the Iberian Peninsula became very real. The kings of León and Castile demanded the payment of tribute from the Moslem rulers, and the Arab and Berber princes complied either because they lacked the strength to fight the Christians or because they would not unite to present a common front against them. Whenever a delay occurred in the payment of tribute, Christian soldiers would attack the plains of Andalusia and the other Moslem regions, wreaking havoc upon them. Thus most of the Moslem kingdoms and principalities became client states of the powerful Christian kingdoms, but at the same time the stronger Moslem states did not desist from a policy of expansion, making great efforts to annex additional regions.

The Moslem kings used Christian assistance in their endeavor to entrench themselves in their positions; they also used it against one another. These kings were not zealous for the glory of Islam but were entirely concerned with enhancing their own might. They yearned only to wax in wealth and to benefit from the advantages of their position. Every governor and deputy, every administrator and noble entertained the hope of throwing off the yoke of his king and establishing a princedom of his own. To achieve this goal, every means was considered proper; and the most effective way was to turn to the Christians, who were excellent soldiers, for help. Moreover, the Moslem rulers and their circles of intimates were far from being devout, whether they merely ostensibly fulfilled the commandments of their faith by way of pro forma observance of customs or, being under the influence of skepticism, openly scorned them.

One consequence of this was that the kings acted in accordance with their selfish impulses in the field of politics. The Moslem sense of unity against the Christian world was weak; indeed, Moslems and Christians cooperated in many wars. Because of their ties with the Christian kings and because of their lukewarm piety, all the heads of Moslem governments became more and more lenient in their attitude toward their Christian subjects. In the kingdom of Seville, the conspicuous change toward Christians and Jews was characteristic of the general change in attitude of the Moslem states toward their non-Moslem subjects. The number of Mozarabs in Andalusia was still great. In all the cities there were Christian communities, and in many villages the Christians constituted a majority.[54] It was thus clear that any injury to them was likely to result in a retaliatory action on the part of the Christian kings.

The Jews in the Hispano-Moslem states derived much benefit from these circumstances. On the one hand, when the rulers had to improve their attitude toward the Christians, the Jews' status was also bettered; and on the other, the Jews could move more freely in the courts of the kings when the spirit of fanaticism that was formerly prevalent there grew weaker. In that period many restrictions in the courts of the Moslem kings were removed, and a certain spiritual laxity prevailed. Feast followed upon feast, and all the nobles drank wine publicly. In one of his poems, al-Mu'tamid, king of Seville, stated that it was a duty to drink wine at the time of public prayer on Friday.[55] All the kings spent vast sums of money to buy female slaves who excelled in singing, and first and foremost they sought to embellish their courts with poets, upon whom they showered numerous gifts. The Moslem kings adorned their palaces with statues of human beings and animals, even though this was forbidden by the rules of their religion.[56] This way of life was the result not of personal inclinations on the part of a few rulers but of a general state of mind among the upper classes of the Hispano-Moslem society. It was apparently a period during which many Spaniards, as part of the human spirit's endless process of searching for the truth and for the meaning of life, shook themselves entirely free of their religious approach and abandoned the laws of their religion.

In those days Jews could appear at the courts of the kings without fear. It was a far cry from the time when the Omayyads occupied the royal throne in Cordova, an era in which the Arab nobles were still proud of their lineage, and their feelings of superiority were very strong. Then the stress on religion prevented the rulers from giving Jews high offices, and consequently Jews had a modest place in the upper echelons of the government. Since the government's income was still large, the kings also had less need of the experience of the Jews in economic matters. Their forays into Christian Spain brought them much booty, which was sold for huge sums. Even in the first half of the eleventh century, when the doors of the royal palace were opened to the Jews, the economic status of the Moslem princes was still sound.

In the middle of that century, however, the relationship between the Moslem and Christian rulers changed to such a degree that the financial position of the Moslem kings became difficult and grew steadily worse. The many Christian incursions, whose purpose was merely the collection of tribute and plunder for its own sake, achieved their ends. One highly edifying fact is that at that time the Moslem rulers, except for the king of Seville, discontinued the minting of gold coins. It seems that, in the second half of the eleventh century, the rulers in Moslem Spain had to contend with many financial difficulties. A collection of responsa dating from the end of that century contains a reference to Jews in a certain city who lent money to a Moslem ruler, who then imposed upon a Jew with an important post in the service of his government in that city the obligation to repay the loan. When he refused to pay it, the Jews who had lent the money turned to the ruler and, assisted by police, obtained pledges from him.[57] This official, who, in the aforementioned responsum, is referred to as "Reuben the Secretary," was one of the many Jews who served the Moslem rulers as tax farmers and treasurers.

The social and economic rise of an important class of Spanish Jews was made possible not only by reason of the hard-pressed condition in which the rulers found themselves. Formerly the Jews of Spain had been, numerically speaking, an isolated minority, but now, after the Berbers and Slavs had established themselves in the provinces of Moslem Spain, their situation was altered. The inhabitants of Moslem Spain had become a mosaic of various national elements. Further, as a consequence of the great changes that began in the first half of the eleventh century, the political and social outlooks of the ruling class underwent a change that was of especially great importance to the position of the Jews. What had been vaguely sensed in the first generation after the breakup of the caliphate became clearly discernible two generations later. The rulers of Moslem Spain of that era, who had attained their positions thanks to their personal talents, did not give consideration to anything except a person's ability. For them, this constituted the determining factor in the struggles among the different social groups. Nor did the kings of Moslem Spain in the second half of the eleventh century depend upon national armies to fight on their behalf with religio-nationalist fervor. Instead, they relied on the warlike prowess of Christian mercenaries.

The courts of these kings were, as it were, animated by the Renaissance spirit; many there shared a personal outlook that was very close to that prevalent in Italy during the fifteenth and sixteenth centuries. This view was most clearly articulated by a writer who was a native of Tortosa and had been educated in Saragossa, which was then ruled by the Banū Hūd. This author, Abū Bakr Muḥammad b. al-Walīd Ibn Abī Randaḳa, later wrote a book of the type of the so-called "mirrors of the kings," which served as handbooks for the rulers of the states in the Middle Ages. In his book, *Sirādj al-mulūk,* he made it plain that whatever the strength of a state, it can only depend upon its elite soldiery, which are few in number.[58] This approach matched the aspiration toward scientific advancement common to most of these rulers, an aspiration that, perforce, resulted in their giving precedence to a man's ability over his origin or his religious and national affiliation. It is quite true that this outlook on political matters was the hallmark of the rulers in Moslem Spain beginning with the second decade of the eleventh century, but as the Moslem states grew weaker and more dependent upon the powerful Christian kings, all the barriers that had been the vestiges of the caliphate tradition disappeared. During the first half of the eleventh century, Jewish statesmen were still relatively uncommon; however, in the second half of that century, the Moslem kings did not hesitate at all to appoint "infidels" to the most estimable assignments.

Thus it came to pass that there developed in Moslem Spain in those days a situation that was particularly congenial for Jews. This became known throughout the lands ringing the Mediterranean Sea, and once again immigrants began to arrive in Spain from various states. Literary sources dating from the beginning of the twelfth century mention names of Andalusian Jews that point to this fact, names such as Joseph Ibn ash-Shāmī and Isaac Ibn ash-Shāmī—the sons of immigrants who came to Spain from Syria or Palestine at the end of the eleventh century.[59] But more numerous than these immigrants who came from faraway countries were, of course, the Jews from the countries of North Africa who came to settle in the cities of Andalusia. A letter written by the head of a Jewish community in one of the cities of Andalusia early in that century mentions "the son of al-Kābisī," in other words, the son of a Jew from the city of Gabes in Tunisia, who had settled in Spain, apparently in Lucena.[60] The members of the old educated, well-to-do families in Spain took the fullest possible advantage of the circumstances. This truly was a golden age for the eminent members of such families. Many mounted higher on the social ladder, becoming wealthy and being welcomed into the ranks of high society; but above all they achieved a new personal and group awareness. They no longer regarded themselves as inferior to the Moslem nobles but as their equals, belonging to the same national group. The riots in Granada seemed like an ephemeral affliction.

To be sure, hostility and envy prevailed among the Moslem

masses, and the Jewish multitudes in Spain were never permitted to forget that they were in exile. The works of Hebrew poets from the last quarter of the eleventh century written in honor of the Jewish "nobles" in Moslem Spain contain ample allusions to hostility toward the Jewish communities. The poets extolled those who held office and defended their people against the enmity of the non-Jews.[61] Even in court society, which professed to be animated by a secular spirit, Jews sometimes heard scornful and provocative remarks, such as those of the vizier Abū Muḥammad ʿAbdalghaffār b. al-Ḳāsim, one of al-Muʿtamid's officers, who told an esteemed Jew that although he was indeed the head of the community and a man of eminence, he was in effect an ignominious person because he did not acknowledge the true faith.[62] But this was mere teasing and did not involve any real action. The rulers needed the educated and affluent Jews, and the rise of Jewish officeholders, who were members of distinguished families, benefited the rest of the Jews both directly and indirectly. It was not for nought that an Arabic author writing in the twelfth century asserted that the Moslem kings had given the Jews dominion over their states in that period,[63] though he was exaggerating more than a little. On the other hand, the geographer ʿAlī b. Saʿīd held that in Spain's Moslem states a Jew or a Christian was never appointed as administrator of the office of the treasury, whose function it was to collect the taxes.[64] This writer was also engaged in wishful thinking, even though on frequent occasions there was a reaction to appointing non-Moslems to high office. However, as advisors and aides, tax farmers and agents, the Jews filled many important roles in those days in all the courts of the Moslem kings in Spain.

The Moslem kings and princes needed the services of the Jews not only in connection with economic activities but also for their diplomatic functions. When they appointed a Jew as emissary to the court of another king, they were not apprehen-

sive that he might try to reach a compromise with that ruler in exchange for a promise of a princedom—the frequent practice of Moslem officials. What was feasible in the days of Joseph the Nagid was practically impossible in the eighth decade of the eleventh century when large kingdoms arose in Moslem Spain. The Moslem kings also had assistance from the Jews in their negotiations with the Christian rulers. Contacts between the Moslem and Christian governments in Spain became very close at that time, and the exchange of emissaries became frequent. However, the members of the Moslem upper class did not know Latin, only Romance, the ancient Spanish tongue, and even in this language they found it difficult to deliver ornate addresses in the presence of the rulers, as was the accepted practice. For their part, the majority of the Christian kings and nobles did not know Arabic.[65] Consequently, for diplomatic activity the heads of both Moslem and Christian governments needed the services of their subjects who were not members of their faith.

Although the Moslem kings did indeed give the Christians important posts and charge them with diplomatic missions to the Christian governments, they were also suspicious of them —not without justification. On the other hand, they did not have many doubts as to the loyalty of the Jews who filled a role in diplomatic contacts. After all, Jews had no consanguineous ties with the Christian princes, nor were they members of their faith. In addition, Spanish Jews were uniquely qualified for this role, for unlike their brethren in most countries, they were steeped in the culture of their environment. Most of the Jewish intellectuals had a command of literary Arabic, and many could converse with the Christians in their tongue, Romance, or even in Latin, whether they acquired their knowledge through study or as a result of many journeys. Even more, the Jews were more acceptable as emissaries and negotiators since they were not members of the warring religions. Thus the Jews

began to participate extensively in Spanish politics and to take part in the general struggle of the Moslem and Christian rulers that spread throughout the Iberian Peninsula in the last third of the eleventh century.

The Jews cooperated willingly and wholeheartedly. The energy the high officials and ambassadors put into their functions and the pleasure they derived from them constituted a reaction to the pessimism that formed the basis of their approach to life. Men of that period were aware that their life span was short and the perils lurking for them were great—ailments for which there was no remedy, or the whim of kings that could raise up the lowly from the rubbish heap and humble the haughty and the mighty. The contemporary Hebrew poets wrote much verse addressing the "censure of the world," poems decrying "perfidious time," which bestows its favors on people planning to change good to evil or may simply replace any good with evil.[66] From this view stemmed the strong desire of the men of that period to benefit from all that was good for as long as good fortune shone upon them. Pursuit of honor, manifest display of social status, and conspicuous show of wealth—all these were really a means of concealing fear of the morrow.

The satisfaction the Jews derived from their political activity was especially great. In point of fact they enjoyed more than others taking part in such matters. Until this time only exceptional individuals like Ḥasdai Ibn Shaprūṭ and the two *nagiddim* of Granada had achieved this status, but in the last third of the eleventh century, the Spaniards had grown accustomed to seeing Jewish statesmen negotiating with kings and princes. Great indeed was the contentment of those Jews from Granada and Seville, from Toledo and Saragossa, who appeared splendidly garbed at the courts of the kings, addressing them and their deputies and governors in vigorous language, making demands and calling for clear replies. It did not even occur to the majority of these officials that they might be meddling in affairs that were not their own and that they were merely instruments of masters of other nations. The intermingling among Arabs, Berbers, Slavs, and native Spaniards was never greater than in the eleventh century; and the Jews thought themselves no less deeply rooted in the soil of the Iberian Peninsula than that admixture of peoples who had crossed the Straits.

The inner attachment of many of those educated and wealthy Jews to their ancestral heritage was not strong. Having enjoyed a sympathetic attitude by the Moslem rulers for some generations, many Spanish Jews had lost sentimental ties with their people, and the intellectuals who came into contact with circles of Arabic skeptics frequently lost their pure faith in the God of Israel. The great experiment to combine Judaism and humanism—the very heart of the history of the Jews in Spain—was foredoomed from the outset. Under circumstances prevailing during the Middle Ages, it seems that it was impossible for relatively large groups of Jews to maintain their ancestral heritage in a foreign land unless they closed themselves away within the narrow confines of talmudic Judaism with all its restrictions and enactments by the ancient rabbis. Instead of combining the achievements of general culture with their heritage, the Jewish members of the upper classes shunned their own people.

Whether they put personal advantage above loyalty to their religion or whether they were consumed by doubts, it is a fact that, by the second half of the tenth century, incidents of apostasy among the Jews of Moslem Spain were common. The rabbis of that era mention such cases in judicial decisions in which they resolve financial disputes or situations involving *ḥalīṣa* (refusal to perform the levirate).[67] During the economic boom of that period, this trouble spread among the Jewish middle classes in Spain; and in the eleventh century, with the rise in social status of the Jewish upper classes in Spain, this tendency grew even stronger. The responsa at the end of that century often deal with disputes that took place when men and women became Moslems. Frequently, these apostates would deny agreements they had made earlier and seek to nullify contracts of purchase and sale they had effected when they were Jews—attempting to do this after many years had passed and the property involved had changed hands.[68] At times the rabbis were queried on other matters connected with instances of conversion to Islam. For example, in the case of a *kōhēn* who had become a Moslem, the question arose whether his sons should be allowed to pronounce the priestly blessing.[69] From the questions put to the rabbis, it would seem that most of the converts were men of property. Even an Arabic source deals with the case of a doctor who was the son of a Jew who had become a Moslem in the beginning of the eleventh century. His name was Abū Dja'far Yūsuf b. Aḥmad, and he was a member of the esteemed Ibn Ḥasdai family.[70] But Arabo-Moslem sources also carry information about mere artisans who became Moslems in the eleventh century, such as a Jewish carpenter called Yūsuf al-Aslamī. He became involved in a dispute with the poet Abu 'r-Rabī' Sulaimān b. Aḥmad al-Ḳuḍā'i, because he refused to lend him a tool.[71]

In the second half of the eleventh century, however, apostasy had not yet reached considerable dimensions. For the majority of the upper stratum of Jewish society, this loosening of their ties to Judaism had not yet resulted in open and avowed abandonment. The sense of honor and tradition characteristic of the inhabitants of the Iberian Peninsula served as a shield; even one whose beliefs were shaken and whose loyalty to the Jewish people was weakened nevertheless outwardly observed the religion of his forebears. Even more, the majority of the Jews who became subordinates of the rulers remained guardians and intercessors on behalf of their people.

At the same time, on the other hand, the distances between

the classes increased in the Jewish communities of Spain. The antagonism grew between the wealthy class, which was closely associated with royalty, and the humble artisans, who were compelled to grit their teeth and accept the authority of the wealthy. In these communities, side by side with the artisan class, there were also actual proletarians, people without any property whatsoever or a regular occupation who hired themselves out to anyone prepared to pay them a wage for unskilled labor.[72] This variegated social stratification was characteristic of a group that had not yet lost its ties with cultivation of the soil and manual labor as means of gaining a livelihood. The strong tie between social stratification and religious points of view, a phenomenon characteristic of the Middle Ages, was laden with dangerous possibilities to the life of faith.

IV

In that generation the most powerful state in Moslem Spain was the kingdom of Seville, whose king had numerous means at his disposal to adopt a vigorous policy. For many years the initiative in the political life of southern Spain lay with him. The immediate goal al-Muʿtamid had set for himself upon ascending the throne was to establish control over the city of Cordova, which his father had desired to conquer for ten years. But the Cordovan vizier Ibn as-Saḳḳā stood as a powerful barrier in the path of his ambition. The vizier established ties with the nagid Joseph and enjoyed the support of the kingdom of Granada for a long time, so that the attempts of the king of Seville came to nought.

Eventually, however, al-Muʿtamid aroused strife between the vizier and ʿAbdalmalik Ibn Djahwar, the ruler of Cordova, who murdered the vizier in 1063. From then on the authority of the Ibn Djahwar family went steeply downhill. Between the two sons to whom the former ruler of Cordova, Abu ʾl-Walīd, had turned over the government in his old age, 'Abdalmalik, the younger, was noted for his great energy and resoluteness, and not many days had elapsed before he had removed his older brother, 'Abdarraḥmān. When he became aware of the dissatisfaction prevalent among Cordova's inhabitants and felt the ground slipping from under his feet, he began to seek help from the king of Seville. The latter was waiting for an opportunity to intervene in the affairs of Cordova and willingly established ties with him. However, al-Ma'mūn, the king of Toledo, also aspired to conquer Cordova, because dominance over it was symbolic of hegemony over all of Moslem Spain. In 1070 al-Ma'mūn began a military campaign, and eventually his army conquered Almodóvar, which is west of Cordova, and ultimately laid siege to the city itself. 'Abdalmalik had to call in help from Seville, and al-Mu'tamid did indeed send troops to defend the city and free it from its state of siege. But the officers of the army conspired with the inhabitants of Cordova, imprisoning the family of Ibn Djahwar and annexing the city to the kingdom of Seville.

The king of Toledo did not, however, abandon his aspirations. He too always sought to enlarge his kingdom, heading his army in military campaigns against the neighboring Moslem states, or sending his regiments to make forays inside their borders. At that time he enjoyed the aid of bands of Christian knights who were experienced soldiers.

Al-Ma'mūn devised many stratagems to subdue the rulers of Cordova. Nevertheless, his plots and the forays into their territory he engaged in with his mercenaries, the Castilians, were, for a long time, to no avail. He eventually discovered a person qualified to help and gave him the task of implementing his objective. This man was Ḥakam b. 'Ukāsha, a Cordovan who was a member of the faction of Ibn as-Saḳḳā. When the vizier was slain, he was imprisoned; he later fled from his prison, no doubt aspiring to take vengeance of his faction's enemies.

Since fickleness had been a conspicuous trait in the character of Cordova's inhabitants from time immemorial, it was not hard for Ibn 'Ukāsha to recruit coconspirators. One night, these disaffected Cordovans opened the gates of the city for him and a band of his companions. Meeting no opposition, he went to the palace of the military governor and surprised him at a feast. Thus, at the beginning of 1075, Cordova was annexed to the kingdom of Toledo. Al-Ma'mūn lost no time in coming to the city to take over the government. But after five months had passed, the Berber king was fatally poisoned. The Cordovan, who now experienced a change of heart, turned to the king of Seville, inviting him to take the government into his hands. Naturally, al-Mu'tamid was glad to accept the invitation. In 1076 he penetrated the city with the help of the faction that supported him.

The Jews in Cordova also participated in the long struggle for dominance. During that period the Jews in the Spanish states believed that they had a share in Spain's destiny. They did not regard themselves as wayfarers or aliens and therefore took part in all the conflicts and intrigues among the rulers and the various factions. In the eleventh century the Jewish community of Cordova was one of the most important in Andalusia.[73] The Jews were deeply and actively involved in the affairs of the city, as were their brethren in the other cities of Andalusia. In fact, a trustworthy Arabic historian wrote that when Ibn 'Ukāsha fled from Cordova, a Jew belonging to the faction siding with the king of Seville pursued and slew him.[74]

V

After Cordova was restored to him, the king of Seville embarked on an expansionist policy in the regions east of the city of the caliphs. As was his habit, he did not spare any effort and eventually achieved success. He contrived to wrest parts of the province of Jaén from the kingdom of Granada in 1074[75] and, after a short period of time had elapsed, managed to annex the entire province. Later he took the initiative to capture Murcia and the districts around it. Murcia, which was one of the important cities in eastern Spain, had been ruled for a long time by an Arabic family, the Banū Ṭāhir. Zuhair, the king of Almería, had appointed Abū Bakr Aḥmad b. Ṭāhir as governor of Murcia. In 1038, after Zuhair was slain, Murcia came under the authority of al-Manṣūr ʻAbdalʻazīz, the king of Valencia, but Abū Bakr retained his post. He was an excellent governor; in his days the city flourished, and its inhabitants were very loyal to him. After his death in 1063, his son Abū ʻAbdarraḥmān Muḥammad, who was renowned as one of the most learned men of his generation, took over as governor. He became an independent ruler of Murcia,[76] but his reign was shaky because his soldiers were few in number.

One day Ibn ʻAmmār, the friend and vizier of al-Muʻtamid, passed through Murcia. Observing the weakness of Ibn Ṭāhir's authority, he entered into a conspiracy with the townspeople. The vizier from Seville then continued on his way to Barcelona and reached an understanding with its prince to conduct a joint campaign to capture Murcia. However, the siege of the city failed; moreover, a conflict erupted between the allies. Ibn ʻAmmār, who had secretly conceived the notion of establishing his own princedom in Murcia, did not resign himself to the failure, but persuaded the king of Seville to send him at the head of his army to make another attempt to capture the city. On the way there he struck up a friendship with ʻAbdaraḥamān Ibn Rashīḳ, the commander of one of the fortresses in that district, and turned over to him the command of the siege of Murcia. After Ibn Rashīḳ succeeded in capturing it and taking its governor, Ibn Ṭāhir, as prisoner,[77] Ibn ʻAmmār arrived and took over as governor. He immediately began to behave like a king and to slight al-Muʻtamid, his former friend and benefactor. When Abū Bakr b. 'Abdal'azīz, the king of Valencia, wanted to obtain freedom for his friend Ibn Ṭāhir and al-Mu'tamid granted his request, Ibn 'Ammār would not obey. He even toyed with the idea of winning control of Valencia and becoming a real king. As was the habit of the Spanish Moslems, derogatory or mocking poems were employed as effective weapons in this political conflict. After Ibn Ṭāhir fled his prison and went to Valencia, Ibn 'Ammār wrote a long poem in which he called upon the inhabitants of Valencia to rebel against their king. Al-Mu'tamid composed a poem in which he mimicked and made sport of Ibn 'Ammār. Ibn 'Ammār responded by writing a poem of reproach criticizing the king of Seville, the king's beloved wife, Rumaikiya, and the entire Banū 'Abbād family.

A Jew also played an important part in this conflict. He was a member of one of the Jewish communities on the eastern coast of Spain and was a frequent visitor to the royal court of Ibn 'Abdal'azīz, the king of Valencia. After Ibn 'Ammār turned his subjects against him, the king burned with a desire for vengeance for himself and for his friend Ibn Ṭāhir. He decided to send one of his trustworthy and shrewd intimates to Murcia to win the confidence of Ibn 'Ammār and then take advantage of a suitable opportunity. To carry out this difficult assignment, the king of Valencia could not find a more able man than the aforementioned Jew; and in truth the latter did not disappoint him. The Jew left for Murcia and succeeded in ingratiating himself with Ibn 'Ammār, who welcomed him into his circle of friends. Ibn 'Ammar showed the Jew the derisive poem he had indited about al-Mu'tamid—but he was not aware that his guest had made a copy and sent it to the king of Valencia. When the copy reached Ibn 'Abdal'azīz, he sent it by carrier pigeon to al-Mu'tamid. Thenceforth, the king of Seville bore a fierce hatred in his heart toward the ungrateful adventurer who had become the ruler of Murcia with his help, and he determined to destroy him when the opportunity offered itself.[78]

VI

At the very time that this conflict was provoking excitement throughout Andalusia and the expansion schemes conceived by the king of Seville were troubling the Moslem rulers, the peril that lurked for them from the Christians grew apace. Dark clouds, harbingers of evil, obscured the blue skies of Andalusia. Incidents warning of the evil that would soon break forth from the north occurred with growing frequency. However, for many years the majority of the Moslem princes did not take proper heed of the situation or even intentionally closed their eyes to it to enjoy their luck in the present.

Fernando I, king of León and Castile, adopted a policy of imposing tribute on the Moslem kingdoms. This policy, which he followed consistently, was designed to break the economic strength of these states so that they would be unable to mobilize strong forces and would fall like ripe fruit into the hands of the Christians. Fernando's method of taking control gradually seemed surer and easier than wars of conquest, which were as yet premature. For their part, the Moslem princes paid these tributes, called *parias,* in the hope that much time would elapse before they became excessively weak and that meanwhile the political situation would change in their favor. But their expectations proved false. Sancho, Fernando's son and heir as king of Castile, increased the *parias,* and this compelled the Moslem rulers to impose heavier and heavier taxes upon their subjects. As the burden on the populace increased, the peasants began to flee from the villages.[79] Sometimes the Christian rulers would attack the Moslem kingdoms in order to wrest some regions away from them and annex them to their own states. In 1057 Fernando drove a wedge south of the Duero River into what is now Portugal, taking the city of Lamego and, in the following year, the city of Viseu. Around 1060 his army penetrated the kingdom of Saragossa and captured the districts of Gormaz and Berlanga in the upper valley of the Duero. Four years later he took the city of Coimbra and annexed all the regions between the Duero and the Mondego rivers to his kingdom. To be sure, these conquests were not as important to the ruler of Castile as the extortion of the tribute designed to overthrow Moslem dominance over southern and central Spain. Nevertheless, they caused strong reverberations in the other countries of Europe.

In those days—the seventh decade of the eleventh century—the spirit of Christian piety grew strong throughout Europe. The popes, acting to strengthen the Church, succeeded in filling all classes with true religious zeal and reinforcing loyalty to the papal throne. In 1063 Pope Alexander II promised absolution from sins to anyone who would go forth to fight the Moslems. Immediately, bands of knights from various countries began to gather to start out on a campaign. The participants in the venture, like the Crusaders in other generations, did not overlook the Jews on account of the Moslems. The Jews are therefore mentioned in the ancient sources in which this Crusade is discussed, though it was mounted thirty years before what came to be called the "First Crusade."

Among the Crusader knights who went to Spain that first year were many French aristocrats—high-ranking nobles such as Guillaume VIII, Count of Poitiers and Duke of Aquitaine, and also renowned soldiers such as Robert Crespin, Baron of Lower Normandy, and his Norman troops. Most of the participants in the campaign came from France, but they were also joined by many from Italy, headed by Guillaume de Montreuil, who commanded the pope's forces.[80] However, not all the Crusaders who came by land and sea to Spain were inspired by religious fervor and the ambition to perform deeds of der-ring-do, for there were also among them adventurers who dreamt of spoils and plunder. When they reached the city of Narbonne, they attacked the ancient Jewish community in that city and, whether motivated by fanaticism or desire for gain, began to plunder and kill. Thanks to the strong stand taken by Wilfred, Archbishop of Narbonne, and the Viscount Berenger, the community was saved.[81] When reports of the deeds of the Crusaders reached Spain, the Jews were seized with fear. Both large and small Jewish communities existed throughout the regions along the banks of the Ebro River, and Jews also lived in the villages. The danger that they would be attacked was very grave.

At the end of 1063 and the beginning of 1064, bands of Crusaders assembled in Catalonia, where they were joined by Spanish warriors led by Sancho Ramírez, king of Aragon, and Ermengaud III, Count of Urgel. In the meantime the papal legate, Cardinal Hugo Candido, arrived there, and under his leadership a provincial council was convened.[82] The commanders of the army took counsel at that time as to what plan of action they should follow, finally deciding to breach the Moslem fortifications in the region of the Esera and Vero rivers, where the Moslems' holdings constituted a bulge into Christian territory. In 1055 Ramiro I, the first king of Aragon, had besieged the city of Graus, a Moslem fortress on the Esera River; a second attempt to subdue it in 1063 cost him his life. Hence, in 1064 his son and heir Sancho, together with the Crusaders, concentrated his forces before that city. When—on their way there—they came upon Jewish communities while passing through regions of the provinces of Barcelona and Lérida, they attacked them; but the Jews had anticipated this evil and had secured for themselves the protection of the authorities in advance. The bishops came to their aid, rescuing them from the wrath of the Crusaders.[83] However, when the Crusaders approached the cities under Moslem dominance, in which larger Jewish communities existed, there was great apprehension.

But the Crusaders did not tarry long before Graus; they descended into the valleys of the Esera and Cinca rivers until they reached the city of Barbastro, some 35 kilometers to the southwest. During the second half of June, they laid siege to it. This city then belonged to al-Muẓaffar, prince of Lérida, but he was not strong enough to defend it against the Crusaders. Aḥmad, king of Saragossa, was vexed with the inhabitants of Barbastro, who had turned their backs on him and recognized his brother as their king; and there were many who even suspected him of secretly supporting the Christians.[84] Thus, the city, inhabited by both Moslems and Jews, was abandoned by the brothers who ruled in Lérida and Saragossa, and an unkind fate awaited it. After the siege had been maintained for more than a month, there was a dire shortage of necessary foods, and the neighborhoods outside the walls were captured by the Christians, who ultimately succeeded in severing the underground conduit that supplied Barbastro with drinking water. Around the beginning of August, Barbastro's inhabitants were forced to surrender, and despite a solemn promise not to harm them, the Crusaders organized a frightful slaughter—killing, according to reports, 6,000 people. They then divided among themselves the houses and their inhabitants within the city, torturing them so that they would reveal the places they had hidden their valuables and raping women in the presence of their husbands and children. The Arabic writers exaggerated in estimating the number of captives who were sent as slaves to other countries. But, for all their exaggeration, it is apparent from their statements that the capture of Barbastro made a strong impression on Christians and Moslems alike. The Christians rejoiced over the capture of an important border fortress, while the Spanish Moslems well knew the cruelty of the Normans and dreaded the continuation of their activities.

Meanwhile, the majority of the Crusaders returned to their own countries, leaving a garrison within the city and handing over the government to Sancho Ramírez, king of Aragon, and Ermengaud, Count of Orgel.

In those first days after the capture of Barbastro, when the inhabitants of the Moslem cities on the banks of the Ebro were stricken with dismay, the Moslems tried to establish contact with the French knights in the city. Many of the Moslems were residents who had been outside the city during the siege, had thus escaped the slaughter, and were concerned about the fate of their families. As was customary in Spain at that time, they could find no better intermediaries than the Jews. A contemporary Arabic chronicler tells a lengthy tale about a Jew who went to the conquered city of Barbastro as the emissary of a Moslem.

This Jew was not a Spanish native but a merchant from one of the countries beyond the Pyrenees who had business dealings with the cities on the banks of the Ebro. When he was asked by one of the inhabitants of Barbastro to obtain the release of his daughters, he entered the city and went to the Moslem's house, which one of the Christian officers had taken for himself. On entering the house, which was well known to him from times past, he realized that no changes had been made in it. The Christian officer sat on the divan upon which the Moslem householder used to sit, and he was also wearing the Moslem's resplendent finery. The Jew asked him what price he demanded for the Moslem's daughters, who were then present and were serving him. The Christian showed the Jew the bags full of gold and silver, the chests of jewelry, and the silk cloth that had come to him as his share of the plunder, making it clear that he had no need of any offer the Jew might propose in exchange for the girls. The Christian knight then asked one of the girls to play an instrument and sing for him, just as she had often done at parties given by the Moslem householder. Tears flowing from her eyes, the girl did as he bade her to do. The knight drank incessantly, listening to Arabic songs whose meaning he—and even the Jew—did not understand. When the Jew saw that he would not attain his objective, he departed.[85]

This Jewish merchant who sought to redeem the daughters of an esteemed and affluent Moslem was but one of many who performed various missions of intermediation between the two large powers that then fought for supremacy in Spain. No matter how severe the struggle grew, the contacts were not broken, and both warring sides needed people to serve as go-betweens. Educated Jews who knew the Moslem and Christian tongues and merchants who came in contact with princes and nobles filled this role, receiving ample emolument for their services and becoming intimates of the rulers.

VII

The Crusade that led to the capture of Barbastro created powerful reverberations in Spain; nevertheless, for practical purposes it had no important results. Before long the energies of the European knights from the lands beyond the Pyrenees were directed into other channels. The war against the Moslems in the Iberian Peninsula remained the objective of the Christian princes in northern Spain. And, indeed, in that epoch rulers from that area who were endowed with initiative and much ability attained this objective. First among them was Alfonso VI, the king of León, who was sent to exile in a Moslem country in 1072, becoming the guest of al-Ma'mūn, the king of Toledo. In that stormy era the turns of fate were frequent, and Alfonso's banishment to Toledo did not last long.

In the summer of that year, his supporters revolted against Sancho, king of Castile, who had supplanted him, and made the city of Zamora their strong point. Sancho set siege to it, but one of the knights of the opposing faction succeeded in penetrating his camp, and slew him. Alfonso was promptly informed of this and left Toledo without delay to return to his kingdom.

As soon as he reoccupied the royal throne, he began to display all the positive aspects of his character. He acted to achieve security on the roads and endeavored to facilitate greatly the functioning of commerce. Like his forebears he deemed it an important goal to strengthen the economic and cultural ties between the countries beyond the Pyrenees and his kingdom, thereby bringing it out of isolation. To this end he fostered pilgrimages to Santiago and prompted Frenchmen to settle along the important road leading to the shrine in Galicia. Alfonso VI also followed in the footsteps of his father, Fernando I, in his policy toward the Moslem states, but he implemented it very forcefully and energetically. He too attempted to weaken these kingdoms by extorting tribute from them, but the kingdoms only became stronger. His political initiative was great, embracing the whole of Spain. In his days there was scarcely a Moslem state in the Iberian Peninsula that was not tributary to the Christians. The most powerful Moslem kingdom, Seville, paid tribute to the Christians beginning from the time Fernando I penetrated it in 1063. Seville's Moslem king was then subjugated and had to agree to allow the Christians to transfer the remains of Isidor, the father of the Spanish Church, from Seville to León, where his burial took place amid ceremonial splendor. This event made a powerful impression upon the Jews; later Jewish historians recorded it among other important occurrences.[86]

Beginning in 1068, the kingdom of Badajoz had to pay tribute to the kingdom of Castile, as did Seville. Granada's ruler was also compelled to pay *parias.* Alfonso himself went to Granada to demand additional payments; after much haggling

'Abdallāh yielded to Alfonso and also obligated himself to make annual payments.[87] In this fashion the Moslem kings became instruments in the hands of the powerful and energetic Christian king.

As a result of this foreign policy, Alfonso VI was confronted with difficult objectives within his own kingdom. When his father conquered the regions between the Duero and the Mondego rivers he expelled all the Moslems, but from other places that were then taken by the Christians, the Moslems often left voluntarily. The Christian rulers brought peasants from various regions in northern Spain to the rural settlements that had been abandoned by the Moslems, but there were not enough Christians to settle the cities. The urban dwellers of Castile and León were too few to be able to provide settlers for abandoned cities. This was one of the reasons that, for many years, the kings of Castile and León did not adopt far-reaching policies of conquest. In his memoirs 'Abdallāh, king of Granada, relates that a man of great influence at the court of Alfonso VI admitted, in a conversation with him, that a lack of manpower deterred the Christian king from conquering the Moslem cities.[88] The number of inhabitants in Alfonso's large kingdom did not exceed three million.[89] This was not a small population for that time, and even today those provinces contain no less than nine million people. However, all the subjects of Alfonso —except the small class of nobles—were peasants, and the urban Christian population was insufficient.

To develop a strong urban population, the kings of Castile and León needed more than the class of foreign merchants and craftsmen that they attracted to their country with privileges; consequently, they began to spread their mantle of protection over the Jews. The city ordinance *(fuero)* that Alfonso VI enacted in 1076 for the city of Najera was typical of the approach of the Christian rulers in the second half of the eleventh century and of Alfonso in particular. This writ of privileges sets forth that the same fine must be paid for the killing or wounding of a knight, a monk, or a Jew.[90] Alfonso VI also awarded privileges to the Jews of Miranda del Ebro that were equal to those of the Christians in the area.[91] He and the other Christian rulers in Spain at that time took this position because their own benefit required that they attract the Jews, whose numbers in the Spanish cities were relatively large. As long as they were favorably disposed toward the Jews, they had no reason to cast suspicion on their loyalty. The Christian rulers therefore made use of them as settlers in the cities they founded, developed, or conquered and, as a matter of course, did not expel the Jews they found in these cities. Whereas the Moslems were suspect because of religio-national ties linking them with their kings beyond the frontier line, the Jews had no political aspirations and asked for no more than a reasonable attitude toward them. The artisans and merchants who dwelt in the cities of the "provincial kings" during the middle and second half of the eleventh century suffered enough from the taxes collected as tribute for the Christian kings. They yearned for a kinder government and above all for security from the forays of alien invaders to which—under Moslem rule—they could look forward every day and every hour.

Hence, the Jews within the borders of Christian Spain benefited greatly from the role designed for them, while those who were in the Moslem cities during their conquest by the Christians gladly welcomed the protection of the new rulers, who could afford them a stable rule, security of life and property, and freedom of movement on the roads. For their part, the Christian rulers had additional reasons to stress a lenient attitude toward Jewish townspeople. Deeply rooted within the provinces of Spain, these Jews knew well the natural environment and the customs of the inhabitants. Because of this they were more successful in developing the various branches of the economy than were those from other lands. Of course, heavy taxes were imposed upon the Jews in exchange for the privileges and special protection granted them. They were regarded as being bondsmen of the king, in keeping with the political views of the feudal era, as these had long since crystallized in France and Germany and carried over, during the days of the Navarrese dynasty of Sancho el Mayor, to León and Castile. Not only did the small group of upper-class Jews benefit from the protection of the rulers of Christian Spain, but so too did the middle classes. In the Moslem states, on the other hand, these classes were in hard-pressed circumstances during that epoch. The favorable situation of the various classes of Jews in northern Spain strengthened the inclination of the Jews of Andalusia and the other Moslem areas to migrate to the regions of Christian dominion, which, from an economic standpoint, constituted a zone with a young, developing economy. The policy of the Christian rulers was therefore well thought out and achieved a number of goals.

But Alfonso VI needed not only diligent and secure craftsmen and merchants to settle the cities in his realm but also educated people who could conduct the affairs of his administration and serve as secretaries in his government bureaus. At a time when the incomes of the Christian rulers increased—due to an increase in taxes because of the development of trade and the expansion of tributes—there was a need for bureaus and departments to deal with the collection of all sorts of taxes and to manage the royal treasury intelligently. The Christian subjects of the kings of Castile and León lacked experience in these matters, whereas the Jews had been expert in them for several generations. Just as quite a number of them conducted the financial administrations of the Moslem princes, they were also trusted by the Christian rulers as able and loyal administrators. To no less a degree, the Christian rulers needed the Jews as political secretaries. In order to carry on negotiations with the Moslem kings, contact the leaders of factions within their states, and maintain ties with discontented circles, they required people who were educated and deeply rooted in Arabic culture, but whose loyalty was not at all in doubt.[92] The Christian kings could find people like these among the Mozarabs who went from the Moslem states to northern Spain—and among the Jews. Both were welcome at the courts of the Christian rulers.

Sisenando, a Mozarab noble at the court of al-Muʿtaḍid, king of Seville, later changed over to the service of Fernando I, becoming his political and military advisor in all that concerned relationships with the Moslem states. It was he who advised Fernando to besiege Coimbra; after its capture he was appointed governor of the districts between the Duero and Mondego rivers. During the reign of Alfonso VI as well, Sisenando for many years played an important part in fashioning policy toward the Moslem kingdoms. It was he who persuaded the ambitious king to act with tolerance and moderation and to be content, for the time being, with their payment of tribute. He also endeavored to persuade the king that it was better for him to take on the role of their protector than to convert the Spanish Moslems into desperate foes who would not flinch from opposing him by any means available to them. Whenever there was any objection to the political line he advocated, Sisenando would point to his years of service with the Moslem king and his expert knowledge of the customs and views of the Arabs. Even in various documents, such as those granting land to monasteries, he identified himself as a former official at the court of the king of Seville, for this was what gave him esteem in the eyes of the other dignitaries.[93]

Because of the dearth of men who were well versed in matters concerning the Arabs, the rulers of northern Spain also had to rely on the services of Jews who came from southern Spain.

To be sure, there also were factors that militated against these rulers' ties with the Jewish intellectuals and men of affairs. All the kings of the dynasty of Sancho el Mayor, who ruled in the second half of the eleventh century, strove to strengthen the ties between Christian Spain and the countries beyond the Pyrenees. By means of marriage with French princesses, they established links of family and friendship with France's upper aristocracy. Knights and priests accompanied the French queens to Castile and Aragon, and these churchmen introduced a new spirit of fanaticism into Spain. They labored to establish the hegemony of the Church over the secular state, opposing, as a matter of course, the rulers' association with Jews, while voicing their objections to the policy of tolerance toward Moslems that had been recommended by the advisors and intimates of the Spanish kings.

Because of the contradiction between what was advantageous for the realm and the demands of the highly influential French clergy, great importance—in regard to the Jews' status—attaches to the personal inclinations of Alfonso VI, the central personality in the struggle for dominion in Spain at the end of the eleventh century.

During the forty-four years Alfonso occupied the royal throne, his inclinations underwent changes; at different periods of his life, disparate elements of his character would stand out. He always showed himself to be a shrewd and multitalented statesman; however, one very conspicuous trait in his character was his tendency to be swayed by influences from without and to change his mind quite frequently, to the point of fickleness. But above all he was intensely egotistical, having been pampered not only by his parents and his sister Urraca but also by destiny. For many years he benefited from events and actions in which he had no hand but which altered the political circumstances in his favor. Because of his successes and talents, he became very haughty, and as a knight there were no limits to his aspirations for glory and praise. Throughout his lifetime he followed his strong passions and was not fastidious in his choice of the means to attain his ends. Unflinchingly, he broke agreements and acted with unconcealed treachery toward his opponents or rivals. Although he was a devout Christian and showed great respect for matters hallowed by his religion, he was far from being a zealot, since as far as he was concerned principles were not important. He acted in accordance with political necessity and self-interest, and when his goals conflicted with the pope's policy, he did not refrain from treating him with hostility.

For all that the ancient documents and the accounts of the chroniclers stress Alfonso's image as a personality devoid of moral principles, it must not be forgotten that in his approach to life he was no different from his contemporaries in both Christian and Moslem Spain. In the eleventh century the majority of the members of the upper classes of the Spanish states put their personal advantage above principles and endeavored to employ every means that seemed useful in attaining their ends. This explains why the Christians could, at a given moment, risk their lives in a war against the Moslems, and then make peace and ally themselves with them against their coreligionists, while showing them respect. This also accounts for their extreme cruelty. Fratricides were a common phenomenon in those days among the royal houses of Christian Spain; for example, the king of Aragon, Sancho Ramírez, threatened to pluck out the eyes of his brother, the bishop of Jaca.

Since a man's worth was determined by his ability, the Moslem rulers gladly welcomed Christian knights into their army, and Christian kings made Jews, who were educated and experienced in the techniques of administration, their close intimates. In the view of Spaniards of that age, personal devotion to their own faith and entering into an association with rulers of another faith were not mutually contradictory. The prince of Castile, Fernán Gomez, served in the army of Cordova's ruler; however, when he returned to Castile in 1060, he demonstrated his loyalty to Christianity by bringing back the remains of two saints. There was surely Christian enthusiasm in the hearts of the Christian kings of Castile and Aragon and the counts of Catalonia, and they regarded the reconquest of all of Spain from the Moslems as their sacred mission. But the realities of the situation prevented them from acting like zealots. Since they were unable to drive out all the Moslems and Jews from the peninsula, they had, perforce, to resign themselves to those groups' continued presence. The totalitarianism of the great states of the later epoch was foreign to their thinking. In this set of circumstances that included weak kingdoms and an atmosphere in which religious enthusiasm and tolerance operated simultaneously, the Jews flourished. The peculiar circumstances of the rule of the "provincial kings" in Moslem Spain and of the first generations of the Reconquista in Christian Spain made possible the economic, social, and cultural advance of the Jews in the Iberian Peninsula. Just as they were made the counselors and administrators of the Moslem kings, the Jews were made the intimates of the Christian kings who fought these Arabs and Berbers. First and foremost in this regard was Alfonso VI, who brought about a new turn in the history of Spain.

A variety of sources provide data demonstrating that throughout the years of Alfonso VI's reign, Jews were close to him and filled important functions in his service.[94] For a long period of time, an Andalusian Jew was his physician and also his advisor on important matters. This physician's first name was Joseph, and his family's name, Ibn Ferrizuel, was apparently a Romance name; however, he was known to the Christians as Cidellus. He originated from the city of Cabra.[95] As in the case of other Jews, he was first received at the royal court as a doctor, for the Christian rulers in Spain greatly esteemed the high professional level of the Jewish and Arabic physicians, preferring them over Christian doctors or over those who had studied in Christian countries. In the course of time, when he became an intimate of the king, he acquired a considerable influence over him and was called upon to affix his seal, as a witness, to royal documents, after the fashion of important nobles. Alfonso bestowed upon him much property, which he held and enjoyed throughout his life.[96] Because of his high station Joseph Ibn Ferrizuel was able to defend the Jews when Christian zealots attacked them, and contemporary Hebrew poets extolled his courage and devotion to his people.[97] As was the custom of the Moslem kings, Alfonso VI recognized the Jewish physician as the *nāsī* of the Jewish communities in his kingdom. For his part Joseph did all in his power to impose religious discipline upon his coreligionists; among other things he harassed the Karaites, who had begun to win converts to their sect. A Jewish historian who lived in Toledo in the twelfth century reports that "he drove them out of all the Castilian fortresses, save one small fortress which he gave them because he did not want to slay them."[98] This item of information stresses the importance of Joseph Ibn Ferrizuel's activities. It demonstrates that the first *nāsī* of the Jews of Castile even obtained from the Christian king the privilege of imposing capital punishment upon heretics, which was similar to the privilege given the Jews by the kings of Moslem Spain. Thus, in those days the juridical status of the Jews of Castile was established for many generations to come, and Joseph Ibn Ferrizuel played an important part in this.

Yet Joseph was only one of the Jews who frequented the palace of Alfonso VI. Already in the early years of his reign some Jews from Castile had become intimates of Alfonso, and after he conquered large areas from the Moslems he brought the Jews there and gave them houses and land in abundance.[99] The great influence the Jews enjoyed at the court of Alfonso

VI was a source of vexation to Pope Gregory VII, and in 1081 he addressed a forceful letter on this matter to the king. He argued that it constituted a degradation of the Church and vigorously demanded that the king not give Jews authority over Christians.[100] But although Alfonso followed the Church of Rome, he did not heed the words of the pope in this matter, retaining the Jewish advisors and officials he had long since grown accustomed to employing in various services. There can be no doubt that the apostate Pedro Alfonso had Alfonso primarily in mind when, in the polemic he wrote at the end of the king's reign, he strongly protested against the high status the Jews in Christian Spain enjoyed and against the honor given them by the Christian kings.[101] To be sure, had this apostate been able to see into the future, he would not have complained so much, for the attachment of many of those Jewish courtiers to the faith of their ancestors was indeed tenuous. They were consumed by doubts and imbued with religious relativism. The views these educated and affluent Jews brought with them from Moslem Spain—from the courts of the Moslem kings and from the circles close to them—led to many of them not having the strength to suffer for their ancestral faith, so that when the day of reckoning came they stumbled and fell. When persecution against the Jews raged throughout New Castile—at the very time that Pedro Alfonso was writing his book—some of the Jews who held royal posts became converts to Christianity. There is proof of this in the fact that King Alfonso VI had to give in to the enemies of the Jews and agree that converts should not be appointed to positions that might give them authority over Christians.[102]

VIII

The united kingdom of Castile and León's ambitions for expansion and the political actions needed to realize them were directed for many years against the Moslem kingdom of Saragossa. This kingdom had borders on all the important Christian states in the Iberian Peninsula, and all of them endeavored to extort tribute from it and wrest whatever portions they could—large or small—away from it. Within the kingdom proper, civil war would erupt from time to time among the princes of the Banū Hūd, and the Christian rulers, of course, hoped to benefit from these conditions. In nearly every one of these struggles, Moslems and Christians joined together to battle against Moslems who had also become linked with, and were aided by, Christians. Jews were among those who pulled the political strings of the kingdom of the Banū Hūd, for Saragossa had been a city of great consequence for the Jews from time immemorial.

Aḥmad I, who occupied the royal throne at Saragossa for an entire generation, was a very energetic and active person. Throughout his reign he sought to widen the borders of his dominion. For many years he carried on a struggle with his brother al-Muẓaffar Yūsuf, the king of Lérida, whom he wanted to dislodge from his small kingdom. The warring that resulted between them led to many vicissitudes. Aḥmad called upon the armies of Catalonia and Navarre for aid, but the Christian troops went over to Yūsuf's side, as did most of the Moslem soldiers. All of them conjointly laid siege to Saragossa in 1051. A short time later Aḥmad obtained permission from the king of Aragon to send his soldiers into that kingdom in order to ambush convoys transporting food supplies from the region of Lérida to Tudela, then also ruled by his brother Yūsuf. After he had succeeded in breaking the tie between the provinces that recognized his brother's authority, a new turn in the relationships among the forces led to all the regions of his father's kingdom, save Lérida, again coming under his dominion. In 1058 he attempted to lay a snare for his brother at a meeting that had been arranged, as it were, to make a peace treaty. But his stratagem came to naught, and consequently Yūsuf, who had become the vassal of the Christian count of Barcelona, occupied for many more years the throne at Lérida.

Ever since around 1060, when the armies of Fernando I had invaded his kingdom and conquered some of the districts in the upper valley of the Duero, Aḥmad himself had been the vassal and tributary of the king of Castile. At the same time he also paid tribute to the Catalan principality of Cerdaña. It is true that for a while being under the aegis of the king of Castile was advantageous for the ruler of Saragossa, since he thereby received protection from the king against his brother Yūsuf, and because at that time the kings of Navarre and Aragon had entered into an alliance that was directed primarily against Aḥmad. When in 1063 Ramiro, king of Aragon, besieged the city of Graus, Castilian troops led by Sancho, the son of Fernando, joined in its defense. At the end of that year, when the aged Fernando divided his kingdom, Sancho received, aside from Castile, the kingdom of Saragossa as a zone of influence and expansion. Henceforth, Aḥmad paid him a yearly tribute. However, in the beginning of 1065 he refused to pay the tribute, entered into an alliance with the king of Seville, and, with the help of troops al-Muʿtaḍid sent him, conquered Barbastro, which had fallen into the hands of the Christians the previous year. In this way Aḥmad purged himself of suspicions that he had wanted to wreak vengeance on the inhabitants of the city—and also earned the laudatory title of *Mudjāhid,* "one who fights a holy war." Henceforth, he was surnamed "al-Muḳtadir Billāh"—"the mighty one, with God's help." Fernando mounted a punitive campaign against the kingdom of Saragossa, but at the end of that year he died without having subdued it.

Fernando's son Sancho, who inherited Castile from him, naturally renewed his demand for tribute, and after two years had passed he set siege to al-Muḳtadir Aḥmad's capital. The

Christian armies closed in upon the city and vigorously attacked its fortifications. Their bands of knights demonstrated a clear superiority over the Moslem forces; particularly conspicuous was the Castilian commander Rodrigo Diaz de Vivar, a valorous young warrior who was destined to win great renown by his heroic deeds in battle against the Moslems. Even the Jews of Saragossa, who witnessed the feats of the "Cid" from the city's walls, were amazed and moved to admiration, and for many years fathers recounted his feats to their sons. Because of the Christians' military prowess, Aḥmad al-Muḳtadir himself elected to halt the war, and he again was obligated to pay tribute. His capitulation was regarded as a crushing defeat. A Hispano-Jewish historian who wrote many generations later recalled that Saragossa was captured by "Cidi Ruy Diaz" in the year 4827.[103] However, Saragossa's Christian neighbors from the north had not quite relinquished their aspirations to conquer parts of it, and thus in the same year a war broke out between Castile on the one hand and between Navarre and Aragon on the other. The Castilians invaded Navarre, and the Moslem troops of al-Muḳtadir, who cooperated with them, mounted an invasion out of Huesca against Aragon, until the Christian king then sued for peace and gave up his ambitions regarding the kingdom of Saragossa.

When Sancho and Alfonso, the other son of Fernando, became embroiled in a quarrel, al-Muḳtadir again ceased paying tribute to the Castilians, who were too preoccupied to be able to defend him against the new attacks of the Aragonese. He sought the protection of the king of Navarre, who had also suffered from the king of Aragon's passion for expansion. In 1073 the pact between the kingdoms of Saragossa and Navarre was renewed and their rulers obligated themselves to defend each other against both Moslems and Christians. But in the meantime Alfonso returned from exile in Toledo, and the plan nearest to his heart was to subdue

Saragossa. Consequently, in 1074 he began a war against Navarre. Two years later the king of Navarre was murdered, his kingdom was divided between Aragon and Castile, and Aḥmad al-Muḳtadir again found himself in a position of independence. He even made a pact with the king of Aragon, frustrating anew Alfonso's aspirations to swallow up the kingdom of Saragossa.

Notwithstanding his dependence upon powerful Christian neighbors and his many wars with them, al-Muḳtadir himself adopted a policy of expansion vis-à-vis the other Moslem states. After having annexed the principality of Tortosa to his kingdom in 1060, he also subdued Iḳbāl ad-daula, the son and heir of Mudjāhid, and added Denia to it. Thus, at the end of the eighth decade of the eleventh century, the kingdom of Saragossa comprised nearly all the regions of what is currently Upper and Lower Aragon—the province of Saragossa and parts of the provinces of Huesca, Pamplona, Logroño, Soria, Guadalajara, Lérida, Teruel, Castellon, Valencia, and Alicante. Some years later he achieved his longtime goal of deposing his brother as ruler of Lérida and annexing this principality to his kingdom as well.[104]

At the ever-stormy and fermenting royal court of Saragossa in the days of al-Muḳtadir, there were men from all over Spain, of various faiths. Some were astute diplomats skilled in intrigue and trickery, and some were men of culture who did not, however, refrain from scheming. In 1081 the "Cid," having been expelled from Castile by Alfonso VI, came to Saragossa. Thenceforth the Castilian hero who had commanded bands of Christian knights became the mainstay of al-Muḳtadir's army and his political advisor.

In addition to his highly ramified political activity, the king of Saragossa was also occupied with the sciences of mathematics and astronomy and with literature. His court was frequented by the Moslem theologian Abu 'l-Walīd Sulaimān b.

Khalaf al-Bādjī and the mathematician 'Umar b. 'Abdarraḥmān al-Kirmānī.[105] Jewish intellectuals were also, no doubt, included within this group.

Particularly conspicuous among them was Abu 'l-Faḍl Ḥasdai Ibn Ḥasdai, the son of the Hebrew poet Joseph Ibn Ḥasdai, author of *Shīra y'tōma* ("Unequalled Verse"). Abu 'l-Faḍl Ḥasdai was born in the middle of the fifth decade of the eleventh century. The father died shortly thereafter,[106] and although he was, consequently, unable to rear his son, he did bequeath to him his talents. The lad devoted himself to the study of the exact sciences with exceptional assiduity. He systematically studied algebra, geometry, and astronomy, and then went on to study medicine and ultimately logic and philosophy. He read Aristotle's books and the books attributed to him, as, for example, the *Physics* (Πεςὶ Φυϐικῆς ἀκροάσεως) and *Heaven and Universe,* which already had been translated in the middle of the ninth century by Yaḥyā Ibn al-Biṭrīḳ, Ḥunain b. Isḥāḳ, and others and also reached the Arabic readers accompanied by commentaries of Greek and Moslem philosophers. After the fashion of the intellectuals in Moslem lands who occupied themselves with the exact sciences, he also acquired knowledge of the theory of music and even extended its theory to practice. Simultaneously, he acquired a complete knowledge of the treasured lore of the Arabic language and its belles lettres. Although Ḥasdai knew Hebrew and was well versed in Hebrew literature, he was fascinated by the brilliance of Arabic literature and was himself a rhetorician and poet in that language. Indeed, with the death of his father, who had been immersed with all his heart and soul in the Arabic heritage and had inspired a love for it in his son, the young man was more and more attracted by the beauty of Arabic culture. On this path he obtained encouragement from various sources. Abu 'l-Faḍl Ḥasdai's talents and profound knowledge quickly became known in Saragossa; he associated with Moslem intellectuals and scientists and joined circles where literary and philosophical questions were debated. When the intellectual and tolerant king learned of his repute, he summoned him to the court and began to befriend him.

In this way the son of the Hebrew poet became a distinguished courtier belonging to the circle closest to the king. Aḥmad al-Muḳtadir, who chose his subordinates from among scholars and writers, appointed him a vizier.[107] Ḥasdai frequented the royal court for many years, serving the Arab king in various ways. As his secretary, he prepared letters in his name to be sent to other rulers and was privy to high state secrets—all the intrigues between the rulers of Saragossa and Navarre and the constant haggling over tribute and military ventures for the sake of conquest, machinations whereby the kings sought to outdo each other in deceit. In the name of Aḥmad al-Muḳtadir, Ḥasdai wrote letters to the king's brother Yūsuf, ruler of Lérida, and to other princes,[108] and, in collections of the rhetorical literature of the Spanish Arabs, fragments remain of the exchange of letters between the Jewish vizier and Aḥmad, the king of Saragossa, himself.[109]

At the time when Ḥasdai became one of the political advisors and close aides of al-Muḳtadir, he was frequently invited to take part in the receptions at the royal court in the course of which the king and his companions would discuss literary subjects—so dear to the upper class in Moslem Spain. He composed laudatory verse for the king and carried on much correspondence with devotees of Arabic literature, sending them his most outstanding poems, whose beautiful language —the hallmark of Arabic rhetoric—amazed them. He wrote them letters in the same ornate language full of allusions and wordplays, all of which the people of those generations enjoyed. Arab writers who had come upon hard times would turn to him for help.[110] The letters he wrote to other scholarly nobles in the kingdom of Saragossa were quite numerous, and are quoted by Arab writers as examples of a distinguished Arabic style.[111] His contemporaries were filled with admiration at his proficiency in Arabic rhetoric; when the prince of Murcia, 'Abdarraḥmān Muḥammad Ibn Ṭāhir, wanted to illustrate the art of Arabic style and at the same time to flatter the king of Saragossa, he mentioned in a letter to him the literary skill of his Jewish vizier Abu 'l-Faḍl Ḥasdai.[112] Ḥasdai also exchanged private letters with kings, such as Ḥusām ad-daula 'Abdalmalik Ibn Razīn, the king of Santa Maria de Levante (1045–1103), who was himself not only a prince experienced in political matters but also a poet.[113] Even the adventuresome vizier Ibn 'Ammār addressed Ḥasdai in poetry, describing to him the appearance of the fortress of Segura, and he also sent him letters couched in ornate language.[114]

The royal court of Saragossa abounded in tolerance and freedom of opinion; it was only on rare occasions that the Moslem nobles would reproach the Jewish vizier for his origins. Once, for example, the writer and vizier Abu 'l-Muṭarrif 'Abdarraḥmān Ibn ad-Dabbāgh asked him in the presence of al-Muḳtadir whether he perused the Bible. But Abu 'l-Faḍl permitted himself to make more than a casual answer; he shot back a stinging reply that, as an Arabic historian reports it, caused the Moslem king to dissolve in laughter.[115] Subsequently, the Jewish scholar seemed to believe that from his very birth he had belonged to the company of Arab nobles and officials, and he began to behave towards people with hauteur, no longer making an effort to conceal his pride. This impulse grew stronger, and he started to seek honors to an extraordinary degree. At this point Ibn ad-Dabbāgh addressed to him a flowery letter written in the best Arabic style, reminding him of his modesty and companionableness in former days and urging him to abandon his haughtiness. Among other things he asked ironically if Abu 'l-Faḍl intended to inherit the office of *kadi* of Saragossa.[116]

Naturally, outside the palaces of the Banū Hūd and the circles of intellectuals who surrounded them, there was in Saragossa, as in other cities in Moslem Spain, a large body of devout Moslems who inveighed against the atmosphere of tolerance at the royal court. These zealots, who could not reconcile themselves to the elevation of a Jew to the rank of vizier, spread the rumor that the Jewish vizier had actually already converted to the Moslem religion. The well informed even disclosed the reason that had motivated him to take this step: He was ablaze with love for, and wanted to marry, a beautiful Moslem girl.[117] To be sure, Ḥasdai himself facilitated matters for those spreading the rumor, for he never stressed his origin, and in his views and way of life did not differ greatly from the other nobles at Saragossa.

At the time that al-Muḳtadir and his companions, among them the Jewish vizier, debated the literary value of new poems and enjoyed discussions about the eternity of the world, *creatio ex nihilo,* and other philosophical and theological problems, there was visible ferment among the lower strata of the populace. In order to amass the huge sums he paid as tribute to the Christian kings and gave as wages to the bands of mercenary knights who served in his army, the king of Saragossa was compelled unremittingly to increase the burden of taxation on all classes of his subjects. The resentment among the people grew, especially as they observed at the same time that the king continued to erect magnificent new palaces. In point of fact, the royal treasury was incessantly overdrawn; indeed, during the reign of al-Muḳtadir, gold coins were no longer minted at Saragossa. The economic plight of the lower classes worsened from year to year, and delegations of peasants appeared before the king, requesting him to lighten the burdens imposed on them by the wealthy and the tax collectors. Once, such a delegation arrived with an ascetic as its leader, a miracle worker who bore the name of a saint. Al-Muḳtadir, who was vexed by his manner of speech, commanded that he be taken away and slain. Arabic historians relate that shortly thereafter the king became severely ill, that he went insane and bayed like a dog; others assert that his malady resulted from the bite of a dog. In this way a curse uttered against him by the ascetic before he was taken away to be slain eventually came to pass. In 1081 his son Yūsuf, surnamed al-Mu'tamin, was crowned as king in Saragossa, and a year later al-Muḳtadir died.[118]

After the death of al-Muḳtadir, the kingdom was once again divided. While al-Mu'tamin reigned in Saragossa, his brother, 'Imād ad-daula Mundhir, received the provinces of Lérida, Tortosa, and Denia, and, as was usual in those days, they began warring against one another. Al-Mu'tamin, relying on the "Cid" and his troops, endeavored to drive his brother out of Lérida, just as his father had done to his uncle. In 1082 the "Cid" and his mercenaries penetrated the principality of Lérida, captured the city of Monzón, and, when Mundhir called upon the armies of Barcelona and the other Catalan principalities for aid, defeated them, taking the count of Barcelona captive. Two years later he again entered Lérida, defeated an army composed of Mundhir's Moslem troops and soldiers of Aragon, and took captive some of the esteemed nobles, among them the bishop of Roda, taking them to Saragossa.

In all things al-Mu'tamin Yūsuf followed in his father's footsteps. Just as he fought his brother with the aid of his Christian knights and was involved in political intrigues, so too did he engage, like his father, in the sciences. He himself wrote a treatise on geometry and optics named *Al-Istiḳmāl wa'l-manāẓir* ("The Book of Supplement and Views"), for which his contemporaries and scholars of later generations praised him highly. Among them was the Jewish writer Joseph Ibn 'Aḳnīn, who numbered the king's book among the classic works on the exact sciences, asserting that there was none to compare with it for brevity and clarity.[119]

The king and scholar of Saragossa retained the Jewish vizier Abu 'l-Faḍl Ḥasdai in his service. But whereas many of the Arabic writers who were intimates of the kings of Spain and served them as secretaries became entangled in intrigues and, as a result, had to wear their feet out moving from court to court, the Jewish vizier remained at his post. His colleague Ibn ad-Dābbagh had already been compelled to flee from Saragossa in the days of al-Muḳtadir after it was reported to the king that the vizier had revealed his plans to foes. Something similar also occurred during the reign of al-Mu'tamin. One day the king learned that the vizier Ibn Royolo had betrayed him. This vizier had formerly been the right-hand man of Iḳbāl ad-daula, king of Denia, and had later transferred to the service of al-Muḳtadir, whom he had prompted to take action to annex that princedom. As a result of the success of that action, he won influence and honor at the court of the Banū Hūd. Later, during the reign of al-Mu'tamin, he made contact with Alfonso VI, who had devised schemes all his life for the conquest of Saragossa. When al-Mu'tamin learned of this, he had his vizier executed.[120] In this Moslem royal court where kings and viziers kept changing, Abu 'l-Faḍl trod securely on slippery ground. As he had done for the father, so he did for the son, composing letters in al-Mu'tamin's name to princes throughout Spain.[121] In the beginning of 1085, when al-Mu'tamin gave his son Aḥmad in marriage to the daughter of Abū Bakr Ibn 'Abdal'azīz, king of Valencia, deciding to conduct these political nuptials amid great splendor, Abu 'l-Faḍl composed the letters of invitation sent to scores of the princes and the most esteemed men in the various states of Moslem Spain.[122]

Abu 'l-Faḍl Ḥasdai was a typical representative of that class of Jewish intellectuals in Moslem Spain who were intimates of the Arabic *haute société* and served the Arabic rulers; that circle of intellectuals who for the most part regarded themselves as real Spaniards and had lost any emotional attachment for their own people; those philosophers who strove to achieve the recognition of a pure faith with no historical or national background and who had attained a greater or lesser degree of significant relativism with respect to all religions. But within the large Jewish community of Saragossa, there were also learned men who were not blinded by the Hispano-Arabic civilization and who adhered firmly to their ancestral heritage. These intellectuals, who were pious and orthodox, strictly observing the religious commandments, saw the reverse side of that social-cultural milieu. They shared the distress of the laboring classes who had to bear the heavy burden of taxation. They felt the pain of their Jewish brethren who suffered because of all the Moslem rulers' wars among themselves, particularly those involving the invasions carried out by the armies of the Christian kings. The Christian knights who served the Arab king of Saragossa for high rewards showed respect toward his Jewish subordinates. However, as they got farther away from the capital, going forth on raids into neighboring Moslem states, they would no longer hide the contempt in their hearts toward the Jews. They often harmed them and at times even attacked those who lived in the cities of the kingdom of Saragossa itself, while exercising care not to maltreat the Moslem natives or—it goes without saying—the Mozarabs. The king of Saragossa's Moslem troops, who witnessed these events, rejoiced at the Jews' distress and did not raise a finger to help them. The Castilian and Aragonese armies, which had penetrated the kingdom of Saragossa and attacked more or less unprotected settlements, wrought havoc on both Moslem and Jewish neighborhoods. When hostile Moslem forces from outside the kingdom's borders would enter the country, they would oppress the Jews in particular. The situation was difficult for ordinary Jews who dwelt in the towns and villages in an area such as the kingdom of Saragossa that was under dispute and destined for calamity. Any man of discernment who beheld it with open eyes could not overlook their suffering—the suffering of a national group considered to be alien by Moslems and Christians alike. The Jewish intellectuals who had not held themselves aloof from their people and who were endowed with the ability to express the sentiments in their hearts bitterly lamented the cruel fate of a nation that dwelt in alien lands.

One such intellectual was Abu 'l-Fahm Levi b. Jacob Ibn at-Tabbān.[123] As one of those scholars who devoted all their time to study and teaching, he eked out a living by teaching, serving as head instructor in a Jewish school in Saragossa similar to the Talmud schools in so many Jewish communities.[124] After the fashion of the Jewish scholars of Spain in those generations, he devoted his free time to the study of Hebrew grammar, systematically going through all that had been written relating to this science up to his day. Eventually, he became a distinguished expert in Hebrew lore, ultimately writing a treatise on Hebrew grammar called *Ha-Mafteaḥ* ("The Key"). The book, which was written in Arabic, selected from and summarized the best studies made in this subject before him, and in various passages the author reached decisions on questions that were matters of controversy for previous grammarians. So, for example, he expressed the opinion that on various matters Samuel the Nagid was right in his dispute with Abu 'l-Walīd.[125] This treatise was lost after Arabic ceased being the language in which Jewish scholars wrote their works. But in that period and in the periods following, many read it, and it achieved great fame for its author.[126]

Levi Ibn at-Tabbān was not a pedantic, dry teacher and grammarian; rather, he was endowed with the talents of a rhetorician and a man of refined and delicate sensitivity. He was also distinguished by an instinct for penetrating observation, and since, in addition, he had a talent for expression, he became one of the great Hebrew poets of that era. Indeed, he knew how to express his strongest feelings in a concentrated style and beautiful language.[127] His contemporaries greatly esteemed his verse, and the eminent Hebrew poets corresponded with him and gave his poetry unusual praise.[128] Levi Ibn at-Tabbān mainly wrote religious poetry, in all its varieties: *m'ōrōt, ahābhōt,* hymns with refrains, penitential and supplicatory hymns for the Ten Days of Penitence, and hymns offered in the event of a drought. These hymns—of which we know about ninety—became very popular with the public, spreading from Spain to the Jewish communities of North Africa, where they were included in the holiday prayerbooks of Tlemcen, Oran, Algiers, Tunis, and Tripoli. Some were even accepted into the rites of Avignon and Rome, as well as in the *Teklāl* of the Yemenite Jews.[129]

Levi Ibn at-Tabbān's hymns deal with themes customarily found in religious poetry: the relations of man to his Creator, sin and retribution, and the marvels of creation. Like the poems by the other authors of hymns, they abound in pleas for the forgiveness of sinners. Nevertheless, they have a special quality that sets them apart from the writings of many other poets. A leitmotiv that recurs throughout the poetry of Levi Ibn at-Tabbān is the expression of profound distress caused by the Jews' protracted exile. The sorrow for the suffering of the nation living in exile on alien soil and enduring the rod of cruel oppressors is expressed in tones that evoke fear and trembling.

Even in verses devoted to other themes, such as the greatness of the Creator, the poet sometimes, without making any real connection, switches to a description of his yearnings for the redemption of the nation that is afflicted with the burdens of exile. In his picturesque language he compares the Jews to a fish caught in a net and laments the fact that "a multitude of aliens is gathered, taking counsel to root out our name." While he gives encouragement to his people, he again returns to speak of its suffering because of Moslem and Christian armies alike:

While I lower my head and walk on my belly
They walk upright and tall and array their prayers:
The one kneels before his cross, the other blesses a false prophet.

Such were the meditations of a Jew who felt and grieved for his people in those troubled years of the ninth and tenth decade of the eleventh century, when Christians and Moslems were locked in a vast struggle for the dominance of the Iberian Peninsula and Jews were trodden upon by the armed forces of both. In those days the incursions by Christian armies into the Moslem realm became ever more frequent. During the first half of the ninth decade of that century, Alfonso VI invaded the kingdom of Saragossa twice, and the second time, in 1085, he laid siege to the city of Saragossa itself. The suffering of the population in general and of the Jews in particular was great, and poets like Levi Ibn at-Tabbān had more than enough reasons to pour out the anguish in their hearts.

However, different themes from the distress over the life of his people in an alien land and their degradation by powerful nations are conspicuous in Levi Ibn at-Tabbān's hymns. It is also evident from them that his faith was not adulterated by philosophic views. The religious feeling that finds expression in his poetry is based on sentiment alone, and it is not for naught that other poets lauded his great piety.[130] This amalgam of national yearnings and folk piety was typical of that era's group of Spanish Jewish intellectuals who were close to the simple folk and remote from the milieu of royal courts, nobles, and their favorites.

IX

The Moslem kingdom of Saragossa, whose ruling class was made up of a multihued mosaic of persons varying in their extraction and character, nevertheless held firm against its many foes. In spite of its difficult struggles, it grew even stronger and larger. Although he made repeated attempts to subdue Saragossa, Alfonso VI did not realize his aspirations in that regard. But the powerful Christian ruler, chief among those active in the conquest of the Moslem states in the Iberian Peninsula, in the meantime achieved many successes in other regions. Thanks to his clever tactics and his highly resourceful and energetic actions, he strengthened the dependent relationships by which the Moslem states were linked to his kingdom. Since this policy continued for nearly twenty years, one of these states had already become weakened to a point where it was ripe for actual conquest. This was the kingdom of Toledo, which shared a long border with Castile.

When al-Ma'mūn, the king of Toledo, died at Cordova in 1075, his was one of the large states in the Iberian Peninsula. To the south it embraced the region of Cordova and to the east it reached the sea, taking in the city of Valencia and its region. But al-Ma'mūn did not leave behind any sons, and the heir to the throne, his grandson al-Ḳādir, was a young prince unequal to his task who was, moreover, under the influence of eunuchs and servants.

Al-Ma'mūn had advised his grandson to rely in all matters on the vizier Abū Bakr Yaḥyā Ibn al-Ḥadīdī, who had served the king for many years. Ibn al-Ḥadīdī, who was the scion of an intellectual Arab family, together with Abū Sa'īd Ibn al-Faradj, the son of the governor of Cuenca, directed all the activities of the government. These viziers consistently implemented the policy formulated by al-Ma'mūn. They sought to keep the tensions between the kingdoms of Toledo and Castile under control and to put off the moment of decision as long as possible. Al-Ma'mūn even encouraged other Moslem rulers to follow this path and acted as intermediary between them and Alfonso VI, with whom he was on terms of personal friendship, since the Christian monarch had been his guest for a protracted period of time. But there was in Toledo a faction of fanatical Moslems who viewed with indignation the relationship between the Moslem king and his Christian neighbors. When al-Ma'mūn was once in Valencia, these fanatics conspired against his rule. Ibn al-Ḥadīdī, however, uncovered the plot, and al-Ma'mūn, who quickly returned to his capital, imprisoned the chief conspirators in the fortress of Huete.

Al-Ḳādir did not carry out the orders of his grandfather. Soon after he mounted the royal throne, he responded to the voice of Ibn al-Ḥadīdī's foes and sent assassins to slay the vizier, who was accompanying the casket of al-Ma'mūn from Cordova to Toledo. Although this design came to nought, he then freed the conspirators imprisoned at Huete, brought them in secret to his palace, and let them murder Ibn al-Ḥadīdī in his presence. This happened three months after the death of al-Ma'mūn. The new king of Toledo even handed over the government to the slain vizier's enemies, who were in fact the foes of his dynasty. It is true that the new authorities continued to pay tribute to the king of Castile, who adopted a strong stand toward al-Ḳādir and increased his demands, and in a general way they seemed, to all appearances, to carry out the traditional policy of the kingdom. But an unrestrained struggle, accompanied by attacks and skirmishes, continued between the faction of new viziers and the one that had been deposed. The governor of Valencia, Abū Bakr Ibn 'Abdal'azīz, who conducted negotiations with the king of Saragossa, proclaimed himself an independent ruler; thus the eastern province was separated from the kingdom of Toledo. Meanwhile, disturbing reports also arrived from the northern and southern borders. Al-Muḳtadir, the king of Saragossa, joined together with Sancho Ramírez, king of Aragon, and their armies penetrated the kingdom of Toledo. The troops of the king of Saragossa captured the cities of Santaver and Molina, while the Aragonese laid siege to Cuenca. At the same time the army of the king of Seville invaded the southern regions of the kingdom of Toledo, capturing a number of districts. Had the king of Seville not feared Alfonso, he would have continued his march of conquest.

Notwithstanding the difficult political situation in which the kingdom of Toledo found itself from the first days of al-Ḳādir's reign, economic activity went on as before in its chief cities. Toledo, the capital, was still large and flourishing. The Jews of Toledo were engaged in every branch of industry and commerce, and the well-to-do continued to acquire property within the city and its environs, including fields and vineyards.[131] Al-Ḳādir and his companions arranged magnificent soirees at the Alcazar in the eastern part of the city, as well as in the palace beyond the Roman bridge called al-Munya al-Manṣūra. They did all this as if they did not see the Sword of Damocles hovering over their heads. Even the Jews of Toledo enjoyed themselves at their parties, the intellectuals finding pleasure in debates on literary matters and the poets continuing to write ornate poetry. A twelfth-century Jewish author who wrote a survey on the chronicles of Hebrew literature in Spain numbered among the important writers the Hebrew poet Abū Harūn Ibn Abi 'l-'Aish, who lived at that time in the city of Toledo.[132]

But while the wealthy reveled and feasted and the scholars listened to the recitation of new poems, trouble was overtaking them.

The payment of tribute to the king of Castile and the outlays related to war with the Moslem kings laid a grievously heavy financial burden upon Toledo's officials and compelled them to extort, by sundry means, ever greater sums from the populace. The dissatisfaction among all classes of the population imperiled the existence of the reign of al-Ḳādir himself. His viziers were disloyal to him and waited for an opportune moment to depose the dynasty they hated. But while they could wait patiently, since they were perfectly well aware of the political situation and could see clearly what could be expected from open conflict with al-Ḳādir and his protector, the king of Castile, the number of extremists in their faction mounted. The *fukarah,* who stemmed from the most highly esteemed families in Toledo, such as the Banū Mughīth and Banu 'l-Lavrānakī, openly incited the populace against the weak king who was tied to the king of Castile by strong bonds and who drained the very lifeblood from his subjects to pay him tribute.

In the eleventh century Toledo was an important center for traditional Islamic studies, and a Toledan writer of that generation, Abū Dja'far Aḥmad Ibn Muṭāhir, was the author of a collection of biographies of Moslem theologians who then resided in the city.[133] Many of these theologians were Cordovans who came to Toledo when they could no longer earn their livelihoods in the diminished capital of the caliphs. These *fukarah,* who had not been reared in an atmosphere of tolerance and were unaccustomed to symbiosis with the Christians, spread an uncompromising spirit of fanaticism throughout the city on the Tagus. Their disciples and the simple folk listened attentively when they heard inimical statements leveled against the traitorous king by the revered sheiks in the porticos of the mosques. This agitation led to revolts, and al-Ḳādir was compelled to call upon the king of Castile for help. Thus it came to pass that in 1079 Alfonso VI, together with his army, crossed the borders of the kingdom of Toledo and initiated a wide range of military actions.

He first directed himself to the western regions of the kingdom of Toledo, where the opponents of al-Ḳādir were concentrated. The rebels were inclined to transfer the dominance of Toledo to the king of Badajo, and in order to inject fear into this faction, Alfonso captured the city of Coria, which belonged to the kingdom of Badajoz. But al-Ḳādir's alerting of the Castilians and their activities inside the kingdom of Toledo increased the rebellious mood against al-Ma'mūn's grandson. Then al-Ḳādir had, perforce, to turn again to Alfonso for support. When the Toledans refused to provide him with the sums the Christian king demanded for further intervention, al-Ḳādir fled from Toledo in 1080 and the city's notables invited al-Mutawakkil, the king of Badajoz, to rule over them. He arrived in the city in June and took over control of the government. But meanwhile al-Ḳādir, from his temporary seat in Cuenca, prompted the king of Castile, in exchange for huge payments, to restore him to his post. Indeed, in April 1081 the king of Castile brought al-Ḳādir back to Toledo and—after al-Mutawakkil left the city—seated him once again on the royal throne. Christian soldiers remained in the kingdom to protect the rule of al-Ḳādir, and a number of fortresses were turned over to them until what had been promised to their king would be paid him.

When al-Ḳādir returned to Toledo, he inaugurated a reign of terror. In order to gather the vast sums he had obligated himself to pay the king of Castile, he did not flinch from using every means available, appointing some of the basest men in the populace as collectors and officials who would obtain for him the money he needed. A contemporary Arabic writer relates that in those days the inhabitants of Toledo were afraid of their own shadows, even when they were among their own families.[134] The resentment in the population reached its climax, and attempts were made upon the life of al-Ḳādir. Meanwhile the kings of Saragossa and Seville again organized forays into the kingdom, which was torn asunder by internal strife.

Among the inhabitants of Toledo and the provincial towns

stood two opposing factions unable to find a common language. One concentrated around those who supported the policy of al-Ma'mūn and around the followers of Ibn al-Ḥadīdī; these were joined by anyone who abhorred the turmoil and the rebellions, the attacks on the lives of people and the strife that had become widespread occurrences within the stormy city on the banks of the Tagus. These people despaired of the rule of the "provincial kings," which depended upon the favors of the Christian rulers and caused so much hardship. They were so weary and desperate that they preferred the direct rule of the king of Castile, in whom they beheld guarantees of tranquil living. The members of this faction were opposed with all their hearts to the suggestion to seek help from the Moslem rulers in North Africa by inviting them to cross the Straits at the head of their armed forces. Like most Spanish Moslems of Iberian or Arab origin, they hated the Berbers as much as they hated the Christians. Even though they had no faith in their ability to defend themselves against the Castilians, they hoped that the submission to the king of Castile was not a final step, but that a change would yet occur that would restore Islam's dominion to its erstwhile eminence. The faction of zealots, on the other hand, blamed the powerless al-Ḳādir for all the troubles that had descended upon the inhabitants, arguing that every added concession would bring catastrophe on the Moslems. They saw no way of living in friendly fashion with the Christian rulers who were guided by fanatical monks from France, and they did not believe that subservience to the king of Castile would enable them to continue their traditional way of life.

The large Jewish community in the city of Toledo proper and in the other cities of the kingdom did not hold itself apart, nor did it view with indifference the conflict of the factions. For a very long time the Jews had, of course, become accustomed to living among the Moslems; Arabic was their language and the Jewish intellectuals felt at home in Arabic culture. But they did not nurse within their hearts the zealous sentiments that inflamed the passions of the Moslems. Unlike the Moslems their pride was not hurt by the payment of tribute, nor were they likely to be affected by changes in dominance; even under the rule of the Arab and Berber kings, they were more than once made to feel that they were not equal in honor or in degree to those who believed in the religion of Mohammed. For their part, therefore, the decisive factors were practical considerations. They sincerely yearned for a stable government that would guarantee them security of life and property and make possible normal progress in the life of the economy. In the fulfillment of this objective—the chief goal of any well-ordered government—al-Ḳādir had failed most decidedly. The Jews of Toledo saw the Moslems' expectations of maintaining their stand against Alfonso VI in their proper light and not through a mirror distorted by hopes and aspirations and begotten by religious and national sentiment. They also knew that the king of Castile did not persecute devotees of other religions and that in his royal court Jews could come and go. The affluent and esteemed members of the Jewish community who were accustomed to serve the Moslem rulers and to benefit from their contacts with the court of the ruler knew quite well that even a Christian king who would replace al-Ḳādir would avail himself of their service. They therefore gave their sympathy to the faction of Toledans that was striving to turn the rule over to the king of Castile, though they took care not to make themselves too conspicuous in order not to bring down upon them the hatred of the Moslem zealots.

In the summer of 1081, the leaders of the compromising faction determined to take a decisive step. They entered into negotiations with Alfonso VI himself and informed him that they were ready to surrender and turn the city over to him—but only after a strong defense that would demonstrate to every reasonable person the Toledans' inability to maintain a stand against Castile.[135] This proposal, which was meant to excuse the Toledans in the eyes of other Moslems, was characteristic of true Spaniards, who believe in honor above all. Even though their spirit was broken and they had no more strength to bear the burden of tribute and carry on a struggle with an enemy who was more powerful, they were unwilling to yield their self-respect. Even al-Ḳādir himself despaired of continuing to rule over Toledo and proposed to Alfonso that he would yield the city and the districts still in his hands if Alfonso would help him obtain anew dominion over Valencia.[136] The Christian king agreed most willingly and increased his military actions throughout the kingdom of Toledo. The chroniclers tell of a siege lasting seven years. They start their count in 1079, the year in which al-Ḳādir first called upon the king of Castile for help and the latter's armies crossed the borders of the kingdom. But the ring of the siege did not tighten until 1081.

The following year, when Alfonso VI appeared in the city's environs, the zealots' faction also endeavored to open negotiations with him. However, by then his confidence and pride were so great that he drove them away in scorn. Many who belonged to this faction then began leaving the city; some went to Ṣaragossa and others fortified themselves in Madrid. In the meantime al-Ḳādir confiscated their property and executed those who fell into his hands. In that year—1082—a report spread throughout Toledo of an incident that removed from the hearts of many, especially the Jews, any doubt as to the stand they must take and erased any of their apprehensions regarding changes in rulers.

Annually, at a fixed time, the king of Castile would send emissaries to Seville to collect the tribute from the Moslem king. That year he sent a Toledan Jew named Ibn Shālīb, who was numbered among his favorite officials. Naturally, he provided him with a heavy guard of horsemen. On reaching Seville, the Jewish emissary encamped before one of the city's gates and requested that the tribute that had been agreed upon be handed over to him. Al-Mu'tamid, the king of Seville, did indeed make ready the required sum, but because it was quite large, he had great difficulty in gathering it and had to impose an extraordinary levy on his subjects. Notwithstanding this action, he did not succeed in gathering the necessary amount in coined money and had to add bars of gold from his treasury. But when a group of nobles led by al-Mu'tamid's first vizier, Abū Bakr Ibn Zaidūn, came to hand over the tribute to Ibn Shālīb, the group suffered a sharp setback. The Jewish emissary of the king of Castile refused to accept the money, claiming that the coins were inferior in value. Ibn Shālīb also used very strong language, garnished with insulting remarks, and voiced harsh threats, such as that henceforth he would only take sections of the cities in the kingdom of Seville. When the Castilian emissary's words were conveyed to al-Mu'tamid, he became very angry and gave orders to destroy the camp of the mission, imprison the emissary's entourage, and execute the Jewish emissary in a most vile manner—by crucifixion. Ibn Shālīb, who earlier had spoken vigorously and haughtily, instantly lost his courage and began pleading for his life, proposing that he redeem himself by paying a ransom equal to the weight of his body. But al-Mu'tamid, whose honor had been impugned, replied that there was no amount in the whole world that he would accept instead of punishing him, and even if all of Spain and the land beyond the Straits were given him, he would not budge. Ibn Shālīb was crucified, and those who accompanied him were thrown into prison.

However, three of the horsemen who had accompanied the Jewish emissary succeeded in making their escape and reaching the king of Castile. When they told him of the open violation of the diplomatic immunity of emissaries—even in those days, an unwritten law—he too was filled with anger. He swore to avenge himself on the Moslem king and to lead a big army on a punitive campaign against the kingdom of Seville that would cross through it from the north to the south and reach the coast at the southern end of the Iberian Peninsula. But meanwhile he was concerned about the horsemen still imprisoned in Seville and therefore sent emissaries to al-Mu'tamid, forcefully demanding that he set them free without delay and send them back to Castile. Al-Mu'tamid, who had in the meantime calmed down and had second thoughts, apologized and did as he was asked.[137] But Alfonso nevertheless carried out his design. He pushed into the kingdom of Seville and his soldiers laid waste the fertile districts north and west of its capital, set siege over a period of time to Seville itself, and eventually reached the seacoast near Tarifa, where Alfonso entered the waters while mounted upon his horse.[138]

This incident made a powerful impression on the Jews of Toledo. They were convinced that Alfonso VI had not forfeited responsibility for the blood of his Jewish emissary and had avenged his murder exactly as he would have avenged that of a Christian noble. They saw in this a clear indication that it was not his intention to discriminate against the Jews who dwelt in the regions he proposed to annex. Indeed, Ibn Shālīb himself was a Jew from Toledo. The fears they had nurtured in their hearts of Toledo's being captured by the Castilians evaporated. In fact, those leaders of the Toledan Jewish community who were farsighted about the situation realized that the Moslem realm was on the wane and started to plan for the future of Jewry in all of Spain. After they became convinced that the Moslems in Spain no longer had the strength to withstand the Christians and that the king of Castile was about to wrest large areas from the Moslems, the Jews began to recognize that their fortunes should be linked with the ascendant might of the kingdom of Castile. The sympathetic attitude of Alfonso VI toward the Jews in his kingdom and his strong ties with officeholding Jews implanted within the hearts of these Toledan Jewish leaders the hope that it would be possible to establish as large a Jewish center in Spain under Christian dominion as had existed in Andalusia in the past under the Omayyad caliphs. They deemed the transfer of the Jewish center to Christian Spain to be an imperative of historical circumstances. In their opinion this transfer demanded the fostering of relationships with the Christian rulers. The acts of oppression by fanatical Christian knights, who more than once maltreated the small Jewish communities in the provincial towns as well as isolated Jews they chanced upon, appeared to them as inevitable birth pangs attending the establishment of a new kingdom.

But in the meantime the siege of Toledo grew increasingly severe. Bands of Castilian soldiers roamed the environs, burning the granaries and the standing corn in the fields. They murdered wayfarers and practically brought traffic on the roads to a halt. With difficulty some small amount of food was brought into the city, to be purchased only at great cost. Whoever could leave the beleaguered city fled while he was still alive and left his possessions behind. The army of the king of Toledo did not dare to sally forth from the gates and could only look on from the walls at what was happening without. The year 1082 went by in this fashion, and the year 1083 arrived without any big battles having taken place around Toledo. Nor had the king of Castile encamped before its gates. Instead, he relied on the actions of his soldiers, who, by their excursions, deprived the Moslems of a sense of security, and he left it to time to take its toll. The king was so certain of success that at the very same time he organized campaigns taking him inside other Moslem kingdoms. In this manner the siege of the city continued until the autumn of 1084.

That autumn Alfonso determined to bring down the final blow upon Toledo. He appeared in the vicinity of the city and pitched his tents one night east of the bend of the Tagus, on the hills upon which his friend al-Ma'mūn had erected his magnificent villa, al-Munya al-Manṣūra. Castilian troops had also ensconced themselves in the hills at a place currently called Puerta del Rey. Thenceforth, Toledo was tightly shut, and none could enter or leave. From time to time the Castilians would mount heavy attacks, using catapults covered by mantelets that were invulnerable to inflammable substances to send huge stones over the city walls. They would also attempt to weaken the walls and breach them from the northern side, where the city was not protected by the river. After they had filled in the moat before the wall, they brought up powerful beams called "rams" made from the stumps of trees whose ends had been clad in iron. Hidden beneath shields moved on wheels, they were fastened on both sides to chains and stretched to the fullest possible extent. When they were released, they shot forward speedily over the wall on which the defenders stood, seeking to restrain the rams by means of sacks of straw and beams they threw below. While the catapults hurled their rams, beating upon the city's fortifications, a rain of arrows poured down from the walls, as did stones and cauldronsful of boiling oil. But the power of the Castilians was superior, and if it were not for the river Tagus that surrounded the city on three sides, the Toledans would have been unable to make any stand at all. In those days it was customary, during a siege against a properly fortified city, for the attackers to assemble movable turrets and bring them close to the walls in order to leap upon the walls and thus carry on the battle against the defenders. The Castilians, however, had no need of this; the Christian commanding officers knew that famine was sapping the strength of the inhabitants and would force them to surrender.

The winter of 1084–1085 was very severe. Tempestuous rains fell almost unremittingly, causing much damage within the city. Great streams of water flowed along the narrow streets descending the hills on which Toledo is perched; the roofs of old houses were blown away, and in the northern neighborhoods the rainwater gathered in many houses, making them vulnerable to collapse. It seemed as if even the heavens were at war with the ailing and beleaguered city. To be sure, the Christian king, too, suffered from the severe winter. The paths of communication between his camp and the Castilian districts from which he received his supplies were flooded because of the heavy snows that fell in the mountains, blocking the passes. But the Moslem kings who wanted to benefit from the assistance of the powerful Christian ruler supplied him with even more than he needed.

When the spring finally came, the city's situation was desperate. Famine and sickness had already inordinately sapped the spirit of the inhabitants, and everyone was aware that the strength of the defenders would not hold out much longer if help from the outside did not arrive. However, the faction of Moslem zealots, which was not prepared to surrender while a spark of hope still existed to save the city, decided to send a mission to the Castilian king, seeking his permission to rally the rulers of the other Moslem states in Spain to their aid. It was an accepted custom to permit this latitude to the defenders of a besieged city. But when the Toledan mission presented itself before the Castilian king, it met in his camp the emissaries of those very kings who had brought their tribute and numerous gifts to Alfonso. Filled with shame and discomfiture, the members of the mission returned to the city. Three days later, on Friday, May 6, 1085, Toledo surrendered.

The leaders of the population made a detailed agreement with the Christian king on the terms of surrender. The conqueror assured the Moslems remaining in the city of security of life and property; he permitted anyone so desiring to depart from the city and even gave an assurance that he would restore the property of anyone who left the city and then returned. It was agreed that the Moslems were to pay to the new government only those taxes they had paid their own king. Moreover, they received a solemn promise that the Great Mosque would remain in their hands in perpetuity. The Arabic and Christian historians who report the terms of the pact do not mention any paragraphs dealing with the Jews; but no doubt their future status was dealt with in the talks preceding the drawing up of the pact. In any event, the Jews remained in their large neighborhood in the western part of the city and also maintained their markets in its center. Alfonso VI was consistent in his attitude toward them; they were not deprived of their privileges, and the conquerors did not inflict any harm upon them.

Thus did the former capital of Spain, once the seat of the Visigoth kings and the city of the Roman consuls, pass once again into Christian hands after having been, for 374 years, under Moslem control.

A long period in the history of Spain had come to its end.

ABBREVIATIONS

AIEO Annales de l'Institut d'Etudes Orientales de l'Université d'Alger

BAC Boletin de la Academic de Ciencias, Bellas Letras y Nobles Artes de Córdoba

BAH Boletin de la Academia de la historia (Madrid)

BH Bibliotheca Hebraea

BJPES Bulletin of the Jewish Palestine Exploration Society

CB Catalogus librorum Hebraeorum in Bibliotheca Bodleiana . . . digessit M. Steinschneider

CHE Cuadernos de historia de España

EEMCA Estudios de edad media de la Corona de Aragón

EI Encyclopedia of Islam, 1st edition

*EI*² *Encyclopedia of Islam,* 2d edition

HB Hebräische Bibliographie

HU Steinschneider, M., *Die hebräischen Ubersetzungen des Mittelalters und die Juden als Dolmetscher,* Berlin, 1893

HUCA Hebrew Union College Annual

JA Journal Asiatique

JJLG Jahrbücher für jüdische Literatur und Geshichte

JJS Journal of Jewish Studies

JQR Jewish Quarterly Review

MAH Memorias de la Academia de historia

MGWJ Monatsschrift für Geschichte und Wissenschaft des Judentums

PAAJR Proceedings of the American Academy for Jewish Research

RABM Revista de archivos, bibliotecas y museos (Madrid)

REJ Revue des Etudes Juives

RIEEI Revista del Instituto Egipcio de Estudios Islamicos en Madrid

SBAW Sitzungsberichte der Philosophisch-Historische Classe der Kaiser Akademie der Wissenschaften

T-S Taylor-Schechter Collections, University Library, Cambridge

ZAW Zeitschrift für die alttestamentliche Wissenschaft

ZDMG Zeitschrift der Deutschen morgenländischen Gesellschaft

ZfHB Zeitschrift für Hebräische Bibliographie

SOURCES

In addition to those given in volumes 1 and 2

1. IN HEBREW

Ibn Djanāḥ, Abū al-Walīd Marwān. *Sefer ha-riḳma,* ed. M. Wilensky and D. Tene. Jerusalem, 1964 *(Sefer ha-riḳma).*

Ibn Djanāḥ, Abū al-Walīd Marwān. *Sefer ha-shōrashīm,* Berlin, 1896; reprinted Jerusalem, 1965 *(Sefer ha-shōrashīm).*

Moses Maimonides. *Ḳōbheṣ T'shubhōt ha-Rambam',* ed. A. Lichtenberg. Leipzig, 1859 *(Ḳōbheṣ).*

Moses Maimonides. *T'shubhōt ha-Rambam,* ed. Blau. Jerusalem, 1957–61 (Responsa Maimonides).

Schirmann, H. *Ha-Shīra ha-'ibhrīt bī-S'fārād u-bi-Provence.* Jerusalem and Tel Aviv, 1955–57 (Schirmann).

2. OTHER

Bacher, W. *Leben und Werke das Abulwalīd Merwan Ibn Ganāḥ.* Budapest, 1885 *(Leben).*

Baer, F. *Die Juden in christlichen Spanien: Urkunden und Regesten.* Berlin, 1929–1936 (Baer, *Unkunden*).

Baron, S. *A Social and Religious History of the Jews.* Philadelphia, 1952– (Baron).

Derenbourg. *Opuscules et traités d'Abu 'l-walid Merwan ibn Djanah de Cordove.* Paris, 1880 *(Opuscules).*

Dozy, R. *Recherches sur l'histoire et la littératur de l'Espagne pendant le moyen âge.* Paris, 1881 *(Recherches).*

Dozy, R. *Supplément aux Dictionnaires Arabes,* 1881–1927 *(Suppléments).*

Graetz, H. *History of the Jews.* Philadelphia, 1891–98 (Graetz).

Levi-Provençal, E. *Histoire de l'Espagne Musulmane.* Paris, 1944–1953 (Levi-Provençal).

Mann, J. *The Jews in Egypt and in Palestine under the Fatimid Caliphs.* New York, 1920–22 *(Jews).*

Mann, J. *Texts and Studies in Jewish History and Literature.* New York, 1931–35 *(Texts).*

Munk, S. *Mélanges de Philosophie Juive et Arabe.* Paris, 1859 *(Mélanges).*

Neubauer, A. *Medieval Jewish Chronicles and Chronological Notes.* Oxford, 1887–95 *(Med. Jew. Chr.).*

Neumann, A. *The Jews in Spain: Their Social, Political and Cultural Life.* Philadelphia, 1942 (Neumann).

Pareja Serrada, A. *Guadalajara y su partido.* Guadalajara, 1915 (Pareja).

Pérès, H. *La nué sic andalouse en arobe classique au XI siècle.* Paris, 1937 (Pérès).

Simonet, F. *Historia de los mozarábes de Espana.* Madrid, 1903 (Simonet).

Steinschneider. *Arabische Literatur der Juden (Ar. Lit.).*

NOTES

See Sources in volumes 1 and 2 for full references

CHAPTER ONE

1. See M. Wilensky, "Über Jekutiel ibn-Hassan," *MGWJ* 70:21, and see G. Margaliouth's interesting conjecture in the introduction to *Hilkhōt ha-nagīd,* that the geonic responsa *Sha'arē ṣedeḳ* and *T'shūbhōt Gĕōnē miz-rāḥ u-ma'rābh* were arranged in Spain in the first half of the eleventh century, since the last rabbinic authority whose responsa they include is R. Ḥanōkh. But of course there is no proof that this was done by the order of Samuel ha-nāgīd and for the purpose of his writings, as Margaliouth maintains.
2. *Sefer ha-riḳma,* p. 338, and note 11. Cf. W. Bacher, "Notes sur Abou 'l Walid," *REJ* 4:273–74.
3. J. Mann, *Jews* 2:228, 231, 233; Mann, *Texts* 1:388–89, and see his paper "Various Questions in the Research of the Geonic Period," *Tarbīṣ* 6:75–76; S. Goitein in *Journ. Econ. Soc. Hist. of Orient* 8:29.
4. Fragments of this commentary were published together with a translation by G. Margaliouth, "Isaac b. Samuel's Commentary on the Second Book of Samuel," *JQR* 10:385–403. See there his persuasive evidence that the author is identical with the R. Isaac b. Samuel who is mentioned as a judge in Cairo in documents from the end of the eleventh century and the beginning of the twelfth century, and see additionally the *Catalogue of Hebrew Manuscripts in the British Museum* 1:125–26. As against Steinschneider, *Ar. Lit.,* no. 181, who inclined to identify the author with a man who lived at the end of the fourteenth century, it should be noted that a Spanish Jew of this late era would not have written his commentary in Arabic. Mann identifies Isaac b. Samuel with Isaac al-Kenzī, who is mentioned in a colophon preserved among the Geniza writings—see *Jews* 2:311—and who wrote a commentary on the tractate *Ḥullīn;* see in a list of books in *JQR* 13:55, and see a quotation in a fragment of a commentary on this tractate published by Lewin in *Ginzē Ḳedem* 3:33. For the fact that Isaac al-Kenzī was also a liturgical poet, see Mann in his aforementioned article, *Tarbīṣ* 6:75.

5. See Mann, *Jews* 1:302–3, and *Texts,* ibid.
6. For the time and place of his work see L. Zunz, *Die gottesdienstliche Vorträge,* 2d ed., pp. 162–65; S. Ochser, *Jewish Encyclopedia* 12:588–89; and see in addition *Joseph u. seine Brüder, ein altjüdischer Roman,* M. J. bin Gorion (Frankfurt a. M., 1917), p. 99. For printings and translations see bin Gorion and in addition Fürst, *Bibliotheca Judaica* 2:111, and Ben Jacob, *Ōṣār ha-se'fārīm,* p. 233.
7. See A. E. Harkavy, *Studien u. Mittheilungen aus der Kais. Bibl. zu St. Petersburg* 3:49.
8. *Sefer ha-shōrashīm,* p. 372.
9. H. Z. Slonimski, *Y'sōdē ha-'ibbūr,* 3d ed. (Warsaw, 1889), p. 47, and cf. *The Jews of Moslem Spain* 1:197, 300.
10. See Steinschneider, *Die Mathematik bei den Juden* (Bibliotheca Mathematica, 1895), p. 48.
11. Al-Maḳḳarī 2:351.
12. Ibid., p. 356. On the name, see Steinschneider, *Ar. Lit.,* no. 228, and see W. Bacher, "Eine jüdische Dichterin im arabischen Spanien," *MGWJ* 20:186–87, and in addition A. S. Yahuda, *'Ēbher we-'arābh* (New York, 1946), pp. 111–12. (Yahuda is incorrect in asserting that the poetess originated from Huesca. Apparently he interchanged her father, Ismā'īl, with Bassām b. Simeon; see *Jews of Moslem Spain* 2:273.
13. Derenbourg, *Opuscules,* p. 344.
14. Ibid., p. 247.
15. See the passage on the subject of grammar in the treatise of R. Isaac Ibn Gayyāt in *Zeitschr. f. jüd. Theologie* 5 (1884): 408.
16. See below.
17. In *Diwan Samuel ha-nagīd,* no. 17, see lines 15–16, 18, 19, 20, 52 and see there line 20 and also line 18, indicating that the poem of R. Nissīm was written in "Ishmaelite [Arabic] meter." Also see *Diwan Ibn Gabirol,* part 6, no. 7.
18. See J. Weiss, *Tarbūt ḥaṣrānīt we-shīra ḥaṣrānīt, bērūrīm l'-habhānat shīrat S'fārād ha-'ibhrīt* (Jerusalem, 1948).
19. *Taḥk'mōnī,* p. 181. Regarding the tendency to write poetry in Hebrew, whereas Arabic was the accepted medium for the other branches of literary creativity, see J. Blau's interesting article " 'Al ma'mādān shel ha-'ibhrīt we-ha-'arabhīt bēn ha-y'hūdīm dōbhrē 'arābhīt ba-mē'ōt ha-rīshōnōt shel ha-Islām," *Léshonēnū* 26:283–84, which explains the flourishing of Hebrew poetry on the grounds of the strangeness of classical Arabic and the Jews' remoteness from the social and aesthetic ideals of Arabic poetry (while admitting that by this era they had already become identified with them in a substantial measure), and see below.
20. Pérès, pp. 55–56, 60.
21. *Diwan Ibn Gabirol,* part 1, nos. 86, 87.
22. Pérès, pp. 367–68; Ibn 'Idhārī, p. 68.
23. J. Marcus, "Shīrē yayin," *Sefer ha-shāna li-y'hūde America* (1935), p. 232.
24. *Minḥat ḳ'nāōt* by Abba Mari, *Responsa of R. Isaac b. Sheshet,* no. 45, and cf. Graetz, *MGWJ* 11:37–38.
25. See below, note 49.
26. Derenbourg, in *Opuscules,* p. vi, conjectures that the name Marwān

(which he always writes minus the *alef*) is parallel to Mar Yōna, which was chosen for its similar ring; and so too in his opinion Marinus is parallel to Mar Yūnus. However, these are remote conjectures, for there is no great similarity between Mar Yōna and Marwān, and Abu 'l-Walīd was, moreover, never called by the name Yūnus. According to Simḥōnī—see *Ha-Teḳūfa* 10:177—he was given the name Marinus because it paralleled his Arabic name, Marwān, and this too is mere conjecture. On the other hand, Wilensky expressed the opinion that the Hebrew grammarian had no Hebrew name whatsoever—that the names Jonah and Marinus were given him by the Hebrew writers; see his article, "Le nom d'Aboū-l-Walīd," *REJ* 92:55–58. This opinion is also subject to doubt. Although Abu 'l-Walīd always refers to himself by his Arabic name, it is hard to assume that a scholar such as he would be called in the synagogue by the foreign name Marwān. The assertion by Bacher in the introduction to *Sefer ha-shōrāshīm,* p. viii, that the name Ibn Djanāḥ was given him because his name was Jonah, is also dubious, since this was the name of his family. For surnames illustrative of the meaning of the original name, the choice was most often made of a cognomen compounded with "Abū." According to a document from the year 1273, a Jew in Jativa was called by the family name Ibn Djanāḥ; see Kayserling, *Jewish Encyclopedia* 7:79.

27. See in Derenbourg, *Opuscules,* pp. 268, 381.
28. See Munk, *Notice,* p. 76. His opinion in this matter was accepted by all the scholars.
29. It is possible that for some reason the entire family of Abu 'l-Walīd moved to Lucena for a certain period, and it is also possible that they sent the youth to the Jewish city in keeping with the custom of sending young men to study in another city. In all truth there were in those days in Lucena more Jewish scholars than there were in Cordova, and therefore this conjecture is more reasonable. In any event, it should not be concluded from the protracted stay of Abu 'l-Walīd in Lucena that he was born in that city, as is done by Wilensky in his article "Le-tōl'dōt R. Jonah b. Djanāḥ," *Tarbīṣ* 4:97–98. Even if Wilensky's opinion is correct —if the name al-Ḳurtubī in the captions of his books (cited above in note 27) was indeed added by the copyists (which is not demonstrated by the eulogy of the dead, which could only have come from a copyist)—as against the absence of any testimony that he was a native of Lucena, the fact that Abraham Ibn Ezra, in the preface to *Sefer ha-moznāyim,* and also the copyists call him by the name "ha-Ḳordōbhī" is decisive.
30. See *Sefer ha-shōrāshīm,* p. 269.
31. Cf. *Jews of Moslem Spain* 1:395–96.
32. *Sefer ha-riḳma,* pp. 226, 284, 300; *Sefer ha-shōrāshīm,* pp. 189, 366, 408; Derenbourg, *Opuscules,* pp. 333, 368, 369. He quotes his poems in *Sefer ha-riḳma,* pp. 275 (without calling him by name) and 278. In the opinion of Derenbourg, *Opuscules,* p. viii, he criticizes stanzas of the verse of Isaac b. Mar Saul also in *Sefer ha-riḳma,* pp. 223 and 306; but see Wilensky's note, p. 306.
33. See *Sefer ha-shōrāshīm,* pp. 94, 226.
34. See *Sefer ha-riḳma,* p. 278, and see Bacher, "Abulwalīd Ibn Ḡanāḥ und die neuhebräische Poesie," *ZDMG* 36:409.

35. *Sefer ha-shōrāshīm,* p. 293; Derenbourg, *Opuscules,* pp. 91, 104 (and the same explanation in *Sefer ha-riḳma,* p. 91, without calling him by name). See furthermore Poznanski, *Mose b. Samuel Hakkohen Ibn Chiquitilla* (Berlin, 1895), p. 8, note 1.
36. Concerning him see *Jews of Moslem Spain* 1:394–95; Munk, *Notice,* p. 79f.
37. See *Sefer ha-riḳma,* p. 175; Derenbourg, *Opuscules,* p. 317; *Sefer ha-riḳma,* p. 279 (without calling him by name).
38. Derenbourg, *Opuscules,* p. 1.
39. *Sefer ha-riḳma,* p. 320.
40. Ibid., p. 319.
41. See Munk, *Notice,* p. 193, note 2.
42. See Derenbourg in the introduction to *Opuscules,* pp. ix–x. However, Derenbourg errs in fixing the date of Ḥayyūdj's death at about 1010 (p. xii) and in his assumption, on the other hand (ibid., p. xiii), that Abu 'l-Walīd had returned to Cordova some years before 1012. If these conjectures were correct, it would not be understandable why Abu 'l-Walīd did not know Ḥayyūdj, a matter that cannot be doubted. There is thus no escaping the assumption that Ḥayyūdj had died earlier still—in about 1006–1007 (and Samuel the Nagid studied with him for but a very short time).
43. See *Sefer ha-shōrāshīm,* p. 48, and cf. *Jews of Moslem Spain* 1:455, note 68. See additionally Simḥōnī in *Ha-Teḳūfa* 10:160.
44. *Sefer ha-riḳma,* p. 319. There is no basis for fixing the year 1012 as the year of his migration, as did Munk, *Notice,* p. 76; yet many scholars who followed him repeated this conjecture. See in particular W. Bacher, *Leben und Werke das Abulwalīd Merwān Ibn Ganāḥ* (Budapest, 1885), p. 1.
45. Derenbourg, *Opuscules,* pp. 3, 5, 243–44.
46. Ibn Ṣā'id, p. 89; Ibn Abī Uṣaibi'a 2:50; and see *Sefer ha-riḳma,* p. 33. Munk's observation, *Notice,* p. 81, that he wrote treatises on logic are, to be sure, merely conjectures.
47. See *Sefer ha-riḳma,* pp. 318–19; *Sefer ha-shōrāshīm,* pp. 62, 76, 77, lines 4–5; 206, 247, 473, line 8 (the universal soul); Derenbourg, *Opuscules,* p. 4.
48. *Sefer ha-riḳma,* pp. 322–23. According to a note in the margin of a manuscript of the *Mōreh n'bhūkhīm,* he also wrote a treatise against the belief in the eternity of the world; see Munk, *Notice,* pp. 82–83, and Derenbourg, *Opuscules,* p. lxxvi.
49. *Sefer ha-riḳma,* p. 282.
50. See Bacher, *Leben,* pp. 73–74.
51. See Ibn Abī Uṣaibi'a 2:50.
52. Schirmann 1:290, line 55, and cf. p. 286.
53. Ibn Ṣā'id, p. 89, and Ibn Abī Uṣaibi'a 2:50. This book of his is cited by Arab authors who wrote on matters dealing with pharmacology; see Munk, *Notice,* p. 81.
54. *Sefer ha-shōrāshīm,* pp. 93, 107. The reference is no doubt to translations into Arabic. Of the translations done in Spain by Christians, the only one known is that of Psalms; see G. Graf, *Geschichte der christlichen-arabischen Literatur* (Rome, 1944–53) 1:87, 124. But it must be assumed that the translations of the other books of the Bible made by Christians in the

Near East in the era of the caliphs reached Spain; concerning these translations, cf. Graf, ibid., pp. 107, 126, 131–32. In any event, in the aforementioned passages Abu 'l-Walīd takes issue precisely with the manner in which the Christians translated the Book of Psalms! For a decision on the question as to which translations Abu 'l-Walīd had in mind—which language the translations were in—importance attaches to the fact that in none of his writings are there any passages indicating a knowledge of Latin. Hence, it is unlikely that he read the Latin translations.

55. The chronological order of his writings is known from the appearance of quotations from the early works in the later ones.
56. Kokowzow reads *Kitāb al-Mustalḥaḳ;* however, according to the context in the passage of the introduction to the book in which Ibn Djanāḥ mentions its name, it is best to read *al-Mustalḥiḳ.*
57. Derenbourg, *Opuscules,* pp. 4, 212.
58. Ibid., p. 244.
59. Ibid., pp. 146–47, 158; see also p. 273.
60. See the introduction to *Sefer ha-riḳma,* p. 11; Derenbourg, *Opuscules,* pp. 311, 313.
61. See what he says about his book in Derenbourg, *Opuscules,* p. 248, line 8.
62. *Sefer ha-riḳma,* p. 320, and see the reaction of R. Moses Ibn Ezra, according to the Arabic text in Derenbourg, *Opuscules,* p. xix.
63. *Sefer ha-riḳma,* p. 253; *Sefer ha-shōrāshīm,* p. 4. See Wilensky, "L'-tōl'dōt R. Jonah b. Djanāh," *Tarbīṣ* 4:100–101.
64. Derenbourg, *Opuscules,* p. 373.
65. All the writings hitherto mentioned are printed together with a French translation by Derenbourg in his *Opuscules.*
66. Ibid., p. 345.
67. Bacher, *Leben,* p. 20, already had noted quite properly that Samuel the Nagid himself wrote the *Iggrōt,* and this is indeed clear from the wording of *Sefer ha-hakhlāma.*
68. See Derenbourg, *Opuscules,* p. xlix.
69. See Bacher, *Leben,* p. 22.
70. See Derenbourg, *Opuscules,* p. li. There, on pp. lix–lxvi, is printed a part of the first "Iggeret" that has been preserved, and, on pp. xlix–liii, is a fragment from *Sefer ha-hakhlāma.*
71. Derenbourg, ibid., p. lxiii. See also p. lxx, note 2; p. 56, note 2.
72. Ibid., p. lix, the second line from the bottom.
73. Ibid., p. liii, lines 4–12.
74. Ibid., pp. l–li, and see *Sefer ha-riḳma,* pp. 319–20.
75. Derenbourg, *Opuscules,* p. lii.
76. Ibid., p. lix, line 5 from the bottom and cf. p. lxvi, note 4, and note 218 of *Jews of Moslem Spain* 2:353.
77. See the quotation from *Kitāb al-Muwāzana* by Ibrāhīm Ibn Barūn in Derenbourg, ibid., pp. xlvi–xlvii.
78. *Shīrat Yisrāēl,* p. 69; at-taḳāna is a linguistic usage of the Spanish Arabs in place of إتقان, see Dozy, *Suppl.* 1:149. According to Halper, *Shīnat Yisrael,* his surname was at-Tayyām—"the twin." However, Stein-

schneider—see *CB* 2318—and Simḥōnī, in *Ḥa-Teḳūfa* 10:174, read al-Tayyāh, which means "he who wanders lost along the paths." This last is compatible with the end of the tale.

79. Schirmann 1:287–91. It is worth noting that even he did not refer to Samuel Ibn Nagrēla by name, which was, after all, more customary in poetry.
80. D. Baneth, "A Fragment from a Polemic Letter to R. Samuel ha-Nagid," *Kirjat Sefer* 2:150–57, and see on p. 150 his conjecture, which is a reasonable one, that it is *Kitāb al-Ḥudjdja* that Ibn Bal'ām mentions. See on him Kokowzow, pp. 78, 85–86. (It is, of course, possible that the "Treatise" Baneth published is a part of *Kitāb al-Ḥudjdja.)* In addition, cf. Wilensky, *Tarbīṣ* 7:585–86, and the reply of Baneth there, pp. 588–89.
81. Since Ibn Djanāh mentions *Kitāb at-Tashwīr* in treatises he wrote in the fifth decade of that century; see in the indices to *Sefer ha-shōrāshīm,* p. 557.
82. *Shīrat Yisrāēl,* p. 67; cf. Simḥōnī, *Ha-Teḳūfa* 10:173.
83. *Sefer ha-riḳma,* p. 24.
84. For establishing the date of the book *Tanḳīḥ,* it is possible to gain support with the addition of ז"ל *(raḥimahu Allāh),* which Ibn Djanāḥ appends after the name of Joseph Ibn Ḥasdai; see *Sefer ha-riḳma,* p. 319. It is known that Ibn Ḥasdai was still alive in 1046; see *Jews of Moslem Spain* 2:258. *Sefer ha-riḳma* was therefore written in about 1048; cf. Bacher in the introduction to *Sefer ha-shōrāshīm,* p. xx.
85. The Arabic original of the grammar was published by Derenbourg in *Le Livre des Parterres Fleuris* (Paris, 1886), whereas the Hebrew translation of Judah Ibn Tibbon was printed by D. Goldberg–R. Kirchheim (Frankfurt a. M., 1856) and later by Wilensky (Berlin, 1929–1931). The Arabic original of the lexicon was published by Neubauer (Oxford, 1875) and the Hebrew translation of Judah Ibn Tibbon by Bacher (Berlin, 1896).
86. See Bacher's survey, *Leben,* pp. 50–51.
87. See Derenbourg, *Opuscules,* p. lxxxix.
88. See the two treatises of Bacher: *Die hebräisch-arabische Sprachvergleichung des Abulwalīd Merwān Ibn Ganāḥ* (Vienna, 1884), *SBAW,* Band 106, Heft 1, pp. 119ff.; *Die hebräisch-neuhebräische u. hebräisch-aramäische Sprachvergleichung des Abulwalīd Merwān Ibn Ganāḥ* (Vienna, 1885), *SBAW,* Band 110, Heft 1, pp. 175ff.
89. It is possible that, aside from the aforementioned writings, he published still others; see the foreword of *Y'sōd Mōra* by Abraham Ibn Ezra where ten of his treatises on the rules governing the Hebrew language are spoken of.
90. See Abraham b. Dā'ūd, p. 73; Ibn Ṣā'id, p. 89: ابن جبرول and p. 120: ابن جبير. Also cf. Neubauer, *MGWJ* 36:499. In a Toledan document of 1200, a Jew is called by the family name Ibn Djābīr; see Gonzalez Palencia, no. 834. The name Djābir appears as a personal name and the family name of Christians; see ibid., nos. 506, 1059. For family names compounded with the suffix -ol, which signifies a diminutive, see ibid., nos. 674, 1146 (Faḳīrol, which was apparently also written erroneously as Fakhīrol) and no. 258 (Fuirol). Also cf. Simonet, *Glosario de voces ibéricas y latinas usadas entre los mozárabes,* pp. xciiff., cxci; Millás Vallicrosa, *Desi-*

nencias adjetivales romances en la onomastica de nuestro judíos, Estudios dedicados a Menendez Pidal 1:132. In a manuscript of *Shīrat Yisrāēl,* the first letter is most often vocalized with a *pataḥ*—see Simḥōnī in *Ha-Teḳūfa* 10:178—and this spelling as well as the Latin erratum Avencebrol (which was apparently pronounced "Avenchebrol") weighs in favor of the pronunciation of "Ibn Djabīrōl" and against "Ibn Djubair" or "Djubairōl"; cf. Simḥōnī, ibid. For the name's existence among Jews in a later era, see David Kaufmann, *Studien über Salomon Ibn Gabirol* (Budapest, 1899), pp. 114–15.

91. The name Ibn Gabriel, by which Hebrew writers occasionally call him, is merely an invented Hebrew form of his name.
92. Of importance for the establishment of the date of his birth is the poem "T'hillat Ēl," *Diwan Ibn Gabirol,* part 1, no. 31, which he wrote—according to its last line—at age 16. In line 105 he speaks of R. Hai Gaon—who died on the eve of the last days of Passover 4798 (March 28, 1038); see Abraham b. Dā'ūd, *Sefer ha-Kabbāla,* p. 66—as one already dead. It can therefore be deduced that the poem was not written before the winter of that year. Consequently, we are led to conclude that the poet was not born before 1022. On the other hand, it is not reasonable to assume that he was born some years thereafter, for if it had been so, he would have been a child in the days of Y'kūṭiēl Ibn Ḥassān, in whose honor he wrote many poems. This conclusion was reached also from the poem "B'ḥar me-ha-ḥalī," *Diwān Ibn Gabirol,* part 1, no. 1, which he wrote at age 17 (see line 71) in honor of the noble Y'ḳūtiēl; however, since the caption over this poem states that it was written in honor of Ibn Ḳaprōn—see note 199 in *Jews of Moslem Spain,* vol. 1, chap. 3—who in my opinion is not identical with Y'ḳutiēl Ibn Ḥassān, who was slain in 1039, we cannot draw any conclusions from it as to the birth date of Ibn Gabirol.

   The source from which we learn where he was born is the book *Shīrat Yisrāēl* by Moses Ibn Ezra. To be sure, in this passage (see *CB* 2314/5) it is only stated *al-Ḳurṭubī nasha'atan Mālaḳa*—نشأ means "to grow up"—but Moses Ibn Ezra also employed the expression in the sense of "to be born," "to be a native of a certain city" (see *The Jews of Moslem Spain* 1:433); moreover, the poet calls himself Mālaḳī, cf. Simḥōnī in *Ha-Teḳūfa* 10:171.

   As for the time when the family moved from Cordova to Malaga, we can only rely on conjecture.
93. See *Diwan Ibn Gabirol,* part 1, no. 39, line 9 and cf. Davidson, "Poetic Fragments from the Genizah," *JQR* n.s. 4:63.
94. Moses Ibn Ezra, *JQR* n.s. 4:63, in the Arabic original and Latin translation; the Hebrew translation in *Shīrat Yisrāēl,* pp. 69–70. Simḥōnī in *Ha-Teḳūfa* 12:151–52 (according to a manuscript in Oxford).
95. See Ibn Ṣā'id, pp. 89, 120, and Moses Ibn Ezra in Steinschneider, *CB* 2314.
96. *Diwan Ibn Gabirol,* part 1, nos. 39, 40 (Bialik-Rawnitzky cast some doubt on its being an elegy for his father; see in the notes and explanations, *Diwan Ibn Gabirol,* pp. 79, 81), 98v, 98vi and see also part 5, no. 69, which includes the fragments in part 1, nos. 98v, 98vi: part 6, no. 92, and the

same elegy according to a Viennese manuscript, B. Klar, *'Ōlēlōt mi-shīrē Ben G'bhīrōl, Minḥa l'-David,* p. 184, and then according to *Maḥzōr Aleppo,* S. Bernstein, "An Unknown Poem of Solomon Ibn Gabirol," *Hadoar* 24:422 and part 5, no. 1; and see the notes and explanations for this poem, which was written at age 16. From the poem "Tūga asher ne'dar," part 1, no. 39, lines 27–28, it can apparently be concluded that the mother died before the father.

97. See Davidson, "Poetic Fragments from the Genizah," p. 64 and Sambari in Neubauer, *Med. Jew. Chr.* 1:127; cf. Simḥōnī in *Ha-Teḳūfa* 10:188.
98. *Diwan Ibn Gabirol,* part 1, no. 19 at the end, and see p. 31, lines 186–87 (written, as stated above, at age 16); 110 (written at the same age); 112, lines 59–60 (written at age 18); 117, lines 93–94.
99. Ibid., part 1, no. 41—see there line 64 and line 5, where he says of himself that he is "unique in his generation"—no. 84.
100. Ibid., nos. 86, 87.
101. On his latent yearnings to enjoy mundane pleasures, see ibid., part 1, no. 10, lines 5–6; on his longing for companionship, see part 5, no. 20, lines 1–5; on his relations with his acquaintances, see part 1, nos. 85, 93. Also cf. Moses Ibn Ezra, *Shīrat Yisrāēl,* p. 71.
102. See *Diwan Ibn Gabirol,* part 5, nos. 54, 55, 56.
103. "T'hillat Ēl," *Diwan Ibn Gabirol,* part 1, no. 31; and see the Arabic caption printed by Davidson in *JQR* n.s. 4:71, in particular lines 61–62, and lines 85–86. Further, see "T'hillat Ēl," part 1, no. 110; in connection with weddings, part 6, no. 16; in connection with elegies, part 1, no. 116, "A Lament for the Māgīd M'bhōrākh," and that poem, part 6, no. 26, and also part 6, nos. 2—an elegy for Solomon b. Moses ha-levi (the editors doubt that it is a poem by Ibn Gabirol)—3, 4, and 5, for a young man named Moses b. Samuel. Also see Schirmann 1:229, an elegy for Abu 'l-Ḥassān Abū Ḥayyīm. (In the opinion of S. Sachs it is an elegy for Y'-ḳūtiēl, but this conjecture is refuted by the superscription, which he had not seen.) See, furthermore, note 8 to chap. 1 in Schirmann and a consolatory poem in part 1, section 71.
104. *Diwan Ibn Gabirol,* part 1, no. 33 and perhaps also no. 46 were written in his honor; see notes and explanations, pp. 92, no. 34, and see line 29, which indicates that he tarried at the poet's place and left it, and perhaps also wrote in his honor part 6, no. 21. The poem in part 5, no. 17 is apparently that of Isaac Ibn Khalfōn, see ed. Mirsky, no. 34; Ibn Khalfōn did indeed praise another man of that family—Abū Sulaimān David Ibn Bābshād—see ed. Mirsky, no. 20, and cf. p. 16, and it is moreover doubtful that a family bearing this Persian name sojourned in Spain. In contrast to Ibn Khalfōn, Ibn Gabirol composed poetry—insofar as is known to us—only in honor of the inhabitants of Spain. As for the poem "Anī 'abhd'khā," part 6, no. 1, which was written in honor of Abū Sulaimān David b. Rāshela from Lucena, in which he calls himself his disciple, the editors had already cast doubt on its being by Ibn Gabirol; see *Diwan Ibn Gabirol,* notes and explanations, p. 3.
105. Ibid., part 1, no. 35. Aḥiya is apparently the son of Ibn Djanāḥ; see Schirmann 1:290, line 55, and also part 1, no. 106, and cf. the notes and explanation. See also Schirmann according to note 7, chap. 1.

106. See *The Jews of Moslem Spain* 2:257 and note 199 to chap. 3. In the opinion of some scholars, the poet also addressed himself to him in the poems in *Diwan Ibn Gabirol,* part 1, no. 57, and part 5, no. 32, but there is no proof for this.
107. *Diwan Ibn Gabirol,* part 1, no. 28.
108. The quarter of it that has been preserved is contained in ibid., part 1, no. 109. The poet wrote this poem when he was 19 years old; see line 34.
109. Ibid., part 1, no. 22, lines 13–17, which were apparently written at age 16 or 17; see note 199 to *The Jews of Moslem Spain,* vol. 2, chap. 3. See no. 112, which was composed at age 18, lines 31–32.
110. *Diwan Ibn Gabirol,* part 1, nos. 13, 15. This poem was published by Schirmann from a corrected manuscript in "A Study about the Life of Solomon Ibn Gabirol," *K'nēset* 10 (1947): 253–54; see there in detail concerning his illness.
111. *Diwan Ibn Gabirol,* part 1, no. 74; and see the poems Schirmann published in *Yūbhal shai* (dedicated to S. J. Agnon), pp. 163–64.
112. *Diwan Ibn Gabirol,* part 5, no. 28.
113. Ibid., part 1, no. 33, lines 2, 4, 6; no. 57, line 2; no. 63, line 15; no. 71, line 21.
114. Ibid., part 1, no. 3, line 10; no. 10, line 20; no. 11, line 6; no. 17, line 2; no. 28, line 28; no. 41, line 11; no. 57, line 1; no. 64, line 12; part 5, no. 32, line 9.
115. Ibid., part 1, no. 26, line 23; no. 69, line 1.
116. Ibid., part 1, no. 35, lines 21, 31; cf. Simḥōnī in *ha-Teḳūfa* 12:185. See also expressions such as *l'khol makka t'rūfa, Diwan Ibn Gabirol,* part 1, no. 1, line 14, and no. 22; *im bo-oniya tirk'bhī,* no. 6, line 29, and cf. notes and explanations, p. 18; *Anshē t'bhūna,* part 1, no. 47, and see line 55, *li-d'rōsh t'bhūna.*
117. *Diwan Ibn Gabirol,* part 5, nos. 35, 38, 39.
118. Ibid., part 1, no. 24.
119. Ibid., part 1, no. 3.
120. Pérès, pp. 219–20.
121. See Schirmann's comment in *Yūbhal shai,* p. 163; *Diwan Ibn Gabirol,* part 6, no. 10, and part 5, nos. 34, 40, 41; "Haḳīṣōtī k'yāshen ahābhīm," in a collection bearing this title, published by S. Z. Shocken under the editorship of M. A. Haberman (Tel Aviv, 1951), no. 6; Schirmann 1:213, 216; Y. Ratzaby, "Shibhrē lūḥōt mi-shīrat S'fārād," *Sinai* 42:116. Cf. Schirmann 1:179, and Simḥōnī in *Ha-Teḳūfa* 17:262.
122. *Diwan Ibn Gabirol,* part 1, nos. 69 (= part 5, no. 5), 130–32; part 5, nos. 46, 47; part 6, nos. 11, 18, 20. Cf. Pérès, pp. 460–61.
123. See also *Diwan Ibn Gabirol,* part 1, no. 9, lines 59–60, and 41, lines 60–61; "Haḳīṣōtī k'yāshen ahābhīm" (see note 21), no. 1.
124. *Diwan Ibn Gabirol,* part 1, no. 123; see Simḥōnī in *Ha-Teḳūfa* 12:155–56, who expresses the opinion that this boastfulness may be explained as an attempt to justify his refraining from engaging in an occupation, on the contention that he was one of the élite.
125. *Diwan Ibn Gabirol,* part 1, no. 93; part 5, nos. 14, 15; part 6, no. 18.
126. See Mirsky in the introduction to the *Diwān Ibn Khalfōn,* pp. 48–49.

127. See Millás Vallicrosa, *Selomó Ibn Gabirol como poeta y filósofo* (Madrid, 1935), pp. 24–27.
128. According to Schirmann 1:182, he is perhaps the first one who described the relationship between Israel and its Creator in the form of folk love songs.
129. *Diwan Ibn Gabirol,* part 3, no. 61.
130. In addition to the sacred verse in ibid., liturgical poems were published by Klar in *Minḥa l'David* (1935), pp. 183–84; in *Hadoar* 30:476–78; and in Schirmann, *Shīrīm ḥadāshīm* (Jerusalem, 1965), pp. 178–79. There are translations into Spanish in Millás, *Poesía Sagrada,* pp. 186–87.
131. Abraham Ibn Ezra on Dan. 11:32.
132. *Diwan Ibn Gabirol,* part 1, nos. 18, 21, 57 (in the opinion of Bialik-Rawnitzky, this poem was written to appease Y'ḳūtiēl, but there is nothing to prove this), 67, 111, 124; part 5, no. 12; part 6, no. 27. Also see below.
133. Ibid., nos. 10, line 74; 24, last line; and see also no. 143, line 47.
134. Ibid., part 1, no. 30.
135. Ibid., part 1, nos. 25, 50, 114. A. Geiger, *Salomo Gabirol u. seine Dichtungen* (Leipzig, 1867), pp. 69–70, holds the view, which Bialik-Rawnitzky also accepted, that he wrote many more poems in honor of the Nagid; however, for some of them there is no proof, and for others this assumption does not hold water at all. To these poems belong part 1, nos. 31, 51, 52, 61, 63 (this is an unlikely conjecture; see lines 31–34), 115, 118, and 166.
136. *Diwan Ibn Gabirol,* part 1, no. 14, line 56; part 5, no. 58.
137. This treatise was first printed by Soncino, 1484, then in a scholarly edition based on a number of manuscripts together with an English translation by Ascher (London, 1859), and last with explanations and references to sources by A. M. Haberman (Merḥabhiya, 1947). Regarding translations see *CB* 2342, to which should be added an English translation, published in New York, 1925. Some scholars have cast doubt on Ibn Gabirol's being the author of the compilation, since this matter is known solely from the book *Shēḳel ha-ḳōdesh* by Joseph Ḳimḥī; however, A. Marx solved the problem in his study "Gabirol's Authorship of the *Choice of Pearls,*" *HUCA* 4:433ff., by demonstrating that the version of *Shēḳel ha-ḳōdesh,* wherein the name of Ibn Gabirol is lacking, is a free adaptation of the compilation, whereas the version in which it is contained is a faithful translation. Fragments of the Arabic original were discovered in collections of the Geniza in Oxford and in the library at Leningrad and were published by M. Sokolow in the *Bulletin of the Russian Academy,* 1929, pp. 287–300, and by N. Braun, "Meḥḳārīm b'-sēfer Mibhḥar ha-p'nīnīm l'rabbi Sh'lōmō b. G'bhīrōl," *Tarbīṣ* 19:45–46.
138. See H. Schirmann, "Solomon Ibn Gabirol and Jonah ibn Djanāḥ" in the *Henoch Yalon Jubilee Volume* (Jerusalem, 1963), pp. 360–61. The appellative *Yāshīsha,* by which the poet calls Abu 'l-Walīd, does not necessarily indicate that the poem was written circa 1050 or thereafter, since it is possible that this is an Aramaic translation of *shaikh* in the sense of "teacher." In Geiger's opinion, *Salomo Gabirol,* he also wrote in his honor the poem "Gefen sh'tūla 'al mayim," *Diwan Ibn Gabirol,* part 1, no. 64,

as he explicitly states in line 19 that he wrote it in honor of his brother Jonah. However, this is not the opinion of Bialik-Rawnitzky (see in the notes and explanations, *Diwan Ibn Gabirol,* p. 108), who make the assumption that "Jonah" is here not a man's name, and Ibn Gabirol was indeed fond of the image of the dove; see the poems that Bernstein published in *Hadoar* 24:422, lines 15–16 and in *Hadoar* 28:538, line 14. On the other hand, Schirmann is of the opinion that in the aforementioned poem the one meant is indeed Jonah Ibn Djanāḥ.

139. The original was published together with an English translation by Stephen S. Wise, *The Improvement of the Moral Qualities* (New York, 1901). The Hebrew translation of Judah Ibn Tibbon was first published in Constantinople in 1550. A new translation, by N. Braun, appeared in Tel Aviv, 5711.
140. *Diwan Ibn Gabirol,* part 1, no. 2, lines 23–26; no. 6, lines 14–17. Concerning the first poem, see Ṣemaḥ in *K'shōresh 'ēṣ* (Jerusalem, 1963), pp. 40–41.
141. In the opinion of Geiger, the diwan's part 6, no. 29 is one of them.
142. *Diwan Ibn Gabirol,* part 1, nos. 26, 27; cf. Simḥōnī in *Ha-Teḳūfa* 10:208.
143. *Diwan Ibn Gabirol,* part 1, no. 21, see line 6 (ben Yōsēf) and line 4, in which the poet states expressly that he left the dwelling place of the Nagid.
144. Ibid., part 1, no. 49 is perhaps such a poem.
145. Ibid., part 1, no. 58; Schirmann, no. 73 (p. 207).
146. *Shīrat Yisrāēl,* p. 194; *Diwan Ibn Gabirol,* part 1, no. 29, and see part 5, no. 31, which is his preface, and the Arabic text of Moses Ibn Ezra in *CB* 2333, which should be amended to read: *wa-ablagha fi 't-takhaṭṭī 'anhu bi-ḳaṣīdatihi allatī ḳasada bihā 'alā ṭūl ash-shikḳa wa-rukūb* [sic!] *al-mashaḳḳa allatī awwaluhā* etc. and should be translated according to this text. Halper, in *Shīrat Yisrael,* did not translate the passage dealing with the journey; see what Geiger cites, *Salomo Gabirol,* p. 139, note 75 in the name of Fleischer, and see in addition Bialik-Rawnitzky in the notes and explanations, *Diwan Ibn Gabirol,* p. 61.
147. *Diwan Ibn Gabirol,* part 1, no. 59, and cf. no. 29, lines 55–58. In the opinion of Geiger and Simḥōnī in *Ha-Teḳūfa* 10:213 (Bialik-Rawnitzy also incline toward this), the poems of part 1, nos. 65, 67, and 85–88 also were composed as a consequence of the controversy—or, more precisely, the controversies—between Ibn Gabirol and the Nagid. But for some of these poems there either is no proof at all or the conjecture is too remote to accept, as in the case of part 1, nos. 86 and 87, in which Ibn Gabirol accuses a man of having stolen his poems from him, i.e., having published verses from poems Ibn Gabirol had composed as if they were his own or included them among his works. It is hard to assume that Ibn Gabirol would be so extreme in his attitude toward the Nagid. On the other hand, it is possible that the following poems are actually related to this episode: part 1, nos. 66, 89, 90, 91; part 5, no. 10. However, in this matter we must fall back on conjectures that are almost impossible to prove, and even if a superscription exists from the hand of the person who arranged the *diwan* in the Middle Ages or from a copyist, this would not prove much since it is possible that even they

indulged in conjecture. So, too, there is no proof that poem no. 149 in the diwan of the Nagid is directed against Ibn Gabirol.

148. Saadya b. Danān, p. 29b. In *Kirjat Sefer* 22:127, Schirmann expresses doubts that Ibn Gabirol really met R. Nissīm after his departure from Saragossa, but Saadya b. Danān states explicitly that this occurred at the time of the wedding of Joseph; see *Diwan Ibn Gabirol,* part 1, no. 32, line 12: "And let him take a blessing [greeting] from his disciple," and line 28, where he mentions the name of R. Nissīm's son, Jacob. The date of Joseph's marriage is not known. It most likely took place in 1053; cf. Abramson in *Tarbīṣ* 26:52–53.
149. A treatise on the question whether the souls were created before the bodies was published by Edelmann in *Ḥemda g'nūza* (Jerusalem, 1863), pp. 2–3, but this is not his treatise on the soul; see further Haneberg, "Ueber das Verhältnis von Ibn Gabirol zu der Encyclopädie der Ichwan uç çafâ," *SB der kgl. bayer. Akad. der Wiss., phil.-hist.* 1866, pp. 98–99.
150. From a quotation in the book *Al-Ḥadīka fī ma'āni 'l-mudjāz wa 'l-ḥaḳīḳa* by Moses Ibn Ezra; see S. D. Sassoon, *Ōhel David,* p. 413.
151. J. Guttman, *Die Philosophie des Salomon Ibn Gabirol* (Göttingen, 1889), pp. 7ff.
152. Ibn Ṣā'id, pp. 70–71.
153. See Haneberg, "Ueber das Verhältnis," and cf. pp. 73ff.; Guttman, pp. 36–37.
154. E. Bertola, *Salomon ibn Gabirol* (Padova, 1953), p. 89.
155. At times Ibn Gabirol does indeed assert that even matter is created by means of the Will. On his theory of the divine Will see also V. Cantarino, "Ibn Gabirol's Metaphysics of Light," *Studia Islamica* 26 (1967): 49ff.
156. Bertola, *Solomon ibn Gabirol* pp. 109–10.
157. S. Munk, *Litbl. des Orients* 7: co. 721ff. Quotations have been preserved in the book *Al-Ḥadīka fī ma'ām* by Moses Ibn Ezra. They were assembled by S. Pines in the *Jubilee Volume in honor of G. Scholem* (Jerusalem, 1958), pp. 92–93. The Latin text of *Fons Vitae* was published by Baeumker in Münster (1895), an English translation in Philadelphia (1954), and a Spanish one in Madrid (1901 [?]).
158. See Kaufmann, *Studien über Salomon ibn Gabirol,* pp. 64–65.
159. This confession was influenced by Saadya; cf. J. Ratzaby in *Orlōgīn* 12 (1956): 247–48.
160. Pérès, p. 222.
161. "Keter Malkhūt" has been translated into European and Islamic languages; see *CB* 2230–31 and the list in *Kirjat Sefer* 32:57, 188. See also the English translation by B. Lewis (London, 1961); the French by A. Chouraqui (*Revue Thomiste* 60:403–40); the Italian by Michele Bolaffi (Livorno, 1863); the Spanish by Millás (*Poesía Sagrada,* pp. 204–5); the German by Hirshfeld (Berlin, 1838); the Yiddish in Vilna, 1874; the Arabic in Alexandria, 1916, and Djerba, 1940; and the Persian in Jerusalem, 1895. Last, the poem was published with a preface and commentary by J. A. Seidman (Jerusalem, 1950).
162. *Shīrat Yisrāēl,* p. 72, and the original in *CB* 2315. As for his observation that Ibn Gabirol "died at the beginning of the eighth century" (the fifth millennium of the Jewish era), whether he erred—which is a likely sup-

position—or he meant a century in which the dates are compounded with "eight hundred," it is certain that what was intended was the ninth century of the fifth millennium. Moses Ibn Ezra's testimony is the most authoritative in fixing the date of his death.

163. On p. 89 of his book, the Arabic writer Ibn Ṣā'id, whose book Moses b. Ezra saw, states that Ibn Gabirol died circa 450 of the *hidjra*—i.e., 1058 C.E.—but this date is surely incorrect. For if this were so, the poet would have passed age 30 by many years, and if we stress the word "circa," there is no great value in this testimony for fixing the exact date.

Nor can reliance be placed on later Hebrew writers who assert that Ibn Gabirol died in 4830 (1070); see "Zēkher ṣaddīḳ," *Med. Jew. Chr.* 1:93; *Sefer ha-ḳabāla* by Abraham b. Solomon, p. 102; *Sefer yōḥasīn,* p. 217a/b; and Sambari, *Med. Jew. Chr.* 1:127. These writers explained those thirty years as the first three decades of the ninth century of the Jewish *acra mundi.* Moreover, a legend had been created that within one year—1070—three of the great rabbis and scholars of that generation had died and that one of these was Ibn Gabirol.

Nevertheless, some scholars of the nineteenth century, relying mainly on the date 1069, which occurs in one of his hymns, maintained the view that the poet did die in 1070; see Munk, *Mélanges,* p. 156; Edelmann, "Ma'mar biḳḳōret," in *Ḥemda g'nūza,* p. xiv; Geiger, *Salomo Gabirol,* pp. 109, 111; Sachs in *Ha-Ṣōfēh,* supplement to *Ha-Maggīd* (1874), p. 313; and also Graetz 6:358–60. Against reliance on that hymn, see Simḥōnī in *Ha-Teḳūfa* 10:219, where he demonstrates that the aforementioned date varies in different *maḥzōrīm* and should not be relied upon. Furthermore, M. Plessner justifiably noted that if Ibn Gabirol had died in 1070, it would be hard to explain how his death was mentioned by Ibn Ṣā'id, who himself died in 1069 or 1070; see his article in *Rivista degli studi orientali* 31:249–50.

Graetz bases himself on the superscription over the poem "Z'manī mah l'khā," part 1, no. 27, which states that it is an elegy upon the death of Samuel the Nagid, but this poem is no more than a hymn on parting and this superscription is an added proof that reliance cannot always be placed upon the assemblers of diwans. Millás, p. 45, makes the same assertion about the poem "L'bhābhī nā' we-nād," part 5, no. 21; this too is a hymn on parting.

In fact, the absence of an elegy for the death of the Nagid in his collected poems (to the extent that they are presumably known to us) demonstrates that Ibn Gabirol died before him. Moreover, Moses Ibn Ezra was surely well versed in the story of his life and he calls him *al-fatā*—the young man. Credence should therefore be given to his account of the death of the poet at about age 30. Such a statement can be made about a person who attained 31 or 32 years. If we assume that he was born in 1022 and was present at the marriage of Joseph when the latter was 18 in 1053, it is probable that he died circa 1054 at age 32. Simḥōnī, in *Ha-Teḳūfa* 10:180–81, arrived at the same conclusion, except that in his opinion Ibn Gabirol was born in 1020.

164. The usual pronunciation of the name בחיי is "Baḥye," and the pronunciation "Baḥyā" is in point of fact a scholar's surmise that finds support for

itself in the pronunciation by Jews of Spanish origin; see Munk, *Mélanges,* p. 482. For the appellation Abū Isḥāk see below, note 170.

165. It appears, for example, in a document from the year 928 in *Cartulario de Santo Torribio de Liébana,* ed. L. Sanchez Belda (Madrid, 1948), no. 37. Concerning a man of the family of Ibn Paḳūda in the village of Alagón west of Saragossa, see *Jews of Moslem Spain* 2:263. In a document written in 1229 in Toledo, there is mention of the house of the heirs of Isaac (R.I.P.) b. Baḳūda; see González Palencia, no. 1048. This house is also mentioned in document no. 674, where the house of Ḥayyim b. Baḳūda is also mentioned, and in this document the name is written . بقوضة .

166. Zunz first commented on this in supplements to a *Catalogue of Hebrew Manuscripts* (Leipzig), p. 318, and concluded therefrom that Baḥyā Ibn Paḳūda dwelt in Saragossa.

167. See C. Ramos Gil, "La Patria de Baḥya Ibn Paqūda," *Sefarad* 11:103–5 (according to a Hebrew translation of his book). After this note was found in a manuscript of the Hebrew translation, I found a similar note in a manuscript of the Arabic original in the collection of T.–S. K 6^{175}. This is apparently an earlier manuscript than the aforementioned Hebrew translation.

168. *Al-Hidāya ilā farā'iḍ al-ḳulūb,* ed. Yahuda, p. 44.

169. Ibid., p. 15.

170. Concerning the time in which he wrote his book, conflicting opinions were expressed by the scholars in preceding generations. Because he does not mention Solomon Ibn Gabirol and there were even passages in the poet's book that parallel passages in his book, some scholars assumed that Ibn Gabirol copied from him, that is to say the one wrote before the other. Those who held this opinion also found support in a list in a manuscript of a late seventeenth-century abridgment of the book; according to the abridgment, the book was written in 1040; see D. Kaufmann, *Die Theologie des Bachja Ibn Paḳuda* (Vienna, 1874), *SBAW Phil.-Hist. Cl.,* Band 77, pp. 3–4 (189–90), 20 (206). On the other hand, A. S. Yahuda argued that Baḥyā wrote his book in the first third of the twelfth century, because he revealed an affinity between it and *al-Ḥikma fī makhlūḳāt Allāh* by al-Ghazzālī (d. 1111); see A. S. Yahuda, *Prolegomena zu einer erstmaligen Herausgabe des Kitāb al-hidāja 'ila farā'iḍ al-qulūb* (Frankfurt a. M., 1904), pp. 9–17. To reinforce his conclusion, Yahuda also relied upon the fact that Baḥyā (on p. 7) mentioned the books of Ibn Djanāḥ. But this problem was solved when Kokowzow published a passage from *Maḳālat al-ḥadīḳa* by Moses Ibn Ezra in which the author mentioned Baḥyā as one who followed in the footsteps of Ibn Djanāḥ in the generation preceding his own; see his article "The Date of Life of Bahya ibn Paqoda" in *Livre d'hommage à la mémoire du Dr. S. Poznanski,* the section on European languages, pp. 13–21. From this passage and from the absence of any mention in *Ḥōbhōt ha-l'bhābhōt* of Isaac Alfasi, the Russian scholar concluded that he did not write his book after the years 1080–1090.

171. See G. Vajda, *La théologie ascétique de Baḥya Ibn Paquda* (Paris, 1947), pp. 88–93.

172. Ibid., p. 105.

173. *Al-Hidāya,* pp. 360–64.
174. Ibid., pp. 392–93, and cf. Vajda, *La théologie ascétique,* pp. 130–31.
175. C. Ramos Gil, "La demonstración de la existencia divina en Baḥya ibn Paqūda," *Sefarad* 11:337.
176. The influence of *Epistles* on Baḥyā was stressed particularly by Kaufmann in *Die Theologie des Bachja Ibn Paḳuda,* pp. 18 (304)–19, whereas Yahuda, in the preface to *Prolegomena,* pp. 70–71, and also Goldziher, *ZDMG* 67:533, expressed the opinion that Baḥyā made use of the sources from which the "Pure Brethren" had drawn and that the views common to him and the brethren were the legacy of all who had a philosophical education in that generation.
177. Yahuda in the preface to *Prolegomena,* pp. 59, 97.
178. *Al-Hidāya,* pp. 194–95, and cf. Vajda, *La théologie ascétique,* p. 74.
179. Ibid., pp. 108–9, and also A. Lazaroff, "Baḥyā's Asceticism against Its Rabbinic and Islamic Background," *Journal of Jewish Studies* 21 (1971): 11ff. About his approach to law and body politic see Fr. Elias de Tejada, "Las doctrinas politicas de Baḥya ben Josef Ibn Paquda," *Sefarad* 8 (1948): 39ff.
180. Cf. Vajda, *La théologie ascétique,* p. 142.
181. See Yahuda in the preface to *Prolegomena,* pp. 72–73.
182. See Goldziher, *ZDMG* 67:531.
183. *Al-Hidāya,* p. 4.
184. See S. J. Ish Horowitz, "Rabbēnu Baḥya w'-sifrō *'Ḥōbhōt ha-l'bhābhōt,*" *Ha-Tekūfa* 10:247–48, 254–55, 257–58.
185. For the printings and translations see *CB* 780; to these should be added one of the early printings, Cracow, 1593. For the translations into Yiddish see A. Yaari, *Kirjat Sefer* 13:398–401; for translations into Spanish and Portuguese see Kayserling, *Bibliotheca Española–Portugueza–Judaica* (1890), pp. 1, 15, 46, 52, 84. Translations into English were published by E. Collins (London, 1904), and M. Hyamson (New York, 1925–1947), and a French translation by A. Chouraqui, *Introduction aux devoirs des coeurs* (Paris, 1950).
186. An analysis of the "Rebuke" was made by C. Ramos Gil, "La Tokeḥá de Baḥya Ibn Paquda," *Homenaje Millás* 2:197–206.
187. Regarding other poems containing the acrostic BHYY, it is difficult to decide whether they are his or the product of another Baḥyā.

CHAPTER TWO

1. The surname of the imaginary person who will constitute below a representative portrait of the day-to-day life of the Jews of Moslem Spain in the middle of the eleventh century was customary among Jews in Arabic-speaking lands. It was also given to men who did not have a son named Ya'ḳūb.
2. Regarding the trade in silk by the Jews of Spain, see *The Jews of Moslem Spain* 1:276, and concerning the eleventh century, see Responsa Alfasi, nos. 77, 137, ed. Bilgoray, no. 149.
3. Concerning houses in Jewish neighborhoods that were the property of non-Jews, see Responsa Alfasi, no. 171 (apparently a question from

Toledo); González Palencia, nos. 605, 635, 648, 669, 674, and, regarding the Alcaná (in Arabic, al-Ḳanāt), nos. 653, 960. To be sure, these documents are from a much later period, but it can be safely assumed that even during the era of Moslem rule, houses in the Jewish quarter passed into non-Jewish ownership; this fact is demonstrated as regards Valencia: *Repartimiento de Valencia,* pp. 240, 261–262, 304; Davila, *BAH* 18:143–44.

4. For methods of construction of dwelling houses in that period, see Torres Balbás, "Restos de una casa árabe en Almería," *Al-Andalus* 10:170–77; "El barrio de casas en la Alcazaba malagueña," ibid., pp. 396–409. Concerning the attics (upper stories), which were called *miṣriyya,* see González Palencia, nos. 674, 676, 710, and cf. Responsa Ibn Migash, no. 133. Sometimes the upper stories were also called *ḥudjra;* see González Palencia, nos. 354, 414. About the practice of renting them to one who was not a member of the family, see al-Maḳḳarī 1:356, line 4, and as for disputes in connection with drainage pipes, see Responsa Ibn Migash no. 132.
5. González Palencia, no. 1135. Concerning the neighborhood, see ibid., no. 1143. This neighborhood was therefore not far from the Church of San Tomé.
6. This is the accepted name in the documents published by González Palencia; see nos. 605, 635, 648, and cf. Torres Balbás, "Estructura de las ciudades hispanomusulmanas," *Al-Andalus* 18:160. A small neighborhood was called *ḥauma*—see González Palencia, nos. 74, 414—or *ḥāra,* see ibid., nos. 605, 710, and cf. Torres Balbás in his aforementioned article, p. 173.
7. Pedro de Alcala, *Vocabulista aravigo in letra castellana* (Granada, 1505), s.v.; Dozy-Engelmann, *Glossaire de mots espagnols et portugais derivés de l'arabe* (Leyden, 1869), pp. 144–45.
8. In Latin script "Call"; for the accepted pronunciation in Barcelona, see *Jews of Moslem Spain* 1:339; for those in other places in eastern Spain, see *Repartimiento de Valencia,* pp. 182, 224, 228, and for the island Mallorca see *Sefarad* 15:69ff.
9. Ibn Ḥayyān in Lévi-Provençal 3:228.
10. See Ibn Ṣa'īd in al-Maḳḳarī 1:135, lines 9–10, and see Torres Balbás, "Les villes musulmanes d'Espagne et leur urbanisation," *AIEO* 6:8ff, 25ff.
11. See *Repartimiento de Valencia,* p. 290; Torres Balbás, "Los Adarves de las ciudades hispanomusulmanas," *Al-Andalus* 12:176, 187; R. del Arco, *Huesca en el siglo* 12:60; and also Millás Vallicrosa, *Documentos del archivo del Pilar, de Zaragoza* (Madrid, 1930), p. 4, and see ibid., p. 14.
12. See Torres Balbás, *AIEO* 6:19.
13. Isaac Alfasi, in *P'ēr ha-dōr,* no. 219.
14. Responsa Yōm Ṭōbh b. Abraham Ish-bīlī, no. 20.
15. See *Ṭūr Ḥōshen Mishpāṭ,* no. 154, in the name of Judah al-Barcelōnī.
16. Responsa Yōm Ṭōbh b. Abraham Ish-bīlī, no. 27.
17. The name "Dona" was widespread among the Jews of Spain; see González Palencia, nos. 258, 635, 674.
18. See González Palencia, nos. 635, 669, 674; cf. Torres Balbás, *Al-Andalus* 12:189ff.

19. See Torres Balbás, *AIEO* 6:17ff.
20. Ibn ʿAbdūn, p. 224, lines 14–15, and see Torres Balbás, "Plazas, zocos y tiendas en las ciudades hispanomusulmanas," *Al-Andalus* 12:438ff.
21. See concerning Saragossa *The Jews of Moslem Spain* 1:276; concerning Valencia, see *The Jews of Moslem Spain* 2:286; about Huesca, see the documents published and cited by R. del Arco, *Archivos historicos del Alto Aragon,* fasc. 2 (Zaragoza, 1930), p. 57, and *Sefarad* 7:288.
22. See González Palencia, nos. 710, 965, 1135, and see also in the Latin document in the introductory volume, p. 76.
23. Ibn ʿAbdūn, p. 224, line 17.
24. Ibid., p. 224; Ibn ʿAbdarraʾūf, *Trois traités,* pp. 110–111.
25. See González Palencia, no. 710, and see, concerning Saragossa, *Jews of Moslem Spain* 1:336, and see below, note 74.
26. Ibn ʿAbdūn, p. 245, lines 21–22; Ibn ʿAbdarraʾūf, *Trois traités,* p. 93.
27. F. Pastor y Lluis, "La Judería de Tortosa," *Boletin de la Sociedad Castellonense de Cultura* 2:327.
28. González Palencia, introductory volume, p. 76.
29. This street is mentioned in the collection of González Palencia, no. 635, and this is apparently the street currently called del Angel.
30. See González Palencia, nos. 635 and 1143, quoted above in note 5, where the street is called *mamarr.*
31. Torres Balbás, "Plazas, zocos y tiendas," pp. 451ff.
32. See *Jews of Moslem Spain* 1:326–27. In the later Middle Ages the shops of the perfumers were located there; see *Cronicas de los Reyes de Castilla, T. I: Cronica de D. Pedro* (Madrid, 1779), p. 184; Amador de los Rios, "La Alcaná de Toledo," *RABM* 24:64ff.
33. Torres Balbás, "Plazas, zocos y tiendas," pp. 463, 468. Concerning the silk scarves, see as-Saḳaṭī, p. 66, line 9.
34. Responsa Alfasi, MS. Bodl. 2794, no. 7, and see the aforementioned article of Torres Balbás, pp. 465–66, and another article by this scholar: "Algunos aspectos de la casa hispanomusulmana," *Al-Andalus* 15:179ff. In it he expresses the opinion that the upper stories over the shops in particular were called *miṣrīyya* and the upper stories of the dwelling houses were called *ghurfa.* However, the documents published by González Palencia show that such a distinction was not always made in the use of these expressions. In nos. 29, 98, and 669 there is reference to upper stories of shops called *ghurfa,* and in no. 461 an upper story in which a craftsman worked is mentioned that is also called *ghurfa.* In documents nos. 674, 676, and 714 upper stories of dwelling houses are mentioned called *miṣrīyya.* Concerning the special entrance leading to the upper stories over the dwelling houses and shops, see González Palencia, nos. 354, 414, 669. See also the information about upper stories above shops in Seville cited by Torres Balbás, "Algunos aspectos," p. 182, and also in a question directed to R. Isaac Alfasi (from Seville) in which the upper story over a shop is called *ghurfa.*
35. Aḍ-Ḍabbī, *Bughyat al-multamis,* pp. 332–33.
36. Ibn Ṣaʿīd, *MS. of the Academy for History in Madrid,* no. 80, p. 35, and see Ribera, Disertaciones 1:24–25. Notwithstanding its anecdotal features, the story demonstrates at least that initially the Moslem judges did not

adopt a posture that would operate to the harm of litigants who were not members of their faith.

37. "Kitāb Aḥkām as-sūḳ," *RIEEI* 4:128, and see there the quotation from the book of 'Abdallāh al-Mālikī, *Riyāḍ an-nufūs* (Cairo, 1951) 1:381. Concerning the history of Yaḥyā, see ibid., p. 64, and concerning 'Abdallāh b. Ṭālib, p. 68. Cf. E. García Gómez, "Unas Ordenanzas del zoco del siglo IX," *Al-Andalus* 22:292.
38. See what is related about Abū 'Āmir Ibn Shuhaid, who died in 1035, in al-Ḥumaidī, p. 127, *Maṭmaḥ al-anfūs,* p. 21, and cf. al-Maḳḳarī 1:345. About Abū 'Umar ar-Ramādī, who died in 1022, see Ibn Ḥayyān in al-Maḳḳarī 2:440; *Maṭmaḥ al-anfūs,* p. 80, and cf. al-Maḳḳarī 2:441. About Abū 'Abdallāh al-Ḥaddād, who died circa 1087, see Dozy, *Recherches* 1:lvi; *Dhakhīra* I², p. 216.
39. P. 241, lines 11–16.
40. Ibn 'Abdūn's demand that non-Moslems be obliged to mark themselves by means of a distinctive sign is one of the demands found in his treatise that have no basis in reality, e.g. the requirement that priests be compelled to marry, see p. 239, line 9.

    In any event, the existence of contradictory information in varied types of sources has resulted in distinguished researchers into Spanish Moslem civilization expressing opposing views in this respect. From the writings of the aforementioned poets, Pérès concluded that in the eleventh century the Mozarabs were required to wear the belt called *zunnār*—see in his book, p. 282. However, Lévi-Provençal rejects this conclusion by Pérès; see Lévi-Provençal 3:224, and cf. p. 429, note 1. The seeming contradiction respecting identifying badges of non-Moslems in the eleventh century is apparently explained by the tendency of the poets of that time to emphasize in a figurative manner former distinctive signs of the Christians, as can be concluded from the statements of Ibn 'Abdūn. F. Simonet, p. 431, and cf. p. 128, already has commented upon the absence of information concerning distinctive signs in Christian literature of the ninth century, but no doubt these badges were introduced into Spain shortly after Eulogius and his colleagues wrote their books. It is unlikely that the theologians did not take advantage of their influence in order to prompt the rulers to impose the observance of this statute on the non-Moslems; this is demonstrated by the information gleaned from the poets.
41. Ibn 'Abdūn, pp. 228, line 18; 239, line 3.
42. *Dhakhīra* II (MS. Oxford), p. 144; and see in Pérès, p. 271.
43. De Pisa, *Descripción de la imperial ciudad de Toledo* (Toledo, 1917), f. 135b; Eulogius, *Mem. Sanct. (Hispania Illustrata IV),* p. 300.
44. Ibn Ḥayyān, cited by Lévi-Provençal 3:224, note 4; J. Briz Martinez, *Historia de la fundación y antiguadedes de San Juan de la Peña* (Çaragoça, 1620), pp. 638–39.
45. Ibn Sahl, cited by Lévi-Provençal 3:224, note 1.
46. See about a new synagogue *Jews of Moslem Spain* 1:159.
47. Eulogius, *Mem. Sanct.,* p. 247; Alvaro, "Indiculus luminosus," *España Sagrada* 11:230.

48. Alvaro, ibid., pp. 272–73; Samson, "Apologeticus," *España Sagrada* 11:380; *Vita Joannis Gorziensis,* cap. 123; Migne 137, col. 303.
49. "Epistola Alvari," *España Sagrada* 11:169; Samson, "Apologeticus," *España Sagrada* 11:377, 381, 384; *Vita Joannis Gorziensis,* cap. 129; Migne 137, col. 307.
50. *Chronicon Moissaciense* PL 98, col. 1425, and see Cassel in the *Encyclopädie von Ersch. u. Gruber,* Sect. II, Bd. 27, p. 206.
51. *España Sagrada* 13:416–17.
52. So it follows that in Aragon, after the reconquest, the Jews' tax was called *aladma (adh-dhimma);* see Eguilaz-Yanguas, *Glosario etimológico de las palabras españolas de origen oriental* (Granada, 1886), p. 82.
53. Eulogius, *Mem. Sanct.,* p. 247; Leovigild, "De habitu clericorum," *España Sagrada* 11:523; Samson, "Apologeticus," pp. 378, 380–81, 385.
54. See Pedro de Alcala, *Vocabulista, item judio,* and cf. Dozy, *Suppl.* 1:415 and cf. E. Strauss–Ashtor, *History of the Jews in Egypt and in Syria under the Rule of the Mamlūks* (in Hebrew) (Jerusalem, 1951), 2:298–99.
55. See *Jews of Moslem Spain* 1:376–77.
56. *Tōrātān shel rishōnīm,* ed. Horowitz (Frankfurt, 1982), 2:58. This is a question to the Gaon R. Hai; see Mann, "Responsa," *JQR* n.s. 10:126.
57. *T'shūbhōt ha-g'ōnīm,* ed. Harkavy, no. 346. This is a question among a collection of questions of R. Jacob b. Nissīm of Kairawān; see there, at the end of p. 179, the date Sh'bhaṭ 4302 (991 C.E.). Many of the questions the *geonim* in Babylonia were asked by the Jews of Kairawān actually originated in Spain; but even if these questions were from the Maghreb, it is possible that they came from the area of Spanish rule, and it is surely permissible to assume that the situations depicted in them were similar to those in Spain proper.
58. *T'shūbhōt GMUM,* no. 201.
59. See responsum of R. Joseph Ibn Abītūr, ibid., no. 193; the translation of Müller, p. 28, is incorrect: *hefsed* is not a damage but rather another epithet for tax, like a "penalty"; see *Tōrātān shel rishōnīm,* vol. 2, no. 9.
60. On this matter see in detail my book, *Jews in Egypt and Syria* 2:222ff.
61. See responsa of Moses b. Ḥanōkh, in *T'shūbhōt GMUM,* nos. 190, 207; of R. Ḥanokh, ibid., nos. 170, 178 (cf. Müller, p. 34), 197, 198 (cf. Müller, p. 35), 202, 203, 209, 211.
62. Lévi-Provençal 3:151–52, and cf. Khalīl b. Isḥāḳ al-Djundī, *Mukhtaṣar* (Paris, 1900), p. 249; Italian translation by Guidi-Santillana (1919), 2:827.
63. Ibn 'Idhārī 2:148; *Vita Joannis Gorziensis,* Migne 137, col. 306; cf. *Jews of Moslem Spain* 1:175.
64. Concerning the appointment of Ardabast, his role in the collection of taxes, and his being the head of the Christian community in all of Spain, see Ibn al Ḳuṭiyya, *Iftitāḥ al-Andalus* (Madrid, 1926), p. 38; Ibn Ḥayyān in *Al-Iḥāṭa,* p. 109. Concerning the holders of this office in a later period of Omayyad rule, see *A'māl al-a'lām,* p. 15; Ibn Ḥazm, *Djamharat ansāb al-'arab* (Cairo, 1948), p. 88, lines 3–4; letter of Alvaro, *España Sagrada* 2:151–52 concerning Romano; and see there p. 155 and cf. p. 14 that Servando was then already *comes;* Ibn al-Ḳūṭīya, p. 5. Concerning judges, see *España Sagrada* 2:155; Ibn 'Idhārī 2:142, al-Maḳḳarī 1:252;

Ibn Khaldūn 4:145. Concerning the assistance of the Moslem authorities in maintaining discipline within the community, see *España Sagrada* 2: 378, and for the role of the *comes* in the collection of taxes, ibid., pp. 380–81, 385.

From the information about the organizational framework of the Christian community—insofar as the history of the Jews in Spain is concerned—special importance attaches to the explicit information that Ardabast became the *comes* of the Mozarabs in the entire country and that he was appointed by the first Omayyad. From this it is apparent that in spite of their anecdotal characteristics one cannot negate out of hand accounts such as those found in later sources regarding the establishment of the office of nagid in Egypt. The data about Ardabast apparently show that every new and powerful Moslem dynasty appointed heads of the community like these for its non-Moslem subjects, so that they would keep an eye on their affairs and also not transfer their allegiance to those who held similar posts in another kingdom; or, at any rate, would have less need of them. Characteristic of these conditions is Alvaro's addressing himself to the *comes* as the superior judge of the community; see *España Sagrada* 2:151–52, and as for the *comes* acting as superior judge, see also Simonet, pp. 103, 112. The small amount of data about the heads of the Jewish community should be clarified in the light of this information.

65. There is no doubt that the words of Abraham b. Dā'ūd, p. 51, should be explained in this fashion. He asserts that al-Manṣūr at first gave Jacob Ibn Djau permission "to fix every tax and every date of payment which they are obliged to meet" and that he later deposed him because "it seemed to him when he appointed him that he would repay him with large gifts and collect money from the Jews, from all communities, properly or improperly." See there that he also appointed him to be a judge.
66. See Dūnash b. Labraṭ (ed. Allōnī), p. 70, lines 34–35; and see S. D. Luzzatto, *Bēt ha-yōṣēr,* p. 27.
67. Documentos, no. 5.
68. See M'naḥem's statement in his letter, in Luzzatto, *Bēt ha-yōṣēr* S. 26f; 28b, lines 2, 19–20, 24–25; 29a, lines 8–10; 29b, lines 1–2, 4, 20. See Luzzatto's explanations, ibid., 33b–c; he endeavors to prove that M'naḥem was accused of heresy.
69. See *Diwan Ibn Gabirol,* part 1, no. 116, line 6; part 5, no. 17, line 3. See also Goitein in *Zion* 27:23, 165.
70. See *The Jews of Moslem Spain* 2:217, according to note 67. Also see above, pp. 171–73.
71. See Responsa Alfasi, no. 173. In the light of the conspicuous parallel between the role of the *comes* and that of the *nāsī,* it is hard to agree with the opinion of Baron 5:44 that Ḥasdai Ibn Shaprūṭ had no official status. As for Ibn Djau, Abraham b. Dā'ūd expressly states that a writ of appointment was given him, but even though such documents have not come down to us and were perhaps not always given to those leaders, the fact is that the information concerning Ḥasdai's use of force against M'naḥem Ben Sārūḳ, Abraham b. Dā'ūd's account of the role of Ibn

Djau, and Alfasi's judgment mentioned above, indicate that the title of *nāsī* was, in these instances, not merely an honorific (which is the opinion of Baron 5:314) but the title of an office recognized by the Moslem government and possessing well-defined functions. The substitution of the title "nagid" in place of *nāsī* was not connected with the downfall of Ibn Djau, as Schirmann assumes (see *JSS* 13:13). The title was not debased inasmuch as it still appears in the days of Samuel the Nagid in Saragossa; see above, p. 32, note 103. Nor should we attribute the title of nagid, which was bestowed on Samuel ibn Nagrēla, to his ancestry, for he was not of davidic descent; indeed, neither were the other community leaders who were given the title of *nāsī* related to the House of David. It would appear that the title nagid was a matter of style and no more than that, and in Spain even styles became passé.

72. Responsa Alfasi, no. 58, and his responsa in *Pe'ēr ha-dōr,* no. 198, and in Harkavy, *T'shūbhōt ha-g'ōnīm,* no. 470.
73. Responsa Alfasi, nos. 67, 302; Responsa Ibn Migash, no. 94; cf. Assaf, *Ha-'On'shīn aḥarē ḥatīmat ha-talmūd* (Jerusalem, 1922), p. 22; and see Aptowitzer, "Malḳot u-makkōt mardūt bi-t'shūbhōt ha-g'ōnīm," *Ha-Mishpāṭ ha-'ibhrī* 5 (1937): 33–104.
74. Responsa Alfasi, no. 146; Responsa Ibn Migash, no. 172. In the main, the prison filled the same function as it did in the Near East; see R. M'shullām of Volterra, ed. Yaari, p. 57 (about Egypt). From a later period there is information that the courts in the Jewish communities of Spain imposed upon offenders beforehand the penalty of imprisonment for a fixed period, and it is possible that they still did this in the days of Moslem rule, as it is known that this penalty was customary among the Moslems in Spain; see Ibn 'Abdūn, p. 108, line 14, and cf. Assaf, *ha-'Ōn'shīn,* pp. 25–26. The Jews' prisons were apparently in those "fortresses" in which were also kept the animals before slaughter in the butcher shops and abbatoirs nearby; see, e.g., A. Vieira da Silva, "A Judiaria velha de Lisboa," *O Archeologo Portugues* 5:322–23.
75. *T'shūbhōt GMUM,* no. 163; Documentos, no. 2.
76. Responsa Ibn Migash in *P'ēr ha-dōr,* nos. 211, 214; cf. a responsum of Alfasi in Harkavy, *T'shūbhōt ha-g'ōnīm,* no. 165.
77. See R. Judah al-Barcelōnī, *Sefer ha-sh'ṭārōt,* pp. 7–8, and cf. p. 131. Assaf, *ha-'On'shīn,* p. 63, conjectured that he found the version of the writ in the *Sefer ha-sh'ṭārōt* of either R. Saadya or R. Hai; but it is not to be found in the remnants of the two treatises he later published. Its discovery there would, however, not prove that in the Near East it was customary to appoint leaders and judges by an elective process, but only this: that Saadya knew of this practice and for this reason included this writ of appointment in his collection.
78. Responsa Alfasi, nos. 80, 106; Responsa Ibn Migash, no. 122.
79. E. Tyan, *Histoire de l'organisation judiciaire en pays d'islam* (Paris, 1938–43) 1:339–48.
80. *T'shūbhōt GMUM,* no. 207 (of R. Moses b. Ḥanōkh); see Assaf, *Batē dīn* (Jerusalem, 1924), p. 104, and Responsa R. Āsher, chap. 13, no. 18; cf. Lévi-Provençal 3:129–30.
81. Responsa Alfasi, no. 248, and cf. *Sefer ha-'iṭṭūr* (ed. Lemberg), folio 62a.

This is the opinion of R. Hai; see *T'shūbhōt ha-g'ōnīm,* ed. Harkavy, no. 180, and cf. Ibn 'Abdūn, p. 202, lines 16–17.

82. Responsa Alfasi, MS. Bodl. 2794, no. 5.
83. Responsa Alfasi, nos. 146, 224, and cf. Responsa Yōm Ṭōbh b. Abraham Ishbīlī, no. 56. Versions of *p'tīḥa* and *aḥramta* issued by the geonic courts were published by Aptowitzer, "Formularies of Decrees and Documents from a Gaonic Court," *JQR* n.s. 4:26–27.
84. See *T'shūbhōt GMUM,* no. 207; Documentos, nos. 8, 9, and see Responsa David b. Zimra, no. 622, concerning the writ of appointment of Joseph ha-levi Ibn Migash. See also Responsa R. Āsher, chap. 55, no. 9: "The Arabic language . . . in which the scribes of our country have become accustomed to write writs of notification and notes on loans and bills of sale and purchase and all manner of enactments for the strengthening of the law is not the vernacular spoken by the masses" but "in the real Arabic wherein were written the books of secular wisdom and the epigrammatic and rhetorical writings."
85. S. Assaf expressed the opinion that the documents in MS. Firkovitch, first collection, no. 240, folios 19b–22a, belong to a formulary compiled in Spain in the eleventh century.
86. Documentos, no. 5.
87. See the amended text of the letter in Mann, *Tarbīṣ* 6, part 1, p. 88. It is remarkable that Mann, in his article in *ha-Ṣōfe l'-ḥokhmat Yisrāēl* 10:206, asks whether this resolute person dwelt in Moslem or Christian Spain. Surely, at that time there were almost no Jews in the Christian principalities of northern Spain, and it is inconceivable that such privileges would have been granted them.
88. Judah al-Barcelōnī, *Sēfer ha-'ittīm,* p. 267.
89. Judah b. Āsher, *Zikhrōn Y'hūda* (Berlin, 1846), folio 55b.
90. See *Jews of Moslem Spain* 1:250, 251. In the light of this parallel there is no room for Mann's doubts in his article in *La-Ṣōfe l'-ḥokhmat Yisrāēl* 10:207, where he inclines to refute the trustworthiness of the information in *Zikhrōn Y'hūda* because of the unusual festival season. Quite the contrary, the information that one could be executed at the holiest hour of the year confirms the trustworthiness of the entire account. See also Responsa R. Āsher, chap. 17, no. 6, which states that it is permissible to punish an informer even on a Yōm Kippūr which occurs on the Sabbath.
91. In the commentary to the Mishna, *Ḥullīn,* chap. 1: "And know that we have a tradition from our teachers that in these times . . . when criminal law is not in effect, this is only in the case of a Jew who committed a capital offense, except for heretics, Sadducees and Boethusians, in view of the multitude of evils perpetrated by them, lest they demoralize the Jews and cause the faith to perish; and this has led to the practical implementation of the law against many men in the cities of the entire West." Mann, in *La-Ṣōfe l'-ḥokhmat Yisrāēl* 10:209, conjectures that these words apply to Christian Spain, but Abraham b. Dā'ūd's account on pp. 69, 72 (see below) refutes this conjecture. See also Maimonides's letter to Phineas, the judge of Alexandria, *Ḳōbheṣ* (Leipzig, 1859), part 1, folio 26b, col. 1.

92. See the statement of Maimonides, in *Hilkhōt ḥōbhēl u-mazīḳ,* chap. 8, par. 11: "In the cities of Maghreb it is a frequent occurrence that informers who are known to reveal people's money are handed over to the gentiles to be punished, beaten, or imprisoned as befits their crime." This passage would seem to apply, in reality, to Christian Spain.
93. Responsa R. Āsher, chap. 17, no. 8, but later he himself pronounced the sentence of death for transgressors; see chap. 17, nos. 1, 3.
94. *Sanhedrin* 37b, 52b; *K'tubhōt* 30a and b.
95. See in detail J. Mann, "Historical Survey of Criminal Law in Our Time" (in Hebrew), *ha-Ṣōfe l'-ḥokhmat Yisrāēl* 10:200–201.
96. *Sha'are ṣedeḳ,* part 4, line 1, no. 9 (of Moses b. Ḥanōkh); Responsa Alfasi, ed. Bilgoray, no. 54.
97. See *Sh'ēlōt u-t'shūbhōt me-ha-g'onīm ha-k'ṣārōt* (Mantua, 5357), no. 182, and cf. Mann, "Responsa," *JQR* n.s. 10:129–30, who is of the opinion that this is a responsum of a Spanish rabbi. Also see Maimonides, *Hilkhōt ḥōbhēl u-mazīḳ,* part 8; Responsa Ibn Adret, part 4, no. 311, and part 5, no. 238; Responsa Isaac b. Shēshet, no. 134. With this reasoning Alfasi justifies all the innovations in the imposition of penalties; see his responsum in Harkavy, *T'shūbhōt ha-g'ōnīm,* no. 165: *fa-yuf'al fī dhalika ḥisba mā taḳtaḍīhi al-maṣlaḥa kamā ḳālū bēt dīn makkīn we-'ōneshīn shelō min ha-tōra.*
98. See *España Sagrada* 11:385. Baron 5:45–46 explains the privilege granted the Jews to pronounce sentence in criminal cases as a parallel to a similar privilege the Mozarab Christians had. He bases himself on a Latin document according to which the Mozarabs did indeed judge criminal cases, though they needed the kadi's approval in each instance. This document is quoted by W. W. Baudissin, *Eulogius u. Alvar* (Leipzig, 1872), p. 13. Also, A. Fattal, *Le statut légal des non-musulmans en pays d'Islam* (Beirut, 1958), p. 349, asserts that the Christians in Moslem Spain could judge a Christian murderer who had slain a member of his community (and it is the days of the Omayyads that he has in mind) and quotes an Arabic translation of A. Mez, *Die Renaissance des Islams* (Heidelberg, 1922), p. 41, who speaks in a general way of permission to judge criminal cases and relies upon the aforementioned quotation in Baudissin's book. However, Baudissin himself notes that that document is, beyond a shadow of a doubt, a forgery, as is demonstrated by the language; see *Eulogius u. Alvar,* pp. 12–13. He quotes Aschbach and Flórez, who also cast doubt upon its authenticity. Therefore, the conjecture of Mann, "Historical Survey of Criminal Law," p. 208, which presumes that the Jews received the privilege of trying criminal cases as loyal allies at the time of the conquest, is a likely one.
99. Responsa Ibn Migash, no. 134.
100. *T'shūbhōt GMUM,* no. 199. From the location of the responsum, i.e., its inclusion in a collection of Spanish responsa, it can be concluded that it, too, is Spanish. Its style at the beginning, the expression "it seems so to me," and the ending all point to its being in reality written by R. Ḥanōkh; cf. nos. 176, 192, 202, 204, 209, and see *Jews of Moslem Spain* 1:451, note 27.
101. See R. Judah al-Barcelōnī, *Sēfer ha-sh'ṭārōt,* p. 13, and cf. p. 83. See also *T'shūbhōt GMUM,* no. 210 (of R. Moses b. Ḥanōkh), in which the rabbi,

in rendering his decision, does not exactly complain against having recourse to non-Jewish courts but against turning to *any* court.

102. See Responsa Alfasi, nos. 156, 221; "The Threats of Ibn Khalfōn," *Diwan Samuel ha-nāgīd,* no. 18; and cf. Schirmann in *Tarbīṣ* 7:300.

103. Cf. Responsa Alfasi, ed. Bilgoray, no. 153.

104. See Lévi-Provençal 3:136–40.

105. Concerning judges who sit (on the judgment bench) in the mosque, see *Akhbār madjmū 'a,* pp. 127, 128; Ibn 'Idhārī, pp. 78–79; and al-Khushanī, pp. 94, 109, 111. Concerning judges who try cases in their homes, see al-Khushanī, p. 90, and in particular see Ibn 'Abdūn, an eleventh-century contemporary, p. 203, line 8, from which it may be inferred that at that time this was an accepted practice because of the great convenience for the judge.

106. From various documents we know of brokers, *dallāl,* who were assigned to the various markets in Toledo, such as those for sellers of vegetables, those for sellers of houses and immovable property, and also those for the market of Alcaná; see González Palencia, no. 659 (a Christian), and see concerning the same agent nos. 476 and 608, where the reading should be القناة and not القنرة, and also no. 653. See also no. 690 concerning the Jewish broker Abū 'Amr b. Israel, who was an agent for slave traders, and see Ibn 'Abdūn, pp. 231, line 6; 232, line 8.

107. Ibn 'Idhārī 2:71, 77, 117, 191, 194, 215; al-Khushanī, pp. 105, 178; Ibn Bashkuwāl 1:30; *Ṭauḳ al-ḥamāma,* pp. 114, 350; an-Nuwairī, p. 38; Ibn al-Abbār in Dozy, *Notice sur quelques manuscrits arabes,* p. 155; the anonymous chronicle of 'Abdarraḥmān 3:73, 76–77.

108. That they had to act thus in lawsuits of this sort—which no doubt were frequently instituted—we learn from law books such as *Risāla of Ibn Abī Zaid al-Ḳairawānī,* ed. Berchet (Algiers, 1949), pp. 262, 264; and Khalīl b. Isḥāḳ al-Djundī, *Mukhtaṣar,* pp. 193, 198, 208, 209, 211, 212, 213. As regards the essence of the problem, i.e., preference of the trial rules, in this respect the presumption that an agreement had been made touching an exact date, e.g., two months, to the inequality between the litigants from the aspect of their civil rights, see in the commentary of al-Kharashī on the *Mukhtaṣar of Khalīl* 5 (Cairo, 1316–1317): 234.

109. Maimonides, *Commentary on the Tractate Aboth,* 4:7, ed. Baneth, *Studies of the Rabbinical Seminary* (Berlin, 1905), p. 31; see Ibn 'Aḳnīn, *Ṭibb an-nufūs,* chap. 27, published by M. Güdemann, *Das jüdische Unterrichtswesen während der spanisch-arabischen Periode* (Vienna, 1873), p. 3; and cf. pp. 187–88, translated into Hebrew by S. Eppenstein in the *Jubilee Book for N. Sokolow* (Warsaw, 1904), pp. 371–88.

110. Concerning monthly payment, see *T'shūbhōt GMUM,* no. 196; on supplying commodities see Loeb, *REJ* 13:198, for the practice in the Jewish communities of Castile in the Middle Ages.

111. See S. Tcharna, "L'tōl'dōt ha-ḥīnūkh b'-Yisrāēl bi-t'ḳūfat g'ōnē Babhel," *Ha-Teḳūfa* 19:224–25.

112. From this epoch in the history of the Jews in Moslem Spain, no information has come down to us on the location of the school, but what is described here was the practice in Spain; see Responsa R. Solomon b. Simeon Duran, no. 192: "For from time immemorial the teachers of the

children taught them in the synagogue"; Assaf, *M'ḳōrōt L'tōl'dōt ha-ḥīnūkh b'Yisrāēl* (Tel Aviv, 5691), 2:4–5; N. Morris, *Tōl'dōt ha-ḥīnūkh shel 'am Yisrāēl* 1:128–29, and 2:198.

113. Also the sons of Samuel the Nagid studied in a school; see *Diwan Samuel ha-nāgīd,* no. 135, lines 24–25. He himself studied in a school in Cordova; see no. 37, line 32.

114. *Baba Batra* 21a, *K'tubhōt* 50a; *T'shūbhōt ha-g'ōnīm,* ed. Harkavy, no. 553; Maimonides, *Hilkhōt Talmūd Tōra* 2, and see there in *Kesef Mishne,* and cf. Zunz, *Zur Geschichte und Literatur,* pp. 167–68, regarding the customs connected with the child's admission to the school. Elyāsāf, a son of Samuel the Nagid, began to study at school at age 3; see *Diwan Samuel ha-nāgīd,* no. 135, lines 24–25, and cf. S. Abramson in the introduction to *Ben Mishlē* (Tel Aviv, 1948), pp. 14–15.

115. See in *Diwan Samuel ha-nāgīd:* "And it came upon him [an illness upon Elyāsāf] while he was reading from his tablet at school. . . ." See there also no. 6, line 10 (condolences to R. Nissīm of Kairawān on the death of a son): "And he was not able to instruct him in the [skill of reading the] tablet"; and cf. Krauss, *Talmudische Archäologie* 3:208. The Hispano-Jewish poet uses the term "tablet" for what was formerly called a pupil's notebook, as distinct from the board on which the teacher writes. Regarding the wooden tablets, see Ribera: Disertaciones 1:265.

116. Judah b. Samuel Ibn 'Abbās, *Yaīr n'tībh,* in Güdemann, *Das jüdische Unterrichtswesen,* p. 58 (Hebrew text). It is true that this author wrote in the middle of the thirteenth century, but the method he recommends was the accepted one for many generations, especially since the Moslems in Spain also employed it; see Ribera: Disertaciones 1:265, who quotes the sources.

117. Regarding these scrolls see *Gittīn* 60a; Morris, *Tōl'dōt ha-ḥīnūkh* 1:138, and Tcharna, "L'tōl'dōt ha-ḥīnūkh," p. 225. However, in Spanish sources it is precisely the tablets that are discussed; see Responsa Simeon b. Ṣemaḥ Duran, part 1, no. 2, where R. Simeon speaks about the teacher who writes on the tablets for the children who have no book, from which it can be inferred that there were boys who did bring books and scrolls with them. Cf. Responsa Ibn Adret, part 5, no. 166. And see in Responsa Simeon b. Ṣemaḥ, part 1, no. 2, where a book in Arabic by R. Maimon, the father of Maimonides, is mentioned. In it Simeon b. Ṣemaḥ speaks on these tablets and bases himself on what was taught in this regard by Joseph ha-levi Ibn Migash, from which it can be inferred that this was the practice in southern Spain in the eleventh and the beginning of the twelfth century. In this same judgment Simeon b. Ṣemaḥ mentions that each week they would study the weekly portion of the Pentateuch. For the entire course of study, see Ibn 'Aḳnīn, ed. Güdemann, pp. 7–8. Regarding the beginning of the study of the Bible with the Book of Leviticus, see Zunz, *Zur Geschichte und Literatur,* pp. 167–68; Morris, *Tōl'dōt ha-ḥīnūkh* 1:171, 2:209; and S. D. Goitein, *Jewish Education in Muslim Countries* (Jerusalem, 1962), pp. 48ff.

118. See *Diwan Samuel ha-nāgīd,* no. 63, the superscription and line 6; and cf. Sassoon's introduction, p. xiv.

119. See responsum of Joseph Ibn Abītūr in *Ginzē Ḳedem* 3:63: "Moreover she spun with them daily, as an equivalent of her sustenance." The reference here is to a 9-year-old girl; see also Responsa Ibn Migash, no. 71.
120. See "Ha-Shīra ha-y'tōma" by Joseph Ibn Ḥasdai in Schirmann 1:174, line 37; and Ibn 'Aḳnīn, p. 7.
121. See Judah Ibn Bal'ām's commentary on Amos 2:8 in Poznanski, *JQR* n.s. 15:29; and Isaac b. Moses, i.e., Profiat Duran, *Ma'asē Ēfōd* (Vienna, 1865), pp. 19, 20.
122. As, e.g., the drinking of *balādhur.* See in the Moslem source: Ibn Bashkuwāl 1:287. The Jews, no doubt, did likewise.
123. See Ibn Djanāḥ in the introduction to *Sefer ha-riḳma.*
124. See the introduction to *Sefer ha-gāluy* by Joseph Ḳimḥī (Berlin, 1887), p. 2, concerning the teachers specially designated for the Hebrew language; *Sefer ha-riḳma,* pp. 227, 310, on the methods of teaching; and further, Ibn 'Aḳnīn, p. 8, regarding the textbooks and the time when a youth should study grammar.
125. See *Diwan Samuel ha-nāgīd,* no. 96, the superscription and line 6, and cf. Ibn 'Aḳnīn, p. 10.
126. Ibn 'Aḳnīn, p. 50.
127. Ibid., p. 11. It should be assumed that this is neither a program nor a recommendation but an opinion based on experience.
128. *Sefer Yā'īr N'tībh* by Judah b. Samuel Ibn 'Abbās, chap. 15, in Güdemann, *Das jüdische Unterrichtswesen,* p. 59.
129. Saadya b. Danān, folio 29a.
130. *Diwan Samuel ha-nāgīd,* no. 73, in particular, line 11; and concerning the Talmud schools of Spain see Abraham b. Dā'ūd, p. 56.
131. See Responsa Alfasi, no. 294; and for the questions they addressed to him, Harkavy, *T'shūbhōt ha-g'ōnīm,* nos. 519, 520, and Responsa Ibn Migash, no. 112.
132. Ibn 'Aḳnīn, p. 52.
133. *Sefer ha-maftēaḥ* (Vienna, 1847), folio 25a: "A student from Spain already addressed a question to me and I answered him"; and cf. S. Assaf, "Sefer m'gillat s'tārīm by R. Nissim b. Jacob of Kairawān," *Tarbīṣ* 12:47: "Some of my students had a difficult question . . . and I resolved it for them," from which it can be inferred that he meant students seated directly before him.
134. *Sefer ha-yāshār* by Rabbēnū Tam, ed. Meḳīṣē Nirdāmīm, p. 90. In his notes (loc. cit.), Rosenthal expresses the opinion that those students from Spain studied with Rabbēnū Gershōm when he was in France and not in Mayence, and this is likewise the opinion of my teacher, the late V. Aptowitzer in the introduction to *R. Eliezer b. Joel ha-levi,* p. 334, whereas B. Z. Benedict conjectures that the meaning of the word "S'fārād" in this passage is "Italia"—see his article "L'Tōl'dōtāv shel merkaz ha-tōra b'-Provence," *Tarbīṣ* 22:108—but this means making geographical names lose their proper identity. S. Assaf had no doubts in this regard; see his article "Ḥalīfat she'ēlōt u-t'shūbhōt bēn S'fārād ve-Ashk'nāz," *Tarbīṣ* 8:162.

The practice of the students to seek out the personal proximity of the teachers paralleled the practice of the young *fukarah,* and Moslem writers of the Middle Ages recommended it in their pedagogical treatises. But this is merely one example of similarity or—to be more precise—identity between the pedagogical approach of the Moslems and that of the Jews.

135. See al-Ḥumaidī, pp. 124–27.
136. *Dhakhīra* I, 1, pp. 199–200.
137. Responsa Alfasi, nos. 75, 133 (ed. Bilgoray, no. 34).
138. Ibid., no. 223.
139. Cf. Ribera: Disertaciones 1:268.
140. *Diwan Samuel ha-nāgīd,* no. 96, line 6.
141. Ibid., 1:173, lines 13–16.
142. Introduction to the *Writings of Ḥayyūdj,* ed. Nutt, p. 1.
143. See Assaf in *Tarbīṣ* 3:214, and regarding this translator, cf. *HÜ* 924. Touching this subject, cf. the article of J. Blau, "Ma'amādān shel ha-'ibhrīt we-ha-'arābhīt bēn Y'hūdīm dōbhrē 'arābhīt . . . ," *L'shōnēnū* 26:282. See also Morris, *Tōl'dōt ha-ḥinūkh* 2:87–88, whose proofs in the matter of the knowledge of Hebrew are convincing only insofar as they relate to the understanding of a sermon by a nonlocal preacher and the like.
144. See J. Blau regarding the half-Arabic known as "Judaeo-Arabic" that the Jewish texts in the Middle Ages contained, *Tarbīṣ* 28:370–71, and see there notes 75, 76.
145. من in the sense of *de* see González Palencia, no. 486, lines 1, 2, 4, 7, and no. 635, line 1; G. S. Colin, "Notes sur l'arabe d'Aragon," *Islamica* 4:166; الى in the sense of *a,* see González Palencia, introductory volume, p. 130.
146. F. I. Simonet, *Glosario de voces ibéricas y latinas usadas entre los mozárabes precedido de un estudio sobre el dialecto hispano-mozárabe* (Madrid, 1889), pp. xciff.
147. G. S. Colin, "Un document nouveau sur l'arabe dialectal d'Occident au XIIe siècle," *Hespéris* 12:6–7.
148. A. Steiger, *Contribución a la fonética del hispano-arabe* (Madrid, 1932), pp. 100, 314; Colin, "Notes sur l'arabe d'Aragon," pp. 164–65.
149. See the passages in Alfasi's responsa that were recorded by Blau; "Hishtaḳfūtām shel lahagīm b'ṭeḳstīm 'arbhiyīm-y'hūdiyīm mi-y'mē ha-bēnāyīm," *Tarbīṣ* 27:86; and cf. Colin in *EI*^{2} (English ed.) 1:502 (*Al-Andalus,* Spanish-Arabic).
150. B. Cohen, "Three Arabic Halakhic Discussions of Alfasi," *JQR* n.s. 19: 392, line 10, and also his responsa in MS. Bodl. 2794, no. 2, p. 1, line 10; also cf. Colin in *EI*^{2}, p. 503.
151. See D. H. Baneth, "The Tanwīn in Its Development to a Separate Word in Judaeo-Arabic Texts" (in Hebrew), *BJPES* 12:141–53, and cf. Colin, *EI*^{2}.
152. Responsa Alfasi, MS. Bodl. 2794, no. 7, line 10, and cf. Blau, *Grammar of Judaeo-Arabic in the Middle Ages* (in Hebrew) (Jerusalem, 1962), § 361, and Colin, *EI*^{2}. Also see González Palencia, no. 2, line 5.
153. González Palencia, no. 193; *Ḳōbheṣ,* part 3, no. 111; Blau, *Grammar,* § 227, 3; Dozy, *Recherches* 2:lxv; and the memoirs of Baidhaḳ that were written in Morocco in the middle of the twelfth century and published

by Lévi-Provençal, *Documents inédits d'histoire almohade* (Paris, 1928), p. 09. See further H. Pérès, "L'arabe dialectale en Espagne musulmane aux X e et XIe siècles de notre ère," *Mélanges W. Marçais,* p. 296.

154. Goitein in *Tarbīṣ* 24:31.
155. Blau, *Grammar,* no. 126.
156. Goitein, *Tarbīṣ* 24:144, line 13; Responsa Alfasi, MS. Bodl. 2794, no. 3, p. 1, line 19.
157. Responsa Alfasi, MS. Bodl. 2794, no. 10, line 8; cf. Blau, *Grammar,* § 219.
158. Cf. Blau, *Grammar,* § 273.
159. Responsa Alfasi, MS. Bodl. 2794, no. 2, p. 1, line 10, and p. 2, line 1; no. 5, p. 2, line 15; no. 6, p. 2, line 7; no. 10, lines 8, 18.
160. Incorrect cases: González Palencia, no. 7, lines 1, 4; no. 10, line 1; no. 476, line 6; no. 504, line 2; no. 589, line 4. Hypercorrections no. 586, line 1; no. 669, line 2.
161. Moses Ibn Djiḳaṭilla, *Translation of the Writings of Ḥayyūdj,* ed. Nutt, p. 64 (*muḥlefet min* corresponding to *mubaddala min*).
162. M'naḥem Ben Sārūḳ, *Maḥberet* (ed. Filipowski), folio 12b (*ṭerem* with the meaning of *ḳabla* instead of *lifnē*); *T'shūbhat talmidē M'naḥem Ben Sārūḳ* (ed. Stern) (Vienna, 1870), p. 28, line 13; Moses Ibn Djiḳaṭilla (trans. of Ḥayyūdj), p. 41, line 22 (*l'ma'an* becomes a purely causal word; *kh'mo* as a conjunction).
163. Dūnash (*'ābhār* in the sense of being permissible, corresponding to *djāza*), see Bacher, *ZDMG* 49:386; *T'shūbhat talmidē M'naḥem Ben Sārūḳ,* p. 72 (*abhnē millūīm yāḳūm m'ḳōm ha-sefer* corresponding to *ḳāma maḳāma*); D. Yellin, "L'hasagat talmidē M'naḥem Ben Sārūḳ," *Jubilee Volume S. Krauss,* p. 128 (*karūt* with the sense of *munfaṣal,* not in the construct state).
164. See Moses Ibn Djiḳaṭilla (trans. of Ḥayyūdj), p. 59, line 2; and cf. M. Gottstein, " 'Iyūnē lāshōn 'al y'sōd targūmē Millōt ha-higayōn l'ha-Rambam," *L'shōnēnū* 15:176.
165. See Dūnash, *Sefer T'shubhat Dunash,* ed. Shroter (Breslau, 1866) p. 76: *v'-etamrūḳē ha-nāshīm hēm ha-sāmīm ha-m'mar'ḳḳōt bahem et gūfōtān.*
166. In the chapters on the influence of Arabic on the Romance dialects spoken in Spain in the days of Moslem rule, Menendez Pidal dwelt, in point of fact, on influence in the lexical area alone; see R. Menendez Pidal, *Los origenes del español,* 3d ed., pp. 453–54, 508–9.
167. Responsa Alfasi in Harkavy, *T'shūbhōt ha-g'ōnīm,* no. 165; MS. Bodl. 2794, no. 5, line 8, and no. 6, p. 1, line 1, p. 2, line 1; Goitein, *JJS* 12:134.
168. Maimonides, *Hilkhōt Matnōt 'Aniyīm* 9:5; Neumann 1:44, 89; Loeb, *REJ* 13:199.
169. Regarding the custom of locating the offices of the community there, see Responsa Ibn Adret, part 5, no. 222.
170. Responsa Alfasi, no. 13; Harkavy, *T'shūbhōt ha-g'ōnīm,* no. 165; Judah al-Barcelōnī, *Sefer ha-sh'ṭārōt,* p. 131. In the sources from the eleventh and the beginning of the twelfth century, the title of *b'rūrīm* was accorded to judges, contrary to what is explained by Neumann 1:35–36, 40, and see the sources he mentions.
171. Responsa Ibn Migash in *P'ēr ha-dōr,* nos. 211, 214.

172. See Responsa Ibn Adret, part 1, no. 617, and part 7, no. 450.
173. Abraham b. Dā'ūd, p. 51, line 8; R. Judah al-Barcelōnī, *Sefer ha-sh'ṭārōt,* p. 131.
174. See the account of R. Nathan the Babylonian in Neubauer, *Med. Jew. Chr.* 1:85; S. Assaf, Iggrūt R. Samuel b. 'Ēlī, Tarbiṣ 1–3.
175. J. S. Reid, *The Municipalities of the Roman Empire* (Cambridge, 1913), p. 448; E. Pérez Pujol, *Historia de las instituciones sociales de la España goda* (Valencia, 1896) 2:260ff., 297ff., 305. Pérez Pujol expressed the opinion that the ancient municipality (the municipium) continued to exist throughout the days of Visigothic rule and extended into the Mozarab community. In contrast to him, Sanchez Albornoz endeavored to prove that the ancient municipium disappeared entirely in the first half of the seventh century and that there is no room for the assumption of continuity in the days of Arab rule; see *Ruina y extinción del municipio romano en España e instituciones que le reemplazaron* (Buenos Aires, 1943), pp. 43, 56ff., 83, 101. But the distinguished Spanish historian only demonstrates the change in the activities of the municipality; see, e.g., p. 52, about elections of officeholders in the later period of Visigothic rule and what the author says about the renewal of the ancient democratic institution of assemblies by the inhabitants that occurred after the liquidation of Visigothic rule; pp. 84–85, 93–94.
176. Simonet, p. 111.
177. See Baron, *The Jewish Community* (1942) 1:204. How great was the continuity of institutions in the Jewish communities of the Greco-Roman diaspora can be concluded, among other things, from the practice—still accepted in the thirteenth century—of choosing those who were to hold office for a period of a Jewish year; see Responsa Ibn Adret, part 3, no. 434, and part 4, no. 312.
178. Responsa Ibn Adret, part 3, no. 434; Responsa Āsher, chap. 7, no. 3.
179. Responsa Ibn Adret, part 1, no. 729; part 3, no. 417; part 4x, no. 260; part 5, no. 126. Cf. Neumann 1:48.
180. Responsa Āsher, chap. 2, nos. 27, 28.
181. Responsa Alfasi, no. 13 (ed. Bilgoray, no. 85).
182. See Baer, *Urkunden* 1:1052; Neumann 1:53–54.
183. Arabic remained the language of the regulations for many generations in the era of Christian rule; see Responsa Ibn Adret, part 3, no. 427.
184. R. Judah al-Barcelōnī, *Sefer ha-sh'ṭārōt,* p. 132; Responsa Ibn Adret, part 3, no. 395: *This* regulation, however, was not read in the synagogue as is customary with all regulations, and see there no. 424, which states that it is precisely the cantor who must read them. This was also the practice with respect to the other announcements; see Responsa Ibn Adret, part 5, no. 150; Responsa Yōm Ṭōbh b. Abraham Ishbīlī, no. 50.
185. Responsa Alfasi, no. 303.
186. Ibid., no. 281.
187. See Neumann 1:46.
188. Responsa Alfasi, MS. Bodl. 2794, no. 5.
189. Ibid., no. 6.
190. Reid, *Municipalities of the Roman Empire,* pp. 450–51; S. D. Goitein,

"Ḥayē ha-ṣibbūr ha-y'hūdiyīm l'-ēr Kitbhe ha-g'nīza," *Zion* 26:173–74. For the later Middle Ages see my *Jews in Egypt and Syria* 2:393.

191. In the Jewish sources of the period of Moslem rule the *ma'ūna* is not mentioned, but its Arabic name, customary for non-Koranic taxes in Moslem Spain (see *A'māl al-a'lām,* p. 15), and its being current in all the Jewish communities in Spain throughout the generations of Christian rule leave no room for doubt that it was already in effect in the days of the Omayyad caliphate. Its importance is demonstrated by the large number of responsa that deal with it. Regarding its collection from the slaughter of animals and the sale of wine, see Responsa Āsher, chap. 6, no. 14, and from business transactions, see ibid., nos. 7, 13, and 17a, col. 1; also cf. Loeb, *REJ* 13:203. As for the *ma'ūna* being designated for the maintenance of the teachers and cantors, see Responsa Āsher, chap. 7, no. 10, and for the fixing of the remuneration of rabbis, see the account of Abraham b. Dā'ūd, p. 68, about R. Moses b. Ḥanōkh.
192. Responsa Alfasi, ed. Bilgoray, no. 38 (included in ed. Livorno, no. 281).
193. R. Judah al-Barcelōnī, cited in *Ṭūr Ḥōshen Mishpāṭ,* no. 9.
194. Responsa Alfasi, no. 160.
195. Documentos, no. 1; see also *T'shūbhōt g'ōnē GMUM,* no. 213, and see there the comment of Müller.
196. Responsa Alfasi, nos. 6, 23, 247.
197. Ibid., nos. 135, 247.
198. Ibid., nos. 23, 247.
199. Lévi-Provençal 3:230.
200. The same as note 198.
201. Responsa Ibn Adret, part 1, no. 617; Baer, *Urkunden* 2:157.
202. Responsa Ibn Adret, part 2, no. 326; part 3, no. 281; part 5, no. 249.
203. Responsa Āsher, chap. 6, nos. 14, 17; chap. 13, no. 20. Also in this context it must be noted that we have no data about this practice among the Jewish communities of Spain during the time of Moslem rule; however, not only do the many data from the time of Christian dominance point to its antiquity, but also so does the fact that the royal administration of the Spanish Omayyads relied on this method.
204. Responsa Alfasi, no. 6, and the opinion of Ibn Migash, which is cited in the Responsa R. Āsher, chap. 13, no. 5. See Maimonides, *Hilkhōt matnōt 'Aniyīm* 9:7, and commentary of R. David b. Zimra, and see, in addition, Responsa Āsher, chap. 6, no. 2, and chap. 13, no. 14.
205. Responsa Ibn Adret, part 4, no. 86, part 3, no. 400, where it is stated that this is an ancient practice, and part 5, no. 220; see also Responsa R. Āsher, chap. 6, no. 29, chap. 7, no. 11: There too there is mention of "a custom that is spread throughout the diaspora."
206. Responsa Ibn Adret, part 4, no. 312.
207. Responsa R. Āsher, chap. 27, no. 1.
208. See *Diwan Samuel ha-nāgīd,* no. 39, line 5.
209. Ibid., no. 36, line 3; no. 38, superscription and line 4.
210. Responsa Ibn Migash, no. 120; and regarding the burial of Moslems in their homes, see Ibn Bashkuwāl 1:130, 300. In the Near East Jews sometimes also buried the deceased person in his home.
211. Abraham b. Dā'ūd, pp. 60–61; *Shīrat Yisrāēl,* p. 72, last line.

212. Concerning the removal of the remains of deceased Jews from Egypt to Palestine see my *Jews in Egypt and Syria* 2:362–63; and on the conveyance of the dead for burial in Nehardea, Mann, *Jews* 2:335. For the transfer of the Moslem dead in Spain, see Ocana Jiménez, "Nuevas inscripciones arabes de Cordoba," *Al-Andalus* 17:387.
213. About Seville, see *The Jews of Moslem Spain* 1:306; for Tarragona, ibid., p. 342; for Tortosa, ibid., p. 343; for Guadalajara, see *The Jews of Moslem Spain* 2:234–35; for Valencia, ibid., p. 281f; and for Alméria, ibid., p. 295f.
214. F. Cantera, "Cementerios hebreos de España," *Sefarad* 13:363–64.
215. F. Balaguer and V. Valenzuela, "Los hallazgos de 'El Fossalé,' " *Argensola* 6:350.
216. Ibn al-Khaṭīb, quoted by Dozy in his introduction to the edition of Ibn 'Idhārī 1:91.
217. Concerning the Jewish cemetery near the Almodóvar Gate, see J. Andrés Vazquez, "La necrópolis hebraica de Cordoba," (in the periodical) *Algo,* May 4, 1935. Also see Cantera in the article mentioned in note 214, pp. 362–63, and cf. R. Romero y Barros, *BAH* 5:248. Concerning the cemetery north of the city, see Ibn Bashkuwāl 1:295, and as for the Moslems' graves in the cemeteries in this part of the city, see the data from the eleventh century, idem, pp. 53, 135, 140, 168, 195, 278; and cf. *Jews of Moslem Spain* 1:298–99. The skeletons fastened by nails found in the old Jewish cemetery right by the Almodóvar Gate or near it—see Cantera—are apparently the skeletons of criminals who were crucified. Their discovery in this location points to its being a cemetery from the days of the Omayyad caliphate, when crucifixion was the accepted method for the execution of robbers and rebels against the government.
218. Cantera-Millás, p. 36.
219. Ibn Bashkuwāl 1:27.
220. "Indiculus luminosus," *España Sagrada* 11:229.
221. See Maimonides, *Hilkhōt Ēbhel* 4:4; Abūdarham (Jerusalem, 1959), p. 371; Cantera, "Cementerios hebreos de España"; further, A. Duran Sanpere–Millás Vallicrosa, "Una necrópolis judaica en el Montjuich de Barcelona," *Sefarad* 7:238ff., 251ff., and 233 for the fact that there were still burials in this cemetery in the eleventh century. Also see p. 248, an explanation of the remains of coffins; M. Castellarnau and J. Grinda, "La cuesta de los hoyos, ó el cementerio hebreo de Segovia," *BAH* 9:267; F. Fita, "El cementerio hebreo de Sevilla," *BAH* 17:174–75, 183; C. Floriano Cumbriano, "Hallazgo de la necrópolis judaica de la ciudad de Teruel," *BAH* 88:845ff. It is true that most of these studies deal with the Jewish cemeteries of the period of Christian rule, but it should not be assumed that any great change occurred in burial customs. Concerning the role of relatives in a burial, see *Diwan Samuel ha-nāgīd,* no. 39, line 7, and on the lack of a coffin, see ibid., no. 41, line 5. Concealment of jewelry in graves was also practiced among the Jews in the other Moslem countries; see the commentary of David b. Zimra on *Hilkhōt Ēbhel* of Maimonides, 4:2.
222. Saadya b. Danān, folio 29b.
223. Millás, "Epigrafia hebraicoespañola," *Sefarad* 5:296, and see there that

in this instance the thing was done after the conquest of Spain by the Arabs or, at least, in the early Middle Ages.

224. Cantera-Millás, pp. 39ff.; F. Fita, *BAH* 17:177ff.
225. A. S. Yahuda, "Inscripción sepulcral hebraica en Toledo," *BAH* 70:323; his opinion in this matter is preferable to that of Cantera-Millás, p. 42.
226. *Abhnē Zikkārōn,* p. 12, lines 5–8, and Responsa Isaac b. Sheshet, no. 114.
227. See *Bēt Yōsēf,* no. 554, and cf. H. J. Zimmels, *Ashkenazim and Sephardim* (London, 1958), p. 219.
228. See a responsum of Natronai in *Sha'arē ṣedeḳ* 3, part 4, no. 12, and cf. D. Kaufman, *Magazin f. d. Wissenschaft des Judentums* 5:72.
229. *Diwan Samuel ha-nāgīd,* no. 36, superscription and line 1, and no. 39, line 6, where it is stated that he rent his garment before the burial.
230. Ibid., no. 36, line 5; cf. *Kitāb al-Uṣūl* by Ibn Djanāḥ, ed. Neubauer, col. 112, which explains *bārōd: laun mukhaṭṭat bisawwād wa-dukhna;* and see the translation of Judah Ibn Tibbon, ed. Bacher, p. 77: "a color flecked with black and dark tints." The custom of wearing black garments during the days of mourning is in accord with the talmudic prescription in *Ēlū m'galḥīn* 23, and see also *Shabbāt* 114.

    However, wearing black garments as a sign of mourning not only was an old Jewish practice, but also was customary among the members of the other faiths in Spain. Dozy first noted that in Moslem Spain white was the color of mourning; see Dozy, *Dictionnaire des vêtements,* pp. 20, 435, and, in particular, *Recherches,* 1st ed. 1:145–46. Later Pérès, pp. 297–98, collected passages from the compositions of poets where this matter is mentioned. However, there are other passages in Hispano-Arabic literature that mention black as the color of mourning, for which reason Pérès inclined to the conclusion that white was the color of mourning for certain classes of society, especially in the ruling circles of the Omayyads.
231. *Diwan Samuel ha-nāgīd,* no. 41, superscription.
232. Responsa R. Āsher, chap. 27, nos. 1, 2.
233. Ibn 'Abdūn, p. 235, line 8; and see Lévi-Provençal, *Séville musulmane au début du XIIe siècle,* pp. 153–54.
234. Ibn 'Abdūn, p. 241.
235. *Vita Joannis Gorziensis,* Migne 137, col. 302.
236. Ibn Ḥazm, *Al-Fiṣal* 2:41, 50, 108.
237. Ibid., 1:142.
238. Ibid., 2:108.
239. Ibid., 1:174, 223.
240. Ibid., 1:135.
241. *España Sagrada* 6:315–16; Simonet, p. 668.
242. García Goméz, "Polémica religiosa entre Ibn Ḥazm e Ibn al-Nagrīla," *Al-Andalus* 4:7; M. Perlmann, "Eleventh-Century Andalusian Authors on the Jews of Granada," *PAAJR* 18:279ff.
243. See al-Maḳḳarī 1:345.
244. Ibn 'Abdarra'ūf, *Trois traités,* p. 114, lines 1–2.
245. See *Jews of Moslem Spain* 1:316 and see, in addition, Ibn Ḥayyān, ed. Antuña, pp. 30, 61, 123.
246. Al-Maḳḳarī 2:428; Pérès, p. 268.

247. See in detail K. Schoy, *Die Gnomonik der Araber (Die Geschichte der Zeitmessung u. der Uhren,* hrsg. von Basserman-Jordan Bd. 1, Lieferung F, Berlin, 1923), pp. 22, 27.
248. Ibn 'Abdūn, p. 224, line 18, and see Lévi-Provençal, *Séville musulmane,* pp. 76, 149.
249. Al-Maḳḳarī 1:126–27, and see in detail Millás, *Estudio sobre Azarquiel,* p. 9.
250. See Schoy, *Die Gnomonik der Araber,* p. 28.
251. Al-Maḳḳarī 1:99, 350.
252. Ibn 'Idhārī 2:232; Al-Maḳḳarī 1:355.
253. See the letter of Maimonides to Pinḥas b. M'shullām, *Ḳōbhēṣ* (Leipzig, 1859), part 1, p. 25; *Mishneh Tōra, Hilkhōt Ḳ'riat Sh'ma'* 4:5; *Hilkhōt T'filla* 4:4.
254. Cf. the detailed description of the bathhouses in Egypt, *Relation de l'Egypte par Abd-Allatif, médécin arabe de Bagdad* (Paris, 1810), pp. 297ff.
255. See Maimonides, *Kesef Mishne* on *Mishneh Tora, Hilkhōt Miḳvaōt* 4:2 (although their opinion is opposed to that of the French rabbis, who held that drawn water is forbidden only on the basis of Oral Law; see *Bēt Yōsēf, Yoreh Deah,* no. 201).
256. M. Gonzalez Simancas, *Las Sinagogas de Toledo y el baño liturgico judío* (Madrid, 1929), pp. 16–18.
257. Gomez Moreno, "Baño de la judería de Baza," *Al-Andalus* 12:154.
258. Torres Balbás, *Zaragoza,* p. 186.
259. See *Jews of Moslem Spain* 1:212.
260. Ibid., p. 339.
261. Ibid., p. 331. Regarding the bathhouse in the Jewish quarter in Seville, see Torres Balbás, "Notas sobre Seville en la época musulmana," *Al-Andalus* 10:182.
262. Al-Maḳḳarī 1:548, 2:259; al-Muḳaddasī, p. 239.
263. Abū Bakr Muḥammad b. al-Walīd aṭ-Ṭurṭūshī, *Kiṭab al-Ḥawādith wa 'l-bida'* (Tunis, 1959), p. 142.
264. See the introduction of Muḥammad aṭ-Ṭālibī, p. 7.
265. Ibn Kathīr 2:339; Ibn Khallikān in the English translation by de Slane, 3:450.
266. Aḍ-Ḍabbī, *Bughyat al-multamis* (Madrid, 1885), p. 332. As aḍ-Ḍabbī reports it, the Moslem theologian who became angry and slew the Jew did this not because the Jew washed himself in the public bathhouse, and apparently not even because the Moslem lad served him, but because he called him *Aḥmadīl,* ("little Mohammed"), and in his opinion this was an act of contempt against their prophet.
267. Ibn 'Abdūn, p. 238, line 18.
268. In the archaeological museum in Toledo there is a bathtub from Moslem times that is 2 meters long, 66 centimeters wide, and 38 centimeters deep.
269. On the bathhouses in Moslem Spain, see J. R. Méleda, " 'El Bañuelo,' Baños arabes que subsisten en Granada," *BAH* 68:503ff.; González Palencia, no. 987; and Torres Balbás, "Los edificios hispanomusulmanos," *RIEEI* 1:102ff.
270. See Responsa Maimonides, no. 185, which states that this was the prac-

tice in Spain, where they had no apprehension about "mingled cloth"; cf. Dozy, *Dictionnaire des vêtements,* pp. 95ff.; and E. W. Lane, *Manners and Customs of the Modern Egyptians* (London, 1954), p. 30. Regarding the *djubba,* worn in Spain at times when it was neither hot nor cold, see Dozy, *Dictionnaire des vêtements,* p. 113.

271. See Cantera, *Sinagogas,* p. 355; Neumann 2:151; and cf. S. Assaf, *T'shūbhōt ha-g'ōnīm mi-tōkh ha-g'nīza* (Gaonic Responsa from Geniza MSS.) (Jerusalem, 1929), pp. 92–93.
272. See the list of the synagogues in Toledo during the era of Christian rule in C. Roth, "A Hebrew Elegy on the Martyrs of Toledo," *JQR* n.s. 39: 123–50.
273. This synagogue was beset by fire in 1250; see Kaufmann, "Les synagogues de Tolède," *REJ* 38:250, and also E. Lambert, "Les synagogues de Tolède," *REJ* 84:24–25.
274. On Tudela see Fr. Fuentes, *Catálogo de los archivos eclesiasticos de Tudela* (Tudela, 1944), no. 91; on Valencia, see J. R. Pertegás, *La judería de Valencia,* in J. Sanchis y Sivera, *La Iglesia parroquial de Santo Tomás de Valencia* (Valencia, 1913), p. 262.
275. Neubauer, *Aus der Petersburger Bibliothek* (Leipzig, 1866), pp. 120–21.
276. N. Wieder, "Islamic Influences on the Hebrew Cult," *Melilah* 2:45–46.
277. An inscription such as one from Tarragona from the sixth century C.E.: Cantera, "Hallazgo de neuvas lápidas hebraicas en el Levante español," *Sefarad* 15:393–94; and another from that city, apparently from the end of the Middle Ages: Cantera, "Neuva lápida hebraica de Tarragona," *Sefarad* 10:173–76, and cf. in his *Sinagogas,* p. 316.
278. See Cantera, "Epigrafía hebraica en el museo arqueologico de Madrid," *Sefarad* 11:108ff. Fita at first thought that this was an inscription from the end of the thirteenth century—see his article "Inscripciones romanas y hebreas," *BAH* 24:30ff. However, see a much later article by him: "Siete inscripciones hebreas de Toledo," *BAH* 47:515–16. Cantera apparently inclines to the view that this is an inscription from a mosque, but this is unlikely, for why should a Hebrew inscription be part of a mosque? If this were not an inscription in two languages (or two inscriptions on the remains of one structure), it would be possible to assume that the stone bearing the Hebrew inscription served as a building block for a non-Jewish structure. But the combination of Hebrew and Arabic in the same line proves that this is a special inscription for a Jewish structure. See, in addition, Millás, "Notas epigráficas," *Sefarad* 11:391–92. For an inscription on the inside of a door of a synagogue in Cordova, see Cantera, *Sinagogas,* p. 10.
279. C. Roth, "The Art of European Synagogues" (G. K. Loukomski, *Jewish Art in European Synagogues* [London, 1947]), p. 17; R. Krautheimer, *Mittelalterliche Synagogen* (Berlin, 1927), p. 116.
280. Cantera, *Sinagogas,* p. 8.
281. Torres Balbás, "La Mezquita mayor de Granada," *Al-Andalus* 10:419.
282. Cantera, *Sinagogas,* pp. 59–60.
283. Krautheimer, *Mittelalterliche Synagogen,* pp. 84–85, 100ff., 140ff.
284. For the popular designation of the pulpit (the people called it *al-minbar*), see Responsa Maimonides, no. 186. For the location of the pulpit, see

Krautheimer, *Mittelalterliche Synagogen,* pp. 87–88, 94, and see the illustrations on pp. 18, 19; and see p. 121 and cf. p. 114. The custom of making the pulpit out of wood, which was maintained until a later period, as is shown by an inscription in the synagogue of Samuel ha-levi Abulafia (see Cantera, *Sinagogas,* p. 97), explains the mishap that caused the death of R. Ḥanōkh; see *The Jews of Moslem Spain* 1:380. And see *The Jews of Moslem Spain* 2:309, note 34.

285. The opinion that the New Synagogue Joseph Ibn Shōshan built, according to the statement of the inscription on his monument—see *Abhnē Zikkārōn,* no. 75—is to be identified with the structure of Santa Maria la Blanca was expressed by Lambert in "Les Synagogues de Tolède," pp. 25–27. This is also the opinion of Kaufmann, see *REJ* 38:252, and Cantera, *Sinagogas,* p. 45. It is true that Lambert relies chiefly upon the embellishments, and following Marçais had indicated their later elements; see G. Marçais, *L'Architecture musulmane d'Occident* (Paris, 1954), p. 366. Lambert observed that some of the embellishments were added at a later time than the construction; see E. Lambert, *Art musulman et art chrétien dans la péninsule ibérique* (Toulouse, 1958), p. 303. Torres Balbás came to the conclusion that the structure was built circa 1260 and inclined to identify it with the synagogue of Ibn Abīdarham; see *Art Hispaniae* 4: *Arte almohade, arte nazarí, arte mudéjar* (Madrid, 1949), pp. 43–46. But from the sequence in which the author of the lament for the incidents of the year 4151 enumerates the Jewish houses of worship in Toledo, it appears quite clearly that there were then in the city four large synagogues: the ancient temple *(ha-hēkhal ha-ḳadmōn),* the Great Synagogue, the New Synagogue, and the synagogue of Samuel ha-levi. Hence it is possible to identify the structure of Santa Maria la Blanca with the Great Synagogue or the New Synagogue. At the outset it should be assumed that the Great Synagogue was built in an earlier period, but certain architectural elements actually demonstrate that Santa Maria la Blanca is an edifice dating from the end of the twelfth century. The bows in the shape of an unpointed horseshoe, the "hidden" bows above them, the octagonal pillars—all these are found in other structures in Castile that were built at the beginning of the thirteenth century; see Torres Balbás, "La Mezquita mayor de Granada."
286. G. Marçais, *L'architecture musulmane d'Occident,* pp. 192, 228, 241.
287. Cantera, *Sinagogas,* p. 62, and cf. p. 11, on the balcony in the synagogue of Cordova.
288. Krautheimer, *Mittelalterliche Synagogen,* pp. 132–33.
289. F. Fita, *BAH* 5:382ff.
290. See Neubauer, *Isr. Letterbode* 4: 333–34, and Berliner, ibid. 5:31–32.
291. See *Jews of Moslem Spain* 1:326.
292. For a superscription such as the one composed by M'naḥem Ben Sārūḳ, see Luzzato, *Bēt ha-yōṣēr* 31a; and see *Diwan Moses Ibn Ezra,* no. 92, *wa-mimmā rasamahu 'ala 't-tēbha,* and on the last line the date (1107), and on line 4, about the designs that were on the ark. Further, see Brody's commentaries, p. 175.
293. Cantera, *Sinagogas,* p. 29.
294. Responsa Ibn Adret, part 2, no. 52: "The places in the synagogue have

owners who are known and each one of them has an established claim on his location and the great early teachers have concurred in this"; see further Responsa Āsher, chap. 5, nos. 3, 4 (from the Moslem area in Spain), 5–7; Responsa Yōm Ṭōbh b. al-Ishbīlī, no. 18; and cf. Neuman 2:148ff., on the synagogues in Christian Spain.

295. *T'shūbhōt GMUM,* no. 171, which, in the editor's opinion, is that of Joseph Ibn Abītūr, and see there the note. Further, see Mann, "Responsa," *JQR* n.s. 10:137.

296. Responsa Ibn Migash, no. 95.

297. Responsa Alfasi, no. 281.

298. *Ha-Manhīg* 19a.

299. *Seder Rabh-Amrām* (Warsaw, 1865) 18b; *Ha-Manhīg* 22b; R. Judah al-Barcelōnī, *Sefer ha-'ittīm,* p. 171; and for the rite in general see *Sha'arē simḥa* (Furth, 1861), part 1, p. 59 (in the middle), and cf. S. Assaf, *T'shūbhōt ha-g'ōnīm mi-tōkh ha-g'nīza,* p. 86. Regarding the worshipers' lack of knowledge of Hebrew that, still in the ninth century, required their reciting the morning benedictions in the synagogue, see S. B. Freehof, "Home Rituals and the Spanish Synagogues," *Studies and Essays in Honor of Abraham A. Neuman* (Philadelphia, 1962), p. 219, who inclines, unjustifiably, to explain this practice as a case of disregard for the religious precepts.

300. Responsa Ibn Migash, no. 86.

301. I. Garbell, "The Pronunciation of Hebrew in Medieval Spain," *Homenaje Millás* 1:647ff. In this paper the passage on the pronunciation of the letter *shīn* on pp. 665–66 should be amended. (According to the author, a printing error occurred, and there should therefore be added to the S a sign emphasizing that the *shīn* was pronounced in a manner approximating our own pronunciation, not as *sin,* as printed.

302. Responsa Maimonides, no. 207. It should be assumed that this custom was widespread throughout the lands ringing the Mediterranean and not just in Egypt.

303. *Sha'arē simḥa,* part 1, pp. 98–99.

304. See *Ha-Manhīg* 64a, and cf. S. Assaf, "li-Ṣmīḥat ha-mer-kāzīm ha-yisrāēligīm bi-t'ḳūfat ha-g'ōnīm," *Hashiloaḥ* 35:508. On the practice in Saragossa in a later era, see Responsa Isaac b. Shēshet, no. 347; cf. also S. B. Freehof, "Home Rituals," pp. 219–20, 225.

305. The *siḳlāṭūn* in the Near East was generally blue, whereas in Spain a greater liking for red was expressed; see Pérès, pp. 320–21. Concerning the chests, see Ibn 'Abdūn, pp. 226, lines 1–2; 250, lines 4–5. For the woods that give forth a scent of perfume, see *Diwan Ibn Gabirol,* part 5, nos. 11, 16. Regarding the many rugs, coverlets, and cushions, cf. the list in the legacy of an Aragonese noble from the middle of the twelfth century in Lacarra 2, no. 280. (It should be assumed that there was a similarity between the furnishing of his house and that of a house in Moslem Spain.)

306. See Lévi-Provençal 3:420. On lettuce and carrots see Ibn 'Abdūn, p. 232, line 18, and concerning the sponge cake, see ibid., p. 234, line 6; p. 235, line 9; and p. 274. Regarding the verses inscribed in the bowls, see *Diwan Moses Ibn Ezra,* nos. 111, 133, 139, 165, 245.

307. See Steinschneider, *Zeitschrift f. d. rel. Inter. d. Jud. v. Frankel* 2 (1845), p. 78, and in his "Introduction to Arabic Literature of the Jews," *JQR* 10:626. See also Ratzaby in *L'shōnēnū* 13:165–66.
308. See Documentos, no. 7; González Palencia, nos. 373, 714, 1141 bis, 1145, 1148.
309. See González Palencia, *Introductory Volume,* p. 58. (The first document in which this market is mentioned is no. 1099 from the year 1142.)
310. See al-Maḳḳarī 1:134–35; Ibn 'Abdūn, p. 244; Ibn 'Abdarra'ūf, *Trois traités,* p. 112.
311. See above p. 93; as-Saḳaṭī, pp. 67–68; Ibn 'Abdarra'ūf, *Trois traités,* p. 87.
312. From Alvaro's letter to the proselyte Bodo, Kayserling concluded that in the ninth century polygamy was uncommon among the Jews of Spain; see *MGWJ* 9:250. In the collection of Alfasi's responsa there are altogether five questions on this subject: Nos. 151 and 282 deal with the arrangements of a family in which there are two wives without mentioning how the second marriage was contracted—whether it was done with the consent of the first wife or when she failed to bear a child over a period of many years; nos. 67 and 188 are apparently two versions of the same responsum, which deals with the case of a man who threatened to marry a second wife but could not; nos. 120 and 185 deal with the departure of the husband to another city where he married a second time without the first wife's knowledge or after she had refused to leave her city. In no. 120 it is related that the first wife claimed the "penalty that is customary in Spain from the earliest times"—i.e., 200 *dīnār ḳāsimiyya* —from which it can be concluded that there existed in Andalusia from ancient times an enactment regarding the penalty imposed upon anyone who takes a second wife in spite of his obligations. According to Vives, this *dīnār* was named after a mintmaster of 'Abdarraḥmān III; see A. Vives, *La moneda castellana* (Madrid, 1901), p. 9.
313. Responsa Ibn Migash, no. 129.
314. Samson, "Apologeticus," Lib. II, praefatio 6, *España Sagrada* 2:381.
315. See Baer, *Urkunden* 1, according to the index, p. 1164; 2, p. 591.
316. See Ibn 'Abdūn, pp. 227, line 17; 228, lines 3, 9; 250, lines 15–17. In Seville, in whose vicinity there were forests, the ovens in the bakeries were also heated with wood; see ibid., p. 231.
317. Ibid., p. 249, lines 11–12; Pérès, pp. 319–20.
318. See Dozy, *Suppl.* 1:76, and see Lacarra 2, no. 280.
319. Responsa Alfasi, no. 252.
320. See *Diwan Moses Ibn Ezra,* nos. 32, 97, 135, 171, 189, 195, 211, 237. (The poems nos. 32, 97, and 135 were written on the occasion of the death of his son, Jacob, as is expressly stated in them, and in Brody's opinion —see the index—the same holds for the rest of the aforementioned poems; however, in those poems the name of the deceased son of the poet is not mentioned.)
321. See Ibn 'Abdūn, p. 241, line 5.
322. Ibid., p. 237, line 9.
323. *Sefer ha-'ittīm,* p. 253–54.
324. *Sha'arē simḥa,* p. 43; *Ha-Manhīg* 55–56.

325. See *Sefer ha-shorāshīm,* p. 226, cf. p. 94, and see p. x to volume 2 of the Hebrew edition on this word.
326. Responsa Alfasi, no. 292.
327. *Likkuṭē R. Isaac Ibn Gayyāt,* ed. Taubes, p. 32.
328. Responsa Ibn Migash, no. 87 (who quotes the opinion of Alfasi).
329. *Sefer ha-'ittīm,* p. 252.
330. Abraham Ibn Ezra on *Ḳōh.* 5:1.
331. Responsa Alfasi, no. 281.
332. Samau'al al-Maghribī, *Ifḥām al-yahūd* (ed. Perlmann), p. 57 (of the Arabic text).
333. *T'shūbhōt talmīdē Dūnash,* ed. Stern (Vienna, 1870), p. 9, line 64.
334. See Abraham Maimuni, cited by Wieder, *Melilah* 2:117; from his words it appears that he had in mind not only what was done in the synagogues in Egypt in his time but for many generations preceding him. See also Responsa Ibn Adret, part 2, no. 52.
335. Responsa R. Āsher, chap. 5, no. 2.
336. F. Sarre, "A Fourteenth-Century Spanish Synagogue Carpet," *Burlington Magazine* 56:89.
337. *Sefer ha-'ittīm,* p. 258, and see the description of the Bible scrolls in the poem of Samuel ha-nāgīd that was published by D. Yellin in *Ha-Teḳūfa* 26/27:607.
338. *Sha'arē simḥa,* part 1, p. 114.
339. See Margaliouth in the notes to Samuel ha-nāgīd, *Sefer ha-halākhōt,* p. 113.
340. Elbogen, *Der jüdische Gottesdienst* (Leipzig, 1913), p. 341.
341. Müller, no. 12, and see in his commentaries, p. 29.
342. Elbogen, *Der jüdische Gottesdienst,* p. 173.
343. *Sefer ha-'ittīm,* pp. 264–65, and cf. Elbogen, *Der jüdische Gottesdienst,* p. 171.
344. *Sefer ha-'ittīm,* pp. 266–68, and cf. Elbogen, *Der jüdische Gottesdienst,* pp. 188–89.
345. See Dozy, *Suppl.* 2:453–54.
346. See Pérès, p. 318.
347. Concerning the inability of most Spanish Jews to read a Hebrew book, see above, note 142. On the Hebrew writing of the Judaeo-Arabic literature in Spain, see Bacher, *JQR* 2:506.
348. See the list of these stories (collections) in the introduction of Ḥ. Z. Hirschberg to his edition of *Ḥibbūr yāfe min ha-y'shū'a,* pp. 44–45, and see, on p. 71, his conclusions as to the source of the tales. Further, see J. Blau in *L'shōnenu* 26:283, on the absence of Arabic books of *Adab* from the lists of Jewish libraries.
349. See Ibn 'Abdūn, p. 243, lines 10–11, and cf. Lévi-Provençal, *Séville musulmane,* p. 118.
350. *Dhakhīra* I, 2, p. 177.
351. F. M. Pareja Casañas, *Libro de ajedrez* (Madrid, 1935) I, p. lxxiv.
352. J. Ferrandis Torres, *Marfiles y azabaches españoles,* pp. 92–93.
353. Tassilo v. der Lasa, *Zur Geschichte u. Literatur des Schachspiels, Forschungen* (Leipzig, 1897), pp. 29ff.

354. Al-Marrākushī, pp. 73–74; French paraphrase is in Dozy, *Récherches* 3: 102–4.
355. H. J. R. Murray, *A History of Chess* (Oxford, 1913), p. 203.
356. N. H. Tur-Sinai, "Abraham Ibn Ezra and the Chess Play" (in Hebrew), *Ha-Yarḥōn ha-yisrāēlī l'-shaḥmaṭ,* Tammuz-Ab 1956, pp. 87–89; cf. Gross, *MGWJ* 65:365–69, and see too *MGWJ* 66:158–60.
357. J. Ferrandis Torres, "Muebles hispanoárabes de taracea," *Al-Andalus* 5:459–65.
358. Pareja 1:lxxvii.
359. P. R. v. Bilguer, *Handbuch des Schachspiels* (Berlin, 1922), p. 24.
360. See Dozy, *Suppl.* 1:68; Ibn 'Abdūn, pp. 233, line 19, and 234, line 6. Cf. Lévi-Provençal, *Séville musulmane,* pp. 152, 153; and Lévi-Provençal, 3: 420.
361. Compare *Tur, Ōraḥ Ḥayyim,* no. 267.
362. In the drawings in Spanish manuscripts in Krautheimer, *Mittelalterliche Synagogen,* pp. 95, 97, and 99, are also depicted unshaven men, but these are drawings from Christian Spain.
363. Castellarnau and Grinda, "La Cuesta de los hoyos," p. 267; A. Prevosti, "Estudio tipológico de los restos humanos hallados en la necrópolis judaica de Montjuich [Barcelona]," *Sefarad* 11:78. Regarding the height, the authors of the first-mentioned study assert that the skeletons in Segovia are those of tall human beings, whereas Prevosti maintains that the height of those interred in the cemetery of Barcelona was generally less than medium.
364. Al-Muḳaddasī, p. 243; Ribera: Disertaciones 1:28–29, 31–32, 111–12, 397–98. For Toledo see idem, p. 109. About Romance in the court of the caliph, see Ibn 'Idhārī 2:226–27.
365. See *Diwan Ibn Gabirol,* part 1, p. 173.
366. The name of a Jew in a document is in González Palencia, no. 1134.
367. The name of a Jew, ibid., nos. 674, 1146.
368. The name of a Jewish family, ibid., nos. 588, 605, 1123. In the beginning of the eleventh century, there dwelt in Huesca a family of *fukarah* bearing this name; see Ibn Bashkuwāl 1:163–64.
369. For nicknames of Jews, see González Palencia, nos. 428, 965, 1138.
370. A list of such nicknames in Simonet, *Glosario de voces ibéricas,* pp. lix, xcii–xciii; Codera, *Discurso de entrada en la Real Academia española,* p. 35.
371. See in the list of the introductory volume of González Palencia, pp. 144–45.
372. *P'ēr ha-dōr,* no. 211.
373. The conclusions of M. Gaster, "Aben oder Ibn in hebräischen Namen," *MGWJ* 77:210–11, are not at all convincing. Gaster bases himself upon the family names of Jews who dwelt a long time in Morocco, and even the spelling of *ben* upon which Herzog relies—pp. 386–87—does not prove anything, since the Hebrew writers wanted to impart a Hebrew pattern to the family names. In the Latin documents Lacarra published, the forms *Aben* and *Ibn* appear in almost equal number; see the indices of *EEMCA* 2:562, 569, and 3:691, 710. It is of course possible that when people came to write a document, they were required to use the literary

form of the name, but it can more likely be concluded from this that both expressions were current.

374. See Ibn 'Abdūn, p. 242, lines 16–18.
375. See *Dhakhīra* IV, 1, p. 105, line 4.
376. See *Dīwān Moses Ibn Ezra,* no. 172, line 14.
377. According to Samuel the Nagid, Karaites were to be found, in his time, only "in a few villages near the land of Edom, of whom it is reported that they incline to heresy in secret"; see *Sefer ha-'ittīm,* p. 267. But this information is contradicted by a letter from Toledo from 1053 (Documentos, no. 2) and by Ibn Ḥazm; see *The Jews of Moslem Spain* 2:222–23. It is, of course, correct that the Karaites settled mainly in northern Spain; see Loeb, "Notes sur l'histoire des juifs," *REJ* 19:208.
378. *Diwan Samuel ha-nāgīd,* no. 107, lines 35–38. Schirmann—13:115—minimizes the spread of Karaism in Spain and explains the stand taken by the Nagid as resulting from the influence of the fanaticism of that era.
379. Poznanski, "Mitteilungen aus handschriftlichere Bibel-Commentaren," *ZfHB* 4:17ff.
380. See Asín 1:252–53, and see about the Jewish skeptic in Alméria *The Jews of Moslem Spain* 2:299.
381. See the questions R. Isaac al-Djayyānī asked R. Isaac Alfasi, *P'ēr ha-dōr,* nos. 177, 178.
382. *T'shūbhōt GMUM,* no. 220 (in Müller's opinion this is a responsum of one of the rabbis of Spain, perhaps that of R. Moses b. Ḥanōkh or his son Ḥanōkh).
383. S. Assaf, "Sources for the History of the Jews in Spain" (in Hebrew), *Zion* 4:33.
384. Pp. 39–40, 125–26, and see about rules and responsa in this matter in his other books, S. Assaf, "Slavery and the Slave Trade among the Jews during the Middle Ages" (in Hebrew), *Zion* 4:107.
385. Responsa Alfasi, nos. 5, 14, 24, 60, 131.
386. As-Saḳaṭī, p. 57, lines 1–2.
387. Responsa Alfasi, no. 166.
388. *Sha'arē ṣedeḳ,* part 3, section 6, no. 15, and Saadyana, no. 36. Apparently, these are two versions of the same question. According to the version in *Sha'arē ṣedeḳ,* the question was put before R. Palṭoi and R. Natronai, whereas according to the version in Saadyana, it was put to R. Palṭoi alone. It is true that R. El'āzār was considered one of the members of the academy in Sura, and it would therefore be reasonable that he should put the question to R. Natronai, who was the head of that academy. However, R. Palṭoi is mentioned in both versions and it is possible that R. El'āzār asked this question before coming to Babylonia or, for some reason, sent it later to the head of the Academy of Pumbeditha.
389. *Dhakhīra* IV, 1, p. 105, line 5, and cf. Pérès, p. 385.
390. Ibid.
391. As-Saḳaṭī, p. 68, line 9.
392. See Lévi-Provençal 3:419.
393. About the Jewish magicians who performed such feats, see Asin 5:4.
394. See Targum Jonathan and *Seder 'Ōlām Zūṭā* in Neubauer, *Med. Jew. Chr.* 2:71, in particular the commentary of David Ḳimḥī on this verse. See

further Abu 'l-Walīd, *Sefer ha-shōrāshīm,* p. 348; Ibn Bal'ām, *JQR* 15: 34–35; *Sefer Yōsīpōn,* cf. Dinaburg, *Yisrāēl ba-gōlā* I², 1, p. 340; and finally, Responsa Maimonides, no. 293: "Moses bar Maimon, one of the exiles from Jerusalem who are in Spain, said thus."

395. *Shēbheṭ Y'hūda,* ed. Shoḥat, p. 120, and the editor's commentary, p. 207; the comments of Zunz on the *Travels of Benjamin of Tudela,* ed. Ascher, 2:6–9.
396. A. Castro, *La Realidad historica de España* (Mexico, 1962), pp. 31ff., 41ff., rightly draws attention to this relationship, without being acquainted with the Hebrew sources from the Middle Ages.
397. Abraham b. Dā'ūd, p. 75.
398. *Diwan Ibn Gabirol,* part 1, no. 29, lines 97, 103; no. 31, lines 91–92.
399. *Shīrat Yisrāēl,* pp. 62–80, and cf. Mann, *Texts* 1:263–64.
400. *Ḳōbheṣ,* part 1, p. 26, col. c.
401. Ibid., part 2, p. 40a. His opinion of the Jews in the Near East was not much better; idem, part 2, p. 44, col. b.

CHAPTER THREE

1. In the writings of the Arabic historians, the dates for the death of al-Mu'taḍid are given as the year 460 of the Hegira (1067–1068)—see Ibn 'Idhārī, pp. 283–84—and 461 of the Hegira (1068–1069); see *Dhakhīra* I, p. 124. As for the month, Ibn Ḥayyān first speaks of the second of Djumādā I, and later of the beginning of Djumādā II; see Ibn al-Abbār in *Abbad.* 2:61. However, Ibn al-Athīr, ibid. 2:34, reports that al-Mu'taḍid died on the second of Djumādā II, and Ibn 'Idhārī also mentions the same month. From this it can be concluded that al-Mu'taḍid died on March 29, 1069.
2. *Maṭmaḥ al-anfus,* pp. 21, 83; cf. al-Maḳḳarī 1:345 and 2:443; *Ṭauḳ al-ḥamāma,* p. 346.
3. Ibn 'Abdūn, p. 245. To be sure, the Arab author speaks of *ḍarb an-nawāḳīs,* but Lévi-Provençal, in his French translation, justifiably renders it "the ringing of the bells"—see *Séville musulmane au début du XIIe siècle,* p. 123—since the author testifies that this denounced matter is the accepted practice in the land of the infidels and that there they did not beat with a clapper but rang bells; cf. the note of Lévi-Provençal in his French translation, p. 159.
4. See Ibn 'Abdūn, p. 239.
5. *Dhakhīra* I, 1, pp. 354–55.
6. *A'māl al-a'lām,* pp. 175, 176, 184. This officer received the title *Dhu 'l-wizāratain;* see Ibn Bassām in *Abbad.* 1:323.
7. Al-Maḳḳarī 2:350–51.
8. *Shīrat Yisrāēl,* p. 72; Abraham b. Dā'ūd, pp. 59–60. On the books of Samuel Ibn Nagrela, see *Kitāb ar-Rasā'il* by R. Meïr b. Todros Abulafia (Paris, 1871), pp. 79–80; Responsa of R. Isaac Ibn Albalia in *Tōrātān shel rishōnīm,* ed. Horowitz, part 2, pp. 35–36; and Responsa Alfasi, no. 134, and cf. ed. Bilgoray, no. 161. There he is called *nāsī,* and this title was also given him by Z'raḥiah ha-levi, *Ba'al ha-mā'ōr* (ed. Lemberg), 5a, col. 1, and also by Abraham b. Dā'ūd (the third) in *T'mīm de'īm,* no. 224.

9. Responsa Alfasi, MS. Bodl. 2794, nos. 8, 9 (referring to the transfers of property that were effected many years before the rabbi who pronounced the decision was queried about them).
10. Ibid., no. 6.
11. *Diwān Moses Ibn Ezra,* no. 39, line 8: "Before he mounts the throne of his forebears and inherits their greatness in his own lifetime."
12. *Ḳiṣṣūr Zēkher Ṣaddīḳ* by R. Joseph b. Ṣaddīḳ, p. 93, line 8, where Shartīḳash should be amended to Shartamīḳash; *Diwān Moses Ibn Ezra,* no. 183, and there, on pp. 297–98, the introduction to *Sefer ha-'ānāḳ.* H. Brody demonstrated with decisive proofs that *Sefer ha-'ānāḳ* was dedicated to Abraham b. Meïr Ibn Muhādjir; see his article "L'mī hiḳdīsh R. Mōshē ben 'Ezrā et Sefer ha-tarshīsh?," *ha-Gōren* (1928) 10:60–80. In his opinion the poem no. 183 is a sort of second dedication of the *'Anāḳ;* see his explanations, p. 344. Moses Ibn Ezra wrote the book in his youth—see *Shīrat Yisrāēl,* p. 171—and from this it may be assumed that the activity of Abraham b. Meïr Ibn Muhādjir belongs to the period of al-Mu'tamid. It is true that in point of fact his place of residence is not mentioned along with his full name in any source, but one branch of the Ibn Muhādjir family did dwell in Seville (see below), and one poem in the *Diwān Moses Ibn Ezra*—no. 261—ends with Arabic verses that contain the words *namḍī bi-Ishbīliya . . . wa-nataḥarrash bi-'bn Muhādjir;* cf. Stern, *Al-Andalus* 13:325–26; Cantera, *Sefarad* 9:225; García Gómez, *Al-Andalus* 15:160–61. Since, from among the members of this family, it was precisely with Abraham b. Meïr that Moses Ibn Ezra maintained a strong contact, it can be assumed that this poem was also dedicated to him.

    For his activities on behalf of Jewish communities, see no. 183, 9, and in *Sefer ha-'ānāḳ,* section I, 26, 37, 61, 124, 136, 137. On his erudition in the field of astronomy, see ibid., 19 (in the opinion of Brody—" 'Ēn Tarshīsh," *JJLG* 18:5 [Heb. section]—this is not an allusion to his erudition in this science), 83 (cf. *Mishbeṣet ha-tarshīsh,* p. 57), 98 (cf. ibid., p. 65).
13. See *Diwān Moses Ibn Ezra,* no. 183, lines 15–16, and cf. Brody's explanation, p. 346, and no. 261, 7. To this dignitary are also dedicated the poems 46, 215, in accordance with what Dov Yarden found in the Moscow manuscript; see the article wherein he published a third poem that was also written by this poet in honor of Abū Isḥāk Ibn Muhādjir: "Two New Laudatory Poems by R. Moses b. Ezra," *Biṣārōn* 23:196–97.
14. Documentos, no. 5.
15. *Shīrat Yisrāēl,* p. 73. Graetz 6:102 conjectures that he was the brother of Abū Isḥāk Ibrāhim Ibn Muhādjir, but this conjecture is without foundation, and indeed in another passage in his book—p. 373—he only states that he was his relative. In the opinion of Graetz and also Neubauer, "Notice sur la lexicographie hébraïque," *JA* 1862, 2:248, this Abū Sulaimān Ibn Muhādjir is identical with David b. Hagar, the judge in Granada who wrote a treatise on laws of divorce and one on grammar (see *The Jews of Moslem Spain* 2:142). This conjecture is also without support. Not only does Graetz amend the name of the Granadan judge that appears in two Hebrew sources in the same form (Hagar) into Ibn Muhādjir, but he also relies on a faulty text of the first source in which

Abū Sulaimān Ibn Muhādjir is mentioned, i.e., *Sefer Shīrat Yisrāēl.* In the quotation from it found in *Sefer ha-yōḥasīn,* it is not asserted that Abū Sulaimān Ibn Muhādjir was from Seville, and it is stated, on the other hand, that he was a disciple of Alfasi instead of being his contemporary, as is reported in *Sefer Shīrat Yisrāēl.* In other words, not only are the names of the two persons different, but so are their places of residence and their literary activities. David b. Hagar was a judge in Granada, and Abū Sulaimān was a poet in Seville; cf. Steinschneider, *Ar. Lit.,* p. 143.

16. *Shīrat Yisrāēl,* p. 73; *Diwān Moses Ibn Ēzra,* no. 225 (where the correct form of the name, Ben Azhar, is found). According to the superscription, the poet wrote the poem in his youth, and there is thus no doubt as to the time in which Abu 'l-Fatḥ lived. His name is in lines 3 and 17. See there line 4: "He is our lord and our commander"; lines 7, 10, 24: "the noble"; and line 15: "when I speak of you in song." For the poet's plea that he speak favorably of him to the *nāsī,* see lines 24f. and 39f. Bialik-Rawnitzky, in their notes and explanations on p. 21, offer the interpretation that Abu 'l-Fatḥ was, as it were, incited to act against the poet. This was not so, and for this reason they met with difficulties in their explanations of those stanzas in which he asks Abu 'l-Fatḥ to speak favorably on his behalf. Concerning the status of the family, see also *Diwān Judah Halevi,* part 1, no. 103, line 8; part 2, no. 93, line 5.

    According to Graetz 6:103, he was one of the disciples of Alfasi and a rabbi in Seville, but this is an error he arrived at from the identification with Abu 'l-Fatḥ ibn Zagora, in whose honor Moses Ibn Ezra wrote poetry; cf. *CB* 1810 and also *JQR* 10:131. However, this is a conjecture that is utterly unfounded. In like manner, there can be no agreement with Graetz's opinion that Abu 'l-Fatḥ Ibn Azhar and Naḥman Ibn Azhar, about whom Judah Halevi poetized, are one and the same person, or that Naḥman was his father. Since the Hebrew name of Abu 'l-Fatḥ was El'āzār, it is impossible that he was identical to Naḥman, and seeing that Judah Halevi was younger than Abu 'l-Fatḥ, it is not to be supposed that he poetized in honor of the father but surely intended this for his son.

17. Abraham b. Dā'ūd, p. 76.
18. His father's name is mentioned in his commentary on Judges (see below), p. 7. About the family name, see Fürst, *Litbl. d. Orients* 12: col. 451.
19. The few data about his biography are given us by Moses Ibn Ezra in *Shīrat Yisrāēl,* p. 73 (the Arabic original, *CB* 1292ff.). In the Leningrad manuscript—see *REJ* 17:176—these words are added: *wa-min dhāwi 'l-aḥsāb al-karīma wa-buyūtāt an-nabāha* ("of distinguished and honored ancestry and from the renowned families"), but this passage can only point to an origin from a family of scholars. That the name Ibn Bal'ām does not appear among names of Jews of Toledo mentioned in the many Arab documents that were preserved in Toledo's archives of the twelfth century and published by González Palencia clearly proves that this family was not one of property. (The name Ibn Bal'ām appears in only one document—no. 38—as a representative of the Jews in Talavera in 1242.) For Ibn Bal'ām's dates see S. Fuchs,

"Studien über Abu Zakariyā Jachjā (R. Jehuda) Ibn Bal'ām," *Magazin f. d. Wissenschaft des Judentums* 20:14ff.

20. See Stern in *Zion* 15: 143; Schirmann 1:298.
21. See at the end of his book on verbs.
22. He mentions the men who turn to him with a request that he clarify the text of the Bible for them. See in Poznanski, *JQR* n.s. 15:2, and also in other passages in his writings; see Abramson, "Sefer ha-tadjnīs etc.," *Sefer Ḥ. Yālōn* (Jerusalem, 1963), p. 58. Because of the multiplicity of these notes, it cannot be assumed that this is mere rhetoric.
23. The full title is *Kitāb at-Tardjīh fī mā wudjida min mukhtalaf arā al-mufassirīn wa-dhikr nukat kathīra fī khilāl dhalika* ("The Book of Reconciliation between What Is to Be Found among the Varying Opinions of the Commentators and the Many Keen Observations Therein"); see there, p. 2.

    His commentaries were published in their entirety: that on Joshua by Poznanski in "Birkat Abraham" *(Festschrift A. Berliner),* Heb. section, pp. 91–107; on Judges, by Poznanski (Frankfurt a. M., 1906); on Isaiah, by Derenbourg in *REJ* 18–20, 22, 23, and cf. Bacher, "Jehuda Ibn Balaams Jesaja-Commentar," *ZAW* 13:129–55; on Jeremiah, by Israelsohn in *Festschrift Harkavy* (Heb. section), pp. 273–308; and on Minor Prophets, by Poznanski in *JQR* n.s. 15:1–53. Of the remaining commentaries of Ibn Bal'ām, only passages have been published; cf. Steinschneider, *Ar. Lit.,* pp. 141–42, and Poznanski, *JQR* n.s. 15:4.

    In addition, see the proofs of Abramson, "Sefer ha-tadjnīs," p. 55, that Ibn Bal'ām had written commentaries on all the books of the Bible.
24. See Israelsohn in *Festschrift Harkavy,* p. 275. This is not the opinion of Abramson, "Sefer ha-tadjnīs," p. 57.
25. See Poznanski in *Festschrift A. Berliner* (Heb. section), p. 93; also, Israelsohn, in *Festschrift Harkavy,* p. 277.
26. Judah Ibn Kuraish: on Isa. 47:13; on Jeremiah, see Israelsohn in *Festschrift Harkavy,* p. 277. M'naḥem Ben Sārūḳ: Judges 5:28, 7:3; Jeremiah, see Israelsohn, *Festschrift Harkavy,* p. 277; Joel 2:6, 4:11; Mic. 5:5, see Poznanski, *JQR* n.s. 15:8. Dūnash b. Labrat: Judges 3:22 and cf. also Israelsohn, *Festschrift Harkavy,* p. 277. Ḥayyūdj: Lev. 18:28, see Poznanski *ZfHB* 4:22; Judges 16:26; Isa. 25:7, 27:8, 30:15, 65; Jer. 6:28 in Israelsohn, *Festschrift Harkavy,* p. 276; Hos. 7:8, 13:7; Mic. 6:6; Hab. 2:7; Zeph. 2:1, 3:6; Zech. 2:2; Mal. 3:20. See also Steinschneider, "Pērūsh R. Y'huda b. Bal'ām be-lāshōn 'Arābhī," *He-Ḥālūṣ* 2:62.
27. R. M'bhassēr: Lev. 13:31, see *ZfHB* 4:19; R. Ḥēfeṣ: see *He-Ḥālūṣ* 2:62, and the commentary on Judges 20:28 *(Kitāb ash-Sharā'i');* Aaron b. Sardjadu: see *He-Ḥālūṣ* 2:61; Samuel b. Ḥofnī: see ibid., p. 62, and see on Lev. 15:3, *ZfHB* 4:19; 1 Sam. 28: see Harkavy, *Zikkārōn la-rishōnīm* I, 3, p. 14 and see his commentary on Isa. 49:17 and further Harkavy, ibid., p. 41 (Gaon Rabbi Samuel in his book *Naskh ash-shar'*).
28. See his commentary on Isa. 1:7, 8, 18; 2:6, 7; 8:3; 29:11; 33:7; 34:14; 49:17; 51:15; 57:10; 64:6; 65:11; 66:8, 9. On the other hand he sometimes accepts his opinion; see ibid. 5:1, 7, 30; 14:23; 18:2; 28:25; 31:4; 38:10, 14; 40:15, 20, 22; 62:2.
29. See the passages from Numbers and Deuteronomy in Steinschneider, *ZDMG* 55:133ff., and see *He-Ḥālūṣ* 2:61, Num. 24:6; for Deut. 14:5, see

Poznanski, "Zu Hai Gaons Kitāb al-Ḥāwi," *ZDMG* 55:599; for quotations of comments on Judges 8:16, 2 Sam. 6:13, see *ZfHB* 1:98; for Isa. 7:19, 24:18,* for his commentary on Jer. 51:34, see Israelsohn, *Festschrift Harkavy,* pp. 276 and 277.

30. See the commentary on Isaiah, the beginning of chapter 38 and the end of Jonah; Poznanski, *JQR* n.s. 15:5; Gaon R. Sh'rīra: concerning the commentary on 2 Sam. 7:23, see Harkavy, *Ḥadāshīm gam y'shānīm,* no. 7 (supplement to Graetz—*Sh'far* 4:32).
31. Lev. 15:23, see *ZfHB* 4:19; 2 Sam. 6:19, see *ZfHB* 1:98, and see Poznanski, *JQR* n.s. 15:9; Isa. 21:4, 27:1, 59:14, cf. Bacher, "Jehuda Ibn Balaams," p. 132.
32. See his commentary on Judges 4:20, 5:28, 20:4; Isa. 51:17, 64:5, and see also *REJ* 22:196, and Bacher, *ZAW* 13:131–32, 134; Jeremiah in Israelsohn, *Festschrift Harkavy,* p. 276; Mic. 2:4, see *JQR* n.s. 15:39, p. 39, and Derenbourg, *Opuscules,* pp. xxi, xxxviii–xxxix, xli, xliii–xlix, and cf. on this matter Fuchs, *Magazin f. d. Wissenschaft des Judentums* 20:30.
33. See in Derenbourg, *Opuscules,* p. xlvii.
34. Koran: Deut. 24:4, Jer. 49:25, see Israelsohn, *Festschrift Harkavy,* p. 276. Arab poets: Judges 7:13, Hos. 8:1, Mic. 2:8, see Poznanski, *JQR* n.s. 15:6. Arab grammarians: Isa. 4:18 (*Kitāb al-'Ain* of Khalīl and *Kitāb az-Zāhir* of al-Anbārī, i.e., Abū Bakr Muḥammad b. al-Ḳāsim al-Anbārī, d. 939, see Brockelman, *Geschichte der Arabische Literatur* 1:119. Historians: Isa. 18:1 (*Ta'rīkh al-Mas'ūdī;* the cited passage is from Masudi, *Murūdj adh-dhahab,* ed. Paris, 1:365), Obadiah 20 (Ibn al-Ḳūṭiyya; however, this passage is not to be found in *Kitāb Iftitāḥ al-Andalus*).
35. Deut. 14:1; Isa. 16:1, 21:22; Hab. 2:4, cf. Poznanski, *JQR* n.s. 15:45.
36. See *REJ* 23:133; Harkavy, *Ḥadāshīm gam y'shānīm* 7:18–19.
37. "Commentary on Joshua," *Birkat Abraham,* p. 103; see there a discussion of the dispute between them with regard to this, and see also *REJ* 17:178.
38. This book is called *Ta'dīd mu'djizāt at-taurāt wa 'n-nubuwwāt,* and it is expressly mentioned in the commentaries on Joel 4:18, on 1 Sam., end of chap. 28. See also *Shīrat Yisrāēl,* p. 188, and cf. *REJ* 17:180, and Poznanski, *JQR* n.s. 15:11.
39. Commentary on Isa. 51:6.
40. See his commentary on Isa. 53:12; 60:12, 15; also Zech. 9:9 and Mal. 3:23. Cf. Poznanski, *JQR* n.s. 15:53, and also p. 9.
41. See on Num. 15:15 in Fuchs, *Magazin f. d. Wissenschaft des Judentums* 20:29; Isa. 9:13; 28:11, 16, 27; 33:1; cf. Bacher, "Jehuda Ibn Balaams," pp. 136–37, also Jer. 8:18, and further Isa. 23:10; Abraham Ibn Ezra, *S'fat Yeter* 38 and his commentary on Ps. 34:4, 84:5.
42. From the *Book on the Particles.* The Hebrew translation was published in part by Fuchs from a manuscript in Paris in *Ha-Ḥōḳēr* 1:133–34, 193–94, 340–41; 2:73–74, and see Derenbourg, *Wiss. Zeitschr. f. jüd. Theol.* 5:408, as to what he writes there against R. Isaac Ibn Gayyāt. From the *Book on the Verbs.* The Hebrew translation was published by Pollak from a Leyden

*29:16, 30:13, 24 (commentary on *Kēlīm*), 34:6, 50:11, 51:17, 30:24 (Gaon R. Hai in the commentary on *Ṭōhōrōt*);

manuscript in *Ha-Karmel* 3:221–22, 229–30, Kokowzow, pp. 52–53, and Poznanski, *REJ* 36:298–301; see also Poznanski, *REJ* 51:152–53. From the *Tadjnīs* (this name was accepted also into the Hebrew literature) were first published various passages by Fürst, *Litbl. des Or.* 7: cols. 466–74, and also there by Fuchs, cols. 659–61, and cf. Steinschneider, *Ar. Lit.* no. 92. Afterwards, Kokowzow published fragments from the Arabic original out of manuscripts in the Firkowitch collection and published the Hebrew translation of the three treatises from a Paris manuscript, pp. 69–152. Finally, S. Abramson published additional fragments from manuscripts out of the Geniza collection at Cambridge, together with fragments Kokowzow had published and with the Hebrew translation, in his study "Sefer ha-tadjnīs etc." in *Sefer Ḥ. Yālōn* (Jerusalem, 1963), pp. 51–149. See there the introduction, pp. 58–59, on the character of the book and p. 63 on its sources. Finally, S. Abramson published a new and complete edition of *The Three Books of Judah Ibn Bal'ām* (Jerusalem, 1967).

43. See *ZDMG* 70:469.
44. See *Shīrat Yisrāēl,* p. 110. In spite of the clear definition of the book's contents by Moses Ibn Ezra, esteemed scholars were misled by the note of a translator (or copyist) who ascribed to Ibn Bal'ām a treatise on the cantillation signs of the Bible called *Horāyat ha-Ḳōre,* and identified it with this book; see Steinschneider, *Ar. Lit.,* no. 92, and cf. Bacher, *MGWJ* 34:46ff., and in particular p. 477.
45. Moses Ibn Ezra: *al-mutafaḳḳih fī ākhir 'umrihi.*
46. See Zunz, *Literatur geschichte der syn. Poesie* (Berlin, 1865), pp. 200–201; *Sha'ar ha-shīr,* pp. 60–61; Schirmann 1:298–99; a Spanish translation is in Millás, *Poesía sagrada,* p. 243.
47. Memoirs of Abdallāh, pp. 66, 70.
48. Dozy, *Recherches* 1:258ff.
49. Responsa Alfasi, no. 131.
50. See *Diwān Moses Ibn Ezra,* nos. 28, 168; *Diwān Judah Halevi,* part 1, no. 119, and see there 16: "A man of the pen, having the power of expression, graced with grandeur and authority"; part 2, no. 21, and see there 1, 35, 61, 65.
51. *Diwān Moses Ibn Ezra,* no. 194, and cf. the superscription of Brody's explanations, *Diwān Moses Ibn Ezra,* p. 364.
52. See *Diwān Moses Ibn Ezra,* no. 168, line 16; *Shīrat Yisrāēl,* p. 74; and the Arabic text in Schirmann, "M'shōr'rīm," *Y'dī'ōt ha-mākhōn* 2:147. See the aforementioned poem, line 19, regarding his expert knowledge in mathematics, and explanations, *Diwān Moses Ibn Ezra,* p. 311.
53. *Diwān Moses Ibn Ezra,* nos. 8, 9, 35f., and see there 36: "Princes begot him"; 71: *wa-rathā R. Abūn bi-ḳaulihi ta'ziyatan fīhi* (for the superscription cf. Brody in explanations, *Diwān Moses Ibn Ezra,* p. 137, whereas in *MGWJ* 40:169 he still explained the poem as being actually an elegy and not a consolatory poem. The poem was sent to Granada to a friend of the deceased Abūn, and hence it appears that Abūn himself dwelt in Granada); 74 (for the name *Madjanīn* cf. Brody's explanations, p. 146; from lines 6–8 we learn that the poet was acquainted with the two scholars in his youth while he was in Granada and associated with them;

and see Brody's explanations, p. 147); 88; 137 (see Brody's explanations, p. 256 and see line 17: "their forebears were chiefs, but they increased the honor"); 205; 224; 235; see also p. 289 and cf. Brody, *Maḥberet mi-shīrē Mōshē b. Ya'ḳōbh Ibn 'Ezrā* (Philadelphia, 1934), p. xxiv.

54. See Memoirs of 'Abdallāh, p. 94, concerning villages in the subdistrict of Malaga whose inhabitants were all Christians.
55. *Abbad.* 1:246.
56. See *Dhakhīra* II (MS. Oxford), p. 124b, and cf. Pérès, pp. 327–28.
57. Responsa Alfasi, no. 281.
58. Ed. Cairo 1935, pp. 330–31.
59. Schirmann, "M'shōr'rīm," *Y'dī'ōt ha-mākhōn* 6:253–60. Joseph Ibn ash-Shāmī died in 1141; see a letter from the Geniza, T.-S., 10 J 24^4, wherein it is related that he died in the month of Nisan and that Joseph Ibn Migash died in the month of Sivan.
60. Documentos, no. 5, p. 1, line 17.
61. See note 12 above.
62. *Dhakhīra* II (MS. Oxford), p. 96b., and see also p. 94a.
63. *Abbad.* 2:16, and see Dozy there, p. 12.
64. Al-Maḳḳarī 1:135.
65. Al-Marrakūshī, p. 74.
66. *Diwān Moses Ibn Ezra,* 168, 41; 207, 18–21; 235, 29; and see notes 113–14 to chap. 4.
67. Ḥanokh b. Moses in *Ṣha'are ṣedeḳ,* part 3, section 1, no. 28; *T'shūbhōt GMUM,* nos. 182, 201; Joseph Ibn Abītūr in *Sha'arē ṣedeḳ,* part 3, section 1, no. 29.
68. Responsa Alfasi, no. 112; ed. Bilgoray, no. 153.
69. Responsa Alfasi, no. 307; ed. Bilgoray, no. 37.
70. Ibn Abī Uṣaibi'a 2:51.
71. *Dhakhīra* III, p. 135b, f, and cf. Pérès, p. 266. In the text of the letter, the Moslem intellectual mentions King Solomon and Moses (although he also includes John the Baptist), and apparently the reference is really to a Jew. The name Joseph, in particular, is proof.
72. See Responsa Alfasi, nos. 67, 173.
73. Documentos, no. 5, p. 1, line 11.
74. *A'māl al-a'lām,* p. 185. In *Dhakhīra* II (MS. Oxford), p. 31a, the poem in honor of al-Mu'tamid is given this superscription: "And to him on the occasion of the return of Cordova to his control and his causing the slaying of Ibn 'Ukāsha"; in f. 73a is found this superscription: "And of what was written on his [al-Mu'tamid's] behalf when Cordova returned to his control and Ibn 'Ukāsha was slain at his behest." However, in the text of this letter it is related how guards were posted around Cordova to prevent Ibn 'Ukāsha from escaping and that he was indeed slain, together with all his men, during the flight, and his head was sent to the king of Seville. Al-Mu'tamid adds as a note to the account that he would have preferred that Ibn 'Ukāsha be brought before him so that he could have slain him with his own hands. From this we infer that there is no contradiction between the accounts in the two sources.

    For the date of this incident, see Prieto y Vives, *Los nayes do taifas* (Madrid, 1926), pp. 54, 75, 235, and cf. Menéndez Pidal, *BAH* 100:517.

75. The king of Granada yielded on Martos in 1075; see Memoirs of 'Abdallāh, p. 75, and cf. Menéndez Pidal, "Leyendo las 'Memorias' del rey zirí 'Abd Allah," *Al-Andalus* 10:3; in 1079 Jaén was already in the hands of al-Mu'tamid; see *Abbad.* 2:86.
76. Ibn al-Abbār in Dozy, *Notice,* pp. 186–87; Ibn 'Idhārī, pp. 191–92, 239–40; Ibn al-Athīr 9:205–6; Prieto y Vives, pp. 40, 62–63, and see there p. 186. In the beginning Murcia still recognized the dominance of al-Muẓaffar, king of Valencia, who had mounted the throne in 1061.
77. According to Abū Bakr Muḥammad Ibn Muzayyin, whose account is cited by Ibn al-Abbār in the aforementioned passage, Murcia was conquered in 471 of the *hidjra* (July 14, 1078–July 3, 1079), and according to a supplement to the history of al-Mu'tamid by Ibn Ḳāsim that was found by Ibn al-Abbār, this occurred three years later; see *Abbad.* 2:87. But Dozy, in *Abbad.* 3:105, justifiably prefers the date Ibn Muzayyin fixed upon, because the development of the events in Murcia since then and until the coming of the Almoravides undoubtedly occupied many years. On the other hand, Dozy states that in 1078 Ibn 'Ammār passed through Murcia, even though Ibn Muzayyin relates that the city was then captured!
78. Ibn al-Abbār, pp. 279–80.
79. *A'māl al-a'lām,* pp. 279–80.
80. In the Arabic source that Dozy had before him (see below), it was stated: *ḳa'id khail Rūmiya,* from which he concluded that the reference was to Guillaume de Montreuil, and this conjecture was accepted by the scholars.
81. This matter is known from the pope's letters to the two persons; see Migne 146, col. 1387, and see Cl. Devic–J. Vaissete, *Histoire générale de Languedoc* (Toulouse, 1872) 3:255–56, who assert that these letters were written circa 1065. But see Jaffé–Wattenbach–Loewenfeld, *Regesta pontificum Romanorum,* nos. 4532, 4533, who establish 1063 as the date.
82. See *España Sagrada* 3:280ff. Fita sought to prove that at that time (in the spring of 1064) the *Cortes* was assembled in which the statutes of Barcelona known as the *Usatges* were established; see his article "Cortes y usajes de Barcelona," *BAH* 17:404ff., where he clarifies the chronological data, such as that the date 7th of October the year IV of King Philip (of France), in which a man declared in his will that it was his desire to join those fighting for the Cross together with the Bishop of Urgol, is 1063. King Philip I did indeed mount the throne on the 29th of August, 1060.
83. See the pope's letter wherein he praises the bishops for this action, Migne 146, cols. 1386–87. It is true that there exists another version of this letter according to which it was also designated for the bishops of Gaul; see ibid. In Fita's opinion—"Cortes y usajes de Barcelona," p. 406—this was the pope's letter to the bishops who took part in the Council of Barcelona and who belonged to the Church province of Narbonne. According to Jaffé, *Regesta pontificum Romanorum,* no. 4528, it was already written in 1063.
84. According to Dozy, al-Muzaffar abandoned the inhabitants of

Barbastro "who wanted to rule over themselves"; see *Recherches* (1st ed.) 1:459. But in the text of Ibn Bassām it is stated: وقصر يوسف ... في حمايتها و وكل اهلها الى نفوسهم. In the third edition of *Recherches* 2:340, Dozy properly translated: "Joseph abandoned the city in such a manner that the inhabitants could rely upon their own strength alone."

85. Ibn Ḥayyān in *Dhakhīra* III, p. 48a, f, the account about the Jew, p. 50a, f; cited in al-Maḳḳarī 2:749–50, and translated into French by Dozy, *Recherches* 2:339–40. On p. 338, Dozy also quotes the book *Al-Ḥulal al-maushiyya.* Other sources: Ibn 'Idhārī, pp. 225–30, and see 253–54; al-Bakrī quoted by Ibn 'Idhārī there and in the book of *Ar-Rauḍ al-mi'ṭār,* p. 4, and cf. J. Bosch Vilá, "Al-Bakri: Dos fragmentos sobre Barbastro," *EEMCA* 3:242–61; *Kitāb al-Iktifā, Abbad.* 2:14; *A'māl al-a'lām,* p. 198. The accounts in these sources are divided into two traditions: One, of which Ibn Ḥayyān is representative, relates that by chance the aqueduct became stopped up and that the city surrendered in exchange for an assurance that the inhabitants would be spared, whereas the other tradition—represented by a source cited by Ibn 'Idhārī (Ibn al-Ḳaṭṭān?)—relates that the water supply was cut off after an act of treachery and that the city was taken by force (عنوة), and that thereafter its inhabitants came out to drink without receiving any assurance whatsoever until, in the end, they were subjected to slaughter. In the second tradition there is no mention of the episode concerning the Jew.
86. Joseph b. Ṣaddīḳ in Neubauer, *Med. Jew. Chr.* 1:92; Abraham b. Solomon, ibid., pp. 107–8; cf. Loeb and Fita, *BAH* 12:170ff.
87. On the fixing of the dates of these events see Menéndez Pidal, "Leyendo las 'Memorias,' *Al-Andalus* 9:3–4.
88. P. 73.
89. Menéndez Pidal 1:92–93.
90. Baer, *Urkunden* 2:11. To be sure, this is a confirmation of privileges that the Jews had enjoyed earlier, but their renewal by Alfonso VI is characteristic of his policy.
91. See Cantera, *Sefarad* 1:89.
92. See Baer, "The Political Situation of the Jews of Spain in the Age of Judah Halevi" (in Hebrew), *Zion* 1:10–11.
93. García Gomez–Menéndez Pidal, "El Conde mozárabe Sisnando Davídiz y la politica de Alfonso VI con los taifas," *Al-Andalus* 12:27–41.
94. *Ar-Rauḍ al-mi'ṭār,* p. 89, quoted by al-Maḳḳarī 2:681–82; another and more detailed version is in *Al-Ḥulal al-maushiyya,* see in *Abbad.* 2:194; this same account is found in Ibn al-Athīr, p. 37, and in an-Nuwairī, p. 135, without mention of any Jews. Notwithstanding the anecdotal character of this account, it demonstrates that the existence of Jews in the circle of Alfonso VI was common knowledge.
95. Abraham b. Dā'ūd, p. 79.
96. See Baer, *Urkunden* 2:29, and also no. 552, and cf. H. Grassoti, *CHE* 29–30, pp. 204–5.
97. See Baer in *Zion* 1:17–18, and cf. Schirmann in *Tarbiṣ* 9:219–20.
98. Abraham b. Dā'ūd, p. 79, and cf. Loeb, *REJ* 18:62; 19:206ff. All these

data relate to the period after 1085, but since they show that this man was active at the royal court for twenty-five years, there is a foundation for the belief that he frequented the king's palace earlier still.

99. See Baer in *Zion* 1:13.
100. Migne 148, col. 604; for the date see Menéndez Pidal 1:249.
101. Migne 157, col. 574.
102. See Baer, *Urkunden* 1:18, and cf. "Political Situation of the Jews," pp. 8–9.
103. Joseph b. Ṣaddīḳ in Neubauer, *Med. Jew. Chr.* 1:93.
104. See Menéndez Pidal 1:159–60, 206–7, and see also J. M. Lacarra, "Dos tratados de paz y alianza entre Sancho el de Peñalén y Moctádir de Zaragoza (1069 y 1073)," *Hamenaje a Johannes Vincke* (Madrid, 1962–1963), pp. 121ff.
105. Bosch Vilá, *El Oriente arabe en el desarollo de la cultura de la marca superior,* pp. 36ff., 42ff.
106. See note 84 of chap. 1.
107. See Ibn Ṣā'id, p. 90, and cf. p. 71. As to his age, Ibn Ṣā'id states that he separated from him in 1066 and that he was then still a youth. With regard to the works on philosophy he studied, there apparently occurred a misunderstanding on the part of the Arab translators (or copyists), and on account of them the modern scholars were led astray. The name of the book Πεςὶ Φυβικῆς ἀκροάσεως (in Latin, *De naturali auditu,* or *Physica auscaltatio*) was translated into Arabic as *As-Samā' aṭ-ṭabī'ī* (it was entitled in Hebrew *Ha-Shema' ha-ṭibh'ī*) or سمع الكيان ; see *Fürst,* p. 250, and *Ḥādjī Khalīfa* 3:619. The Arab translators who did not understand this name changed the text in Ibn Ṣā'id's passage and wrote فبدأ منه بسمع كتاب الكيان, and hence the also erroneous translations of Orientalists such as Finkel, *JQR* n.s. 18:53–54. (The sequence according to which Abu 'l-Faḍl studied was the traditional one; see *Ṭibb an-nufūs* by Joseph Ibn 'Aḳnīn in ed. Güdemann, p. 40).

    An error also occurs in yet another passage in Ibn Ṣā'id's book in which Abu 'l-Faḍl Ḥasdai's name is mentioned. The statement made on p. 71 that there was none comparable to him in the speculative sciences refers to Abu 'l-Faḍl and not to al-Kirmānī. Yet earlier it had been asserted that al-Kirmānī did not know logic or astronomy, and if this is so, it is impossible that there was none to compare to him in the speculative disciplines.

    His appointment as vizier no doubt occurred after 1066, inasmuch as this matter is not mentioned by Ibn Ṣā'id, who parted from him in that year and relates, as aforesaid, that he was still a youth.
108. *Dhakhīra* III, pp. 128a, 129a, 131b.
109. Ibid., 128a, 134a.
110. Al-Fatḥ Ibn Khāḳān, *Ḳalā'id al-'iḳyān* (ed. Paris), pp. 209, 211, line 6f.; Al-Maḳḳarī 1:351; *Dhakhīra* I, pp. 197–98.
111. *Dhakhīra* III, pp. 132a, correspondence with Abu 'Ammār Ibn al-Faradj; p. 133a, correspondence with Ibn al-Marshānī when he went to visit him at Rueda; 133bf., a letter to Abū Muḥammad Ibn Siḳbāl.
112. *Dhakhīra* III, p. 125a.
113. J. Bosch Vilá, *Albarracín musulmana,* p. 169; and see further Ibn Ṣa'īd,

Al-Mughrib fī ḥula 'l-Maghrib 2:441, and see there in the editor's comments quotations from biographical notes on Ḥasdai b. Joseph in works that have not yet been published.

114. *Dhakhīra* (MS. Paris) II, p. 126b; III, p. 127b.
115. Al-Makkarī, p. 273, and there: Abu 'l-Faḍl Ibn ad-Dabbāgh (since the reference is to Abu 'l-Faḍl Ḥasdai!). On Ibn ad-Dabbāgh see the biography in Ibn Bassām in Dozy, *Recherches* (1st ed.) 1:163–64.
116. *Ḳalā'id*, p. 122. A reply to a letter of Ibn ad-Dabbāgh, see *Dhakhīra* III, p. 76a, f.
117. *Dhakhīra* III, p. 125a; *Ḳalā'id*, p. 209. Munk, who translated (or copied) these texts in his *Notice*, believed the information regarding the conversion to Islam by Ḥasdai; see there p. 208, as well as Pérès, p. 267. According to the unproved conjecture of a Spanish scholar, Ḥasdai did indeed convert to Islam in order to obtain the office of vizier; see J. Bosch Vilá, "El reino de taifas de Zaragoza," *Cuadernos de historia Jeronimo Zurita* (1960), 10—11:30.

    However, Saadya b. Danān expressly denies this rumor; see "She'ēla 'al d'bhar ha-anūsīm," *Ḥemda G'nūza* 16a, and surely Moses Ibn Ezra, who was almost the same age, would not have mentioned him or spoken of him respectfully in his book, *Shīrat Yisrāēl*, p. 69, if he had become a Moslem. As mentioned above, Graetz, 6:49, had already commented on this quite correctly. Even the taunts of his colleague Ibn ad-Dabbāgh point to his being a Jew. See also A. S. Yahuda, "Ḥasdai b. Joseph b. Ḥasdai," in the collection of his articles *'Ebher w'-'arābh*, pp. 113–14.
118. Prieto y Vives, p. 47; Bosch Vilá, "El reino de taifas," p. 18.
119. Al-Makkarī 1:288; *Ṭibb an-nufūs*, ed. Güdemann, pp. 28–29.
120. Dozy, *Recherches* (1st ed.) 1:163–64; Memoirs of 'Abdallah, p. 78.
121. *Dhakhīra* III, p. 127a.
122. *Ḳalā'id al-'iḳyān*, p. 210, cited by al-Makkarī 1:424 and cf. the words of Anonymous in the *Supplement to Ibn 'Idhārī*, p. 304.
123. In the manuscript of *Shīrat Yisrāēl*, MS. Bodl. 1074, folio 42b., and see ed. Halper, pp. 75–76, there is the vowel sign of the Arabic *u* over the *tav* in the family name; however, the reading should undoubtedly be *al-Tabbān* ("seller of straw"). Cf. *CB* 1616. The name of his father, Jacob, is known from his signatures, for he calls himself Levi b. Jacob. It is true that Alḥarīzī states in *Taḥk'mōnī*, p. 39, "And like the poems of Ben Joseph Tabbān there is none so beloved," and later on p. 41, "and R. Levi and R. Jacob, the sons of Tabbān, produce flowery language as though it were thrashed from straw." This version—"Ben Joseph"—is found in the old printed editions such as Constantinople, 1578, folio 9a, and Amsterdam, 1729, folio 50b. But MS. Almanzi, British Museum, Add. 27, 113, folio 17a, reads only "As the poems of Ben Tabbān," as it does in MS. Oxford, Neubauer, 1977, folio 22a; MS. Neubauer, 2517, folio 20b; MS. Paris, 1285, folio 14b. From the second passage in which Levi and Jacob, "the sons of Tabbān," are mentioned, Landshuth concluded that he had a brother named Jacob who was a poet; see *'Amūdē ha-'abhūda*, Maḥbereṯ II, pp. 154–55. On the other hand, there is in the *Diwān Moses Ibn Ēzra*, no. 239, a poem that, according to the superscription, he wrote as a reply to Abū Yūsuf Ibn Abi 'l-Fahm, and

there in line 4 the man is called Jacob; Brody had already conjectured there, in the index of names, p. 430, that Abū Yūsuf Ya'aḳōbh Ibn Abi 'l-Fahm was the son of Levi Ibn at-Tabbān. It should be added that the poem is written in the manner of an old person addressing a young one. D. Yarden, moreover, discovered in the Ginzburg MS. that the poem no. 187 in that *diwan* is not of Moses Ibn Ezra but of Jacob Ibn at-Tabbān; see his article "Nine New Poems of R. Moses Ibn Ezra etc.," *Mōlād* 19:630–33. In truth, there is no necessity to conclude from the words of Alḥarīzī that Jacob was Levi's brother and the superscription Abū Yūsuf Ibn Abi 'l-Fahm reinforces the opinion that this Jacob (as far as the man who assembled the *diwan* knew) was the son of Levi. The agnomen *Abū Yūsuf* of that Jacob b. Levi could have been a mere supplementary name, as was the practice with the Arabs and the Jews who dwelt among them, but it is also possible that he really had a son called Yūsuf, and if this is indeed so, he may have been called by the name of his grandfather, in which case there is no error in the version "Ben Joseph Tabbān" in the *Taḥkemōnī.* According to this conjecture Levi was a son of Jacob b. Joseph, and he himself had a son whose name was Jacob who begot Joseph (Yūsuf). Much weight should be attributed to the superscription on the poem no. 239 in *Diwān Moses Ibn Ezra* that shows that Jacob Ibn at-Tabbān was the son of Levi; in any case, it is not to be assumed that in the same generation there were two poets named Jacob Ibn at-Tabbān.

For the time in which he lived, see Brody, "Moses ibn Esra und Levi al-Tabban," *MGWJ* 71:52, and also *Encyclopedia Judaica* 2: cols. 473–74.

124. See Brody, "Moses ibn Esra," note 42.
125. Derenbourg, *Opuscules,* pp. xlv–xlvi, xlviii.
126. Abraham Ibn Ezra in the introduction to *Sefer ha-Moznayim;* Ibn Barūn, *Kitāb al-Muwāzana,* ed. Kokowzow Къ исторiи еврейской филологiи (St. Petersburg, 1916), pp. 12, 14, and see there in the Russian section pp. 6–7, and also Brody in *Encyclopedia Judaica* 2: cols. 473–74, about possible quotations in the commentary of Abraham Ibn Ezra on Ps. 7:10, 35:13.
127. See the words of the assembler of the *Diwān Judah Halevi* in Geiger, *Divan des Castilliers Abu 'l-Hassan Juda ha-Levi* (Breslau, 1851), p. 169. Alḥarīzī's evaluations are susceptible to various explanations; see Graetz 6:110; Zunz, *Literaturgeschichte der syn. Poesie,* p. 217.
128. See Brody, "Moses ibn Esra," and *Diwān Judah Halevi,* part 1, nos. 14, 22; part 2, no. 15, and cf. Brody's remarks in the notes, p. 176.
129. The edition of his *diwan* by D. Pagis, *The Poems of Levi Ibn at-Tabbān* (Jerusalem, 1967) comprises 72 pieces.
130. *Diwān Moses Ibn Ezra,* no. 57, 7.
131. See *The Jews of Moslem Spain* 2:226–27.
132. *Shīrat Yisrāēl,* p. 74.
133. He died in 1066; see Pons Boigues, p. 168, and see regarding the aforementioned families Ibn Bashkuwāl 1:63, 64, 67, and also Memoirs of 'Abdallāh, p. 77, and further Lévi-Provençal in *Al-Andalus* 4:41, notes 27, 28.
134. *Dhakhīra* IV, 1, p. 127.
135. Rodrigo Jimenez de Rada, *Rerum in Hispania gestarum chronicon* 6: cap. 23

(Granada, 1545), folio 54b; Menéndez Pidal, "Adefonsus imperator toletanus, magnificus triumphator," *BAH* 100:526ff.

136. See "Kitāb al-Iktifā," *Abbad.* 2:18; Ibn 'Alḳama as it was translated (or copied) in *Primera cronica general,* ed. Menéndez Pidal, p. 537; and also *Dhakhīra* IV, 1, p. 126, lines 2–3, which relate that al-Ḳādir suggested the exchanges even before Alfonso VI returned him to Toledo, but apparently these were *post factum* guesses. What Ibn Bassām asserted, namely that this was a secret agreement, would prove this supposition.

137. According to Ibn al-Khaṭīb (see *Abbad.* 2:174) al-Mu'tamid sought from Alfonso the return to him of the Almodóvar fortress; this is apparently the fortress north of Cordova called by this name (Almodóvar del Campo).

138. The slaying of the Jewish messenger of the king of Castile was an event that had powerful reverberations throughout Spain because of the connection between him and al-Mu'tamid's turning to Yūsuf b. Tāshfīn, and therefore many Arabic historians mentioned it and also embellished the account by the addition of various details, some heard from narrators and read in their sources and some stemming from themselves. Thus it turns out that even among modern scholars there are varying versions of this account. These versions touch upon the name of the emissary, the purpose of his mission and particularly its timing. See al-Iḥāta in *Abbad.* 112:174ff.; *A'māl al-a'lām,* pp. 185, 280ff.; Ibn Khaldūn in *Abbad.* 2:211; Al-Makkarī 1:782, 2:598, 676; *al-Ḥulal al-maushiyya* in *Abbad.* 2:187; an-Nuwairī, ed. Gaspar Remiro, p. 97; Ibn al-Athīr 10:92–93, cf. Fagnan, p. 481.

It is apparent that we have here accounts of two different events: The account of the mission of the Jew, Ibn Shālīb, before the conquest of Toledo, of which the purpose was to receive the tribute of the king of Seville, a mission that culminated in his being slain after he refused to accept the coins that had been brought out to him; and a second account of the demands of Alfonso VI, after the conquest of Toledo, that the provinces that had formerly belonged to the kingdom of Toledo be delivered up to him. Apparently the Arabic historians confused the two incidents, some of them erroneously setting as the date of the first mission the time after Toledo was taken and some attaching the account of the slaying of the Jewish emissary to the account of the mission connected with the handing over of the aforementioned regions.

Graetz 6, note 4, assumed that Alfonso did not wish to turn the king of Seville into his avowed enemy until he had subjugated the kingdom of Toledo, and Graetz was therefore of the opinion that those Arabic historians who set the period after 1085 as the date of the Jew's mission were right. But in point of fact, the Arabic historians present information about the aforementioned campaign of Alfonso in the very year of 1082; see *Rauḍ al-ḳirṭās,* ed. Tornberg, p. 92. Among the dates the writers present, the year 1082 is to be preferred. The writer Abū Bakr Muḥammad b. 'Isā Ibn al-Labbāna, who fixes upon this date, was an inhabitant of Denia and lived at the time of these events. He was a high officer in the service of one of the Moslem princedoms in Spain and was therefore called a vizier; was a frequent visitor at the courts of the kings in

Spain, such as the court of al-Mu'taṣim in Almería (al-Maḳḳarī 2:453 and cf. 1:250) and the court of Seville, where he was in 1090; and became one of those close to al-Mu'tamid (ibid. 1:439; 2:486, 578, 623). He also visited him in Aghmāt (ibid. 2:487, 578) and was on the island of Mallorca in August 1096 (*Abbad.* 2:233). From this we can infer that the account of this writer is an authentic source. On the other hand, the book *Al-Ḥulal al-maushiyya* was written at the end of the fourteenth century; see *Abbad.* 2:182.

The messenger's name is given in the Arabic sources in various forms: Ibn Shālīb, by Ibn al-Labbāna—see in al-Maḳḳarī 2:598—and Ibn al-Khaṭīb—see *A'māl al-a'lām,* p. 185; Ibn Shālib, see *Al-Ḥulal al-maushiyya* in *Abbad.* 2:187; Ibn Shālbīb, by an-Nuwairī, p. 97 (in the other sources there is only reference to a Jewish emissary without mention of his name). In this matter it is also proper to depend upon Ibn al-Labbāna, who was an intimate of the king of Seville and wrote a special treatise on the history of his family.

Concerning the status of Ibn Shālīb, the author of *Al-Ḥulal al-maushīyya* relates that he was not the emissary of the king of Castile but accompanied him as a financial adviser. This report is not reasonable, for if he were only the adviser to the emissary, he would not have arrogated to himself the right to speak in the matter of not receiving the tribute.

Detailed information on the personality of the Jewish emissary is presented by Leo Africanus, who had early Arabic sources before him. He reports that the name of the emissary was 'Amrām b. Isaac of Toledo, and that he was a physician, philosopher, and astronomer. After the conquest of Toledo, Alfonso VI engaged him as a secretary, turned over to him functions in the local administration, and charged him with writing letters to the Moslem rulers. The purpose of his mission to Seville was the collection of the tribute, which ended with his being slain because of his forceful speech. When news of his execution reached Alfonso VI, he decided to mount a campaign against the kingdom of Seville, and then al-Mu'tamid turned to the Moslems of North Africa with a request for help. This account, which is found in his book *De viris quibusdam illustribus apud Arabis,* Jo. Alberti Fabricii Bibl. Graeca 13 (Hamburg, 1726), p. 295, was accepted by Graetz 6, note 4.

INDEX OF PERSONS AND PLACES

Names beginning with al-, ar-, as-, etc. are listed under the second element of the name. Entries in *italics* refer to specific works of literature.

Note: For general subject references, see under *Spain (Moslem);* for subjects related to lifestyle, see under *Abū Ya'ḳūb Yūsuf.*

INDEX